The HERITAGE *of the* ULTIMATE LAW *of* LIFE

DAISAKU IKEDA

World Tribune Press

Published by

World Tribune Press
606 Wilshire Blvd.
Santa Monica, CA 90401

Printed in the United States of America.

This book is printed on Glatfelter Thor PCW paper.
It contains 30% post-consumer waste and is
SFI (Sustainable Forestry Initiative) certified.

Design by Lightbourne, Inc.

ISBN 978-1-932911-77-0

10 9 8 7 6 5 4 3

CONTENTS

EDITOR'S NOTE

This series of lectures by SGI President Ikeda was published in SGI-USA's *Living Buddhism* from the May–June 2007 issue through the May–June 2008 issue.

Please also see *The Writings of Nichiren Daishonin*, vol. 1, pp. 216–19, for "The Heritage of the Ultimate Law of Life."

- GZ, page number(s)—refers to the *Gosho zenshu*, the Japanese-language compilation of letters, treatises, essays and oral teachings of Nichiren Daishonin.
- LS, page number(s)—refers to *The Lotus Sutra*, translated by Burton Watson (New York: Columbia University Press, 1993).
- OTT, page number(s)—refers to *The Record of the Orally Transmitted Teachings*, translated by Burton Watson (Soka Gakkai: Tokyo, 2004).
- WND, page number(s)—refers to *The Writings of Nichiren Daishonin*, vol. 1 (WND-1) (Tokyo: Soka Gakkai, 1999) and vol. 2 (WND-2) (Tokyo: Soka Gakkai, 2006).

The Heritage of the ULTIMATE LAW *of* LIFE

SGI PRESIDENT IKEDA'S STUDY LECTURE SERIES

This is a series of lectures by SGI President Daisaku Ikeda on "The Heritage of the Ultimate Law of Life." Nichiren Daishonin states: "Shakyamuni Buddha who attained enlightenment countless kalpas ago, the Lotus Sutra that leads all people to Buddhahood, and we ordinary human beings are in no way different or separate from one another. To chant Myoho-renge-kyo with this realization is to inherit the ultimate Law of life and death."

[1]

The Ultimate Law of Life and Death

Striving in the Spirit of the Oneness of Mentor and Disciple To Open the Way to True Happiness for All Humanity

Life and death are the greatest mysteries, and they form the primary focus of religion. Where have we come from, and where do we go? Why are human beings born? Are our lives just random events or do they have some greater purpose? What is the meaning of death? Are we merely reduced to meaningless nothingness, as so many people in our modern world vaguely believe? Or are we restored to a luminous immortal "soul," as many time-honored religious traditions of East and West maintain? Or, as Shakyamuni Buddha teaches [in expounding the Middle Way], is it neither?

The Wisdom of Buddhism Transcending the Extremes of the Views of Annihilation and Permanence

Nichiren Daishonin's writing "The Heritage of the Ultimate Law of Life" expounds a matter of ultimate importance relating to life and death. The use of the word *ultimate* suggests the crucial nature of this subject, as it is also the essential purpose of Buddhism and the foundation of religion.

The Lotus Sutra uses the term *one great reason* to express the ultimate purpose for Buddhas to appear in the world—to enable all living beings to realize the Buddha wisdom and attain enlightenment. The matter of ultimate importance relating to life and death that Nichiren teaches in this writing is closely connected to this ideal of universal enlightenment in the Lotus Sutra.

Based on the Buddhist concept of dependent origination[1]—one of the truths to which Shakyamuni became enlightened—the sufferings of aging and death arise from innate darkness or ignorance within the individual. The Buddha teaches that these sufferings can be overcome by extinguishing this inner benightedness.

The wisdom or insight that enabled Shakyamuni to attain enlightenment represents the wisdom that conquers the delusion and suffering related to death. Based on this wisdom, the Buddha rejected the two most common views of death, which represented two extremes, and both of which he considered erroneous. Neither could fully enable people to transcend the fear and uncertainty of death. One of these was the view of death as the annihilation or complete cessation of self (the view of annihilation), while the other was the view of death as the self continuing in the form of an unchanging immortal soul or spirit (the view of permanence). Both views consider the question of life and death only from the point of birth until one's demise, with life and death seen as opposites. As such, neither view embodies the wisdom that correctly perceives the true reality of life and death.

It seems that most people, conscious as they are of their mortality, hold one of these two views in some form or other. The view of annihilation, however, gives rise to fear and anxiety about death. And the view of permanence, we find, is the product of self-attachment.

Nichiren also indicates that these two views cannot help people gain true happiness. For instance, in "Letter from Sado," he writes that human beings tend to be terrified of death and attached to life: "The most dreadful things in the world are the pain of fire, the flashing of swords, and the shadow of death. Even horses and cattle fear being killed; no wonder human beings are afraid of death. Even a leper clings to life; how much more so a healthy person" (*The Writings of Nichiren Daishonin,* vol. 1, p. 301).

Then, to describe the wisdom of Buddhism, he cites a lesson from Shakyamuni's Lotus Sutra: "The Buddha teaches that even filling the entire major world system with the seven kinds of treasures does not match offering one's little finger to the Buddha and the [Lotus] sutra. The boy Snow Mountains gave his own body, and the ascetic Aspiration for the Law peeled off his own skin [in order to record the Buddha's teachings]. Since nothing is more precious than life itself, one who dedicates one's life to Buddhist practice is certain to attain Buddhahood" (WND-1, 301).

The first sentence in this quote refers to a passage from the "Former Affairs of the Medicine King" chapter of the Lotus Sutra, indicating that using our individual lives—which each of us prizes and cherishes—for the sake of Buddhism is the highest form of offering we can make. Based on this, Nichiren declares that by selflessly dedicating ourselves to Buddhism, just like the boy Snow Mountains and the ascetic Aspiration for the Law, we can gain enlightenment. He says, therefore, that this course of practice is the supreme path for attaining happiness.

In the same writing, Nichiren highlights the folly of a life that mirrors the thinking of the two views, annihilation and permanence. He does so by describing how fish and birds, fearful for their safety, go to great lengths to hide themselves from predators but are nevertheless haplessly tricked by bait or traps and end up losing their lives.

Seikyo Press

SGI President and Mrs. Ikeda taking a commemorative photo on the occasion of receiving honorary professorships from South Korea's Dongju College. President Ikeda has received more than 200 academic honors from around the world and Mrs. Ikeda has received seven.

In "Letter from Sado," Nichiren describes the Buddha's wisdom, which transcends the views of annihilation and permanence, as living and taking action with the spirit of selfless dedication for the sake of Buddhism. This is an important point (see WND-1, 301–07).

By its very nature, a view of life and death considered only from the point of birth onward causes people to focus on whether their present self will end at death or continue. Not surprising, perhaps, since human beings, though keenly aware of their mortality, cannot personally experience what death or the afterlife is like while alive. But no matter how we may debate this issue from this perspective, it will not produce supreme wisdom or understanding. The view of annihilation, the complete cessation of existence, for instance, will never free people from fear of or anxiety over death. On the other hand, the view of permanence, which sees the self continuing as an unchanging, everlasting soul, often comes from one's simple desire for immortality; ultimately, it does not constitute the wisdom for elevating one's spiritual state, instead serving only to strengthen self-attachment and to deepen delusion.

Of course, many philosophies and religious traditions of East and West espouse the existence of some eternal spiritual entity that transcends the present self. But even if those doctrines are effective in providing some peace of mind regarding death, they fall short of being the supreme wisdom for elevating the way people live. Rather, as I mentioned earlier, they cause people to be caught up in the delusions of self-attachment and the sufferings of aging and death.

Buddhist scriptures show that when Shakyamuni was asked whether his life would continue after death, he did not answer one way or the other. Because his doing so would not have contributed to helping people elevate their lives and might only have added to their delusion and suffering about death.

In "Letter from Sado," Nichiren taught his followers, who were then struggling bravely amid persecution, the way of selfless dedication to Buddhism (see WND-1, 301–07). In other words, he taught them the spirit of not begrudging their lives and the basic criteria for leading lives that value the Law above all. In this way, he aimed to help his followers break through to the source of delusion and suffering concerning death—their narrow attachment to ego—and cast off that delusion and suffering.

Unless we are free of the suffering of death, we cannot savor true happiness. But liberating ourselves from this suffering cannot be achieved through theorizing or intellectualizing. Life and death make up the great, eternal rhythm of the universe itself. When we come to apprehend the greater self within us that is part of this rhythm—and feel in the depths of our being that this rhythm is the fundamental pulse sustaining our lives—we can overcome the suffering of death. The path of this inner liberation lies in chanting Nam-myoho-renge-kyo and teaching others to do the same. In "The Heritage of the Ultimate Law of Life," Nichiren explains this fundamental view of life and death.

Life and Death As Functions of the Mystic Law

In this writing, Nichiren Daishonin explains that the Mystic Law (Jpn *myoho*) itself embodies the phases of life and death: "*Myo* represents death, and *ho*, life" (WND-1, 216). He also says that all life, all phenomena, are subject to and undergo these two phases, which are functions of the Mystic Law. He indicates that birth and death are an inherent part of life. In this way, he seeks to prevent people from making the mistake of abhorring life and death or from having a strong attachment to either.

The Mystic Law is the eternal, infinite Law of the universe. This eternal Law embodies the phases of life and death. In other words, the two phases are themselves the rhythm of the eternal Law and appear as the life and death of countless living entities—as the arising and extinction of all phenomena, as all kinds of causes and effects in every dimension, as the harmony and dynamism of the universe as a whole.

This concept of life and death as functions of the Mystic Law constitutes the matter of ultimate importance in our lives, because true happiness can only be found in living in accord with this great rhythm of life and death.

Mentor and Disciple in Buddhism Transmit the Heritage of Attaining Buddhahood

So far I have summed up the meaning of "the matter of ultimate importance concerning life and death," one main theme of "The Heritage of the Ultimate Law of Life." Next, I will confirm the meaning of *heritage*, another major theme, while going over the essential points of the entire writing.

"The ultimate Law of life and death as transmitted from the Buddha to all living beings is Myoho-renge-kyo. The five characters of Myoho-renge-kyo were transferred from Shakyamuni and Many Treasures, the two Buddhas inside the treasure tower, to Bodhisattva Superior Practices, carrying on a heritage unbroken since the infinite past" (WND-1, 216).

"*Myo* represents death, and *ho,* life. Living beings that pass through the two phases of life and death are the entities of the Ten Worlds, or the entities of Myoho-renge-kyo" (WND-1, 216).

"Life and death are simply the two functions of Myoho-renge-kyo" (WND-1, 216).

"Shakyamuni and Many Treasures, the two Buddhas, are also the two phases of life and death" (WND-1, 216).

"Shakyamuni Buddha who attained enlightenment countless kalpas ago, the Lotus Sutra that leads all people to Buddhahood, and we ordinary human beings are in no way different or separate from one another. To chant Myoho-renge-kyo with this realization is to inherit the ultimate Law of life and death" (WND-1, 216).

"For one who summons up one's faith and chants Nam-myoho-renge-kyo with the profound insight that now is the last moment of one's life, the sutra proclaims: 'When the lives of these persons come to an end, they will be received into the hands of a thousand Buddhas, who will free them from all fear and keep them from falling into the evil paths of existence'" (WND-1, 216).

"The heritage of the Lotus Sutra flows within the lives of those who never forsake it in any lifetime whatsoever—whether in the past, the present, or the future" (WND-1, 217).

Nichiren Daishonin begins by saying that the "ultimate Law of life and death" is Myoho-renge-kyo, and that Myoho-renge-kyo is the heritage that Bodhisattva Superior Practices [the leader of the Bodhisattvas of the Earth] received from Shakyamuni Buddha and Many Treasures Buddha.

As mentioned earlier, only through living and taking action with the spirit of selfless dedication for the sake of Buddhism can Myoho-renge-kyo be transmitted as the ultimate Law of life and death. Therefore, Nichiren cites the name of Bodhisattva Superior Practices as the teacher or mentor who takes on the commitment to live and take action with this spirit. He explains that the "heritage of the ultimate Law of life and death" only flows in faith based on the oneness of mentor and disciple.

With faith and chanting with clear belief, we can inherit the ultimate Law of life and death.

Next, he clarifies that the Mystic Law embodies the phases of life and death, and that the life and death of all living entities, the arising and extinction of all phenomena, constitute life and death as functions of the Mystic Law. The living beings of the Ten Worlds and the two Buddhas Shakyamuni and Many Treasures embody life and death as functions of the Mystic Law.

Based on this, Nichiren then declares that there is absolutely no distinction among "Shakyamuni Buddha who attained enlightenment countless kalpas ago," "the Lotus Sutra that leads all people to Buddhahood" and "we ordinary human beings" as entities of Myoho-renge-kyo, the Mystic Law (WND-1, 216). And he explains that only through faith and chanting Myoho-renge-kyo with clear belief in this can we inherit the "heritage of the ultimate Law of life and death." Faith—chanting

Myoho-renge-kyo with the conviction that Buddhas and the Law for attaining enlightenment are both Myoho-renge-kyo, that Myoho-renge-kyo exists nowhere but within our lives—is the essence of accepting and upholding the Mystic Law, which is the fundamental practice of Nichiren Buddhism.

Nichiren further explains, in terms of life and death, that the essence of faith in the Mystic Law is having the attitude that "now is the last moment of one's life" (WND-1, 216). This means steadfastly upholding genuine faith at each moment of our lives so that even if we were faced with our death, we would have no regrets and would calmly transcend the suffering of death. And when we carry out such genuine faith until the last second of our lives in this existence, we can "accept and uphold" the Lotus Sutra across the three existences—past, present and future. This, Nichiren says, is what it means for the "heritage of the Lotus Sutra to flow within our lives" (see WND-1, 217).

When we uphold correct faith until our last moment in this world, the "heritage of the ultimate Law of life and death" will flow in our lives continually throughout the cycle of birth and death, across past, present and future. This is the epitome of life and death as functions of the Mystic Law.

Therefore, continuing faith throughout our lives, throughout our existence in this world, is crucial. Our remaining steadfast in correct faith until our final moment is itself the attainment of Buddhahood in this lifetime. At that time, death will not signify the cessation of life but the completion of one life and the start of a new, even profounder, existence. Such a death will be totally free of all fear and anxiety. We will savor joy in both life and death.

The Great Vow of *Kosen-rufu* and the Path of Mentor and Disciple

"All disciples and lay supporters of Nichiren should chant Nam-myoho-renge-kyo with the spirit of many in body but one in mind, transcending all differences among themselves to become as inseparable as fish and the water in which they swim. This spiritual bond is the basis for the universal transmission of the ultimate Law of life and death. Herein lies the true goal of Nichiren's propagation. When you are so united, even the great desire for widespread propagation can be fulfilled" (WND-1, 217).

"Nichiren has been trying to awaken all the people of Japan to faith in the Lotus Sutra so that they too can share the heritage and attain Buddhahood. But instead they have persecuted me in various ways and finally had me banished to this island. You have followed Nichiren, however, and met with suffering as a result. It pains me deeply to think of your anguish" (WND-1, 217).

"It must be ties of karma from the distant past that have destined you [Sairen-bo] to become my disciple at a time like this. Shakyamuni and Many Treasures certainly realized this truth. The sutra's statement, 'Those persons who had heard the Law dwelled here and there in various Buddha lands, constantly reborn in company with their teachers,' cannot be false in any way" (WND-1, 217).

In the first half of this writing, as I've just outlined, Nichiren Daishonin sets forth the requirements for us as the disciples of Bodhisattva Superior Practices—as Bodhisattvas of the Earth—to establish faith through embracing Myoho-renge-kyo. In the latter half, Nichiren's focus shifts to the practice of *kosen-rufu* aimed at sharing with all people faith that accepts and upholds the Mystic Law.

In other words, he is saying that when we cherish the great desire for *kosen-rufu* and chant Nam-myoho-renge-kyo with the unity of "many in body, one in mind," the heritage of the ultimate Law of life and death will flow in our lives. He adds that the true goal of his propagation efforts lies in this struggle for *kosen-rufu*.

Kosen-rufu is a struggle to help all people transcend the suffering of death and actualize lives of genuine happiness.

When we focus on the great desire for *kosen-rufu* and its attainment, the bond of mentor and disciple, and the unity of "many in body, one in mind" hold crucial importance.

Further, Nichiren declares that the heritage of the Law that enables all people to attain enlightenment is found in the path he opened for *kosen-rufu*, or widespread propagation, in the Latter Day of the Law.

Nichiren then emphasizes the profound karmic bonds of mentor and disciple that link him and Sairen-bo, to whom this writing is addressed and who had weathered persecution on account of upholding Nichiren's teaching. To cherish the same great desire and to fight with the same spirit of selfless commitment as the mentor, even in the face of arduous difficulties, is the path of the oneness of mentor and disciple in the struggle for *kosen-rufu* in the Latter Day of the Law.

It is the mentors and disciples of the Soka Gakkai who have revived the great path of Nichiren Buddhism in the present age, widening and expanding it further so that today it connects people throughout the world.

The mentor of the "*kosen-rufu* of the entity of the Law (the Gohonzon)" is Nichiren Daishonin—the Buddha of the Latter Day who revealed the Law of Nam-myoho-renge-kyo for the enlightenment of all humanity into the eternal future and set forth the method for its propagation.

The Soka Gakkai is an organization carrying out the Buddha's will and decree. It is a harmonious gathering of believers directly connected to Nichiren and has spread Nichiren Buddhism throughout the world while overcoming countless hardships and obstacles.

Kosen-rufu is a struggle to help all people transcend the suffering of death and actualize lives of genuine happiness, thus establishing a world in which genuine peace prevails. This is the true purpose of Nichiren's propagation.

The Soka Gakkai's founding president, Tsunesaburo Makiguchi, fully inherited this spirit and set an example of selfless dedication to Buddhism by giving his life for his beliefs. The second president, Josei Toda, carried on Mr. Makiguchi's struggle with the same unwavering commitment. He established the ideals and practice of the Soka Gakkai and laid the framework for the harmonious community of believers founded on the spirit of "many in body, one in mind."

Earnestly following this great path of mentor and disciple, upholding the principles of humanism and pacifism that are the essence of Nichiren Buddhism, I have spread its essential message across the globe through the pursuit of dialogue. When this path followed by the first, second and third presidents of the Soka Gakkai flows vibrantly as the lifeblood transmitting the philosophy and practice of Nichiren Buddhism throughout the world, the foundation of *kosen-rufu* in the present age will have been completed. The crucial five-year period for completing this process has now begun.

"Attain a state of life of true happiness based on the heritage of faith, and enable others to do the same."

The True Meaning of Heritage Is the Heritage of Faith

"The important point is to carry out your practice confident that Nam-myoho-renge-kyo alone is the heritage that was transferred from Shakyamuni and Many Treasures to Bodhisattva Superior Practices" (WND-1, 217).

"Be resolved to summon forth the great power of faith, and chant Nam-myoho-renge-kyo with the prayer that your faith will be steadfast and correct at the moment of death. Never seek any other way to inherit the ultimate Law of life and death, and manifest it in your life. Only then will you realize that earthly desires are enlightenment, and that the sufferings of birth and death are nirvana. Even embracing the Lotus Sutra would be useless without the heritage of faith" (WND-1, 218).

At the conclusion of this writing, Nichiren Daishonin emphasizes the "heritage of faith." Again, he says, "Even embracing the Lotus Sutra would be useless without the heritage of faith" (WND-1, 218).

Exactly 50 years ago, my mentor, Josei Toda, lectured on this writing in Kansai, where our organization's motto is "Ever-victorious." During that stirring lecture, he said to the members so dear to him: "Please attain a state of life of true happiness based on the heritage of faith, and please enable others to do the same."

The heritage of the ultimate Law of life and death starts to flow and spread throughout society when we make a vow to join our mentor in joyfully propagating the Mystic Law.

I deeply believe that the present emergence of a great global network of Bodhisattvas of the Earth will lead to a profound change in the way humanity perceives life and death; it will cause the heritage of peace, humanism and happiness to flow swift and strong throughout the world; it will spark a fundamental transformation in the life-state of all humankind.

And I entrust the realization of this noble mission to my fellow members throughout the world. I have faith in my disciples. Above all, I am counting on the youth.

1. Dependent origination: A Buddhist doctrine expressing the interdependence of all things. It teaches that no beings or phenomena exist on their own; they exist or occur because of their relationship with other beings and phenomena.

KEY POINTS

Transcending the Extremes of Annihilation and Permanence

The wisdom or insight that enabled Shakyamuni to attain enlightenment represents the wisdom that conquers the delusion and suffering related to death. Based on this wisdom, the Buddha rejected the two most common views of death, which represented two extremes, and both of which he considered erroneous. Neither could fully enable people to transcend the fear and uncertainty of death. One of these was the view of death as the annihilation or complete cessation of self (the view of annihilation), while the other was the view of death as the self continuing in the form of an unchanging immortal soul or spirit (the view of permanence). Both views consider the question of life and death only from the point of birth until one's demise, with life and death seen as opposites. As such, neither view embodies the wisdom that correctly perceives the true reality of life and death. (p. 3)

Functions of the Mystic Law

The Mystic Law is the eternal, infinite Law of the universe. This eternal Law embodies the phases of life and death. In other words, the two phases are themselves the rhythm of the eternal Law and appear as the life and death of countless living entities—as the arising and extinction of all phenomena, as all kinds of causes and effects in every dimension, as the harmony and dynamism of the universe as a whole. (p. 5)

Mentor and Disciple Transmit the Heritage

Nichiren Daishonin begins by saying that the "ultimate Law of life and death" is Myoho-renge-kyo, and that Myoho-renge-kyo is the heritage that Bodhisattva Superior Practices [the leader of the Bodhisattvas of the Earth] received from Shakyamuni Buddha and Many Treasures Buddha.

As mentioned earlier, only through living and taking action with the spirit of selfless dedication for the sake of Buddhism can Myoho-renge-kyo be transmitted as the ultimate Law of life and death. Therefore, Nichiren cites the name of Bodhisattva Superior Practices as the teacher or mentor who takes on the commitment to live and take action with this spirit. He explains that the "heritage of the ultimate Law of life and death" only flows in faith based on the oneness of mentor and disciple. (p. 6)

The Great Vow of *Kosen-rufu*

Nichiren declares that the heritage of the Law that enables all people to attain enlightenment is found in the path he opened for *kosen-rufu*, or widespread propagation, in the Latter Day of the Law.

Nichiren then emphasizes the profound karmic bonds of mentor and disciple that link him and Sairen-bo, to whom this writing is addressed and who had weathered persecution on account of upholding Nichiren's teaching. To cherish the same great desire and to fight with the same spirit of selfless commitment as the mentor, even in the face of arduous difficulties, is the path of the oneness of mentor and disciple in the struggle for *kosen-rufu* in the Latter Day of the Law. (p. 8)

DIALOGUE AND REFLECTION

1) "Both views [annihilation and permanence] consider the question of life and death only from the point of birth until one's demise, with life and death seen as opposites. As such, neither view embodies the wisdom that correctly perceives the true reality of life and death" (p. 3). How has the Buddhist view of life and death affected your own view?

2) "Nichiren declares that the heritage of the Law that enables all people to attain enlightenment is found in the path he opened for *kosen-rufu*, or widespread propagation, in the Latter Day of the Law" (p. 8). How has your dedication to *kosen-rufu* changed and how has that affected your practice and faith?

The Heritage of the ULTIMATE LAW *of* LIFE

SGI PRESIDENT IKEDA'S STUDY LECTURE SERIES

This is a series of lectures by SGI President Daisaku Ikeda on "The Heritage of the Ultimate Law of Life." Nichiren Daishonin states: "Shakyamuni Buddha who attained enlightenment countless kalpas ago, the Lotus Sutra that leads all people to Buddhahood, and we ordinary human beings are in no way different or separate from one another. To chant Myoho-renge-kyo with this realization is to inherit the ultimate Law of life and death."

[2]

The True Heritage

Freeing Humanity From the Sufferings of Birth and Death by Bringing the Wisdom of the Mystic Law To Flow Forth

The Passage From "The Heritage of the Ultimate Law of Life"

I have just carefully read your letter. To reply, the ultimate Law of life and death as transmitted from the Buddha to all living beings is Myoho-renge-kyo. The five characters of Myoho-renge-kyo were transferred from Shakyamuni and Many Treasures, the two Buddhas inside the treasure tower, to Bodhisattva Superior Practices, carrying on a heritage unbroken since the infinite past.

(The Writings of Nichiren Daishonin, *vol. 1, p. 216)*

Nichiren Daishonin wrote "The Heritage of the Ultimate Law of Life" in response to a question from Sairen-bo, a learned priest, formerly of the Tendai school, who had become a follower of Nichiren while Nichiren was on Sado Island. It would seem Sairen-bo had written asking him about the "heritage of the ultimate Law of life and death," a term used in the esoteric doctrine of the Tendai school at the time.

"I have just carefully read your letter," Nichiren writes, indicating that he has closely examined Sairen-bo's concerns (WND-1, 216). Perhaps Sairen-bo had written to him in great detail about the teachings he had learned thus far, expressing his thoughts, questions and problem areas. Nichiren acknowledges that he has read Sairen-bo's letter carefully and that he understands his query. We get a clear sense of the mentor's compassionate spirit to respond to the disciple's concerns.

Myoho-renge-kyo Is the Ultimate Law of Life and Death

In response to Sairen-bo's question, Nichiren Daishonin first clarifies the most essential point—that the ultimate Law of life and death, which is the heritage transmitted by the Buddha, is Myoho-renge-kyo (see WND-1, 216). This is a declaration that the supreme teaching enabling people to fundamentally overcome the sufferings of birth and death is none other than Myoho-renge-kyo (the Mystic Law). As the basis for this claim, Nichiren makes two principal points in this writing.

First, he shows the legitimacy of the heritage of the Lotus Sutra, which is seen in the Buddhas Shakyamuni and Many Treasures entrusting Myoho-renge-kyo to Bodhisattva Superior Practices, the leader of the Bodhisattvas of the Earth. In this installment, I will discuss the significance of this point.

Second, Nichiren considers why Myoho-renge-kyo is the supreme teaching for surmounting the sufferings of birth and death. In the course of that discussion, he indicates that the birth and death of all living beings, the arising and extinction of all phenomena, constitute life and death as functions of Myoho-renge-kyo. In other words, all birth and death, all occurring phenomena, represent transitions or instances of emergence and extinction, which are part of the rhythm of the great Law of the universe itself. We need to reappraise the meaning of birth and death in the context of human beings from this all-encompassing perspective of existence. I will take this up for discussion in the next and subsequent installments.

The Legitimacy of the Heritage of the Lotus Sutra

Next, Nichiren Daishonin writes, "The five characters of Myoho-renge-kyo were transferred from Shakyamuni and Many Treasures, the two Buddhas inside the treasure tower, to Bodhisattva Superior Practices" (WND-1, 216). Here, he clarifies, in terms of the legitimacy of the heritage, that Myoho-renge-kyo is the ultimate Law that can free people from the sufferings of birth and death, and that it is the heritage to be passed on. In other words, he indicates that the supreme legitimacy of Myoho-renge-kyo rests on the fact that it is the teaching or Law that was transferred from Shakyamuni and Many Treasures, seated side by side in the Treasure Tower, to Bodhisattva Superior Practices during the Lotus Sutra's Ceremony in the Air.

In the Ceremony in the Air, Buddhas and bodhisattvas from throughout the entire universe—hailing from the ten directions and the three existences of past, present and future—assemble before the two Buddhas Shakyamuni and Many Treasures. It is a solemn ceremony conducted on a gigantic scale, centering on the enormous Treasure Tower adorned with the seven kinds of treasures, which is suspended in the air.

In the centuries after the Buddha's passing, few people delved closely into why and for whom this ceremony was conducted. Only Nichiren Daishonin directly focused on these questions and interpreted them in terms of his life.

What was the purpose of the Ceremony in the Air? It was to actualize the Buddha's great wish of universal enlightenment. To realize this goal, it was vital to enable people in the evil age after the Buddha's passing to attain Buddhahood. The Ceremony in the Air was thus an event in which this mission of universal enlightenment was entrusted to the Bodhisattvas of the Earth. Since attaining Buddhahood, at the essential level, means overcoming the sufferings of birth and death, the true heritage that is the ultimate Law of life and death is found in the Ceremony in the Air, where this entrustment takes place.

To recap, at the outset of this writing, Nichiren first affirms that Myoho-renge-kyo is the ultimate Law of life and death and the heritage passed on by the Buddha, offering as proof its entrustment to Bodhisattva Superior Practices by Shakyamuni and Many Treasures. These opening passages therefore seem designed to underscore the legitimacy of the heritage of Myoho-renge-kyo.

I will clarify this point by considering the respective roles or functions of Shakyamuni, Many Treasures and Superior Practices.

The Functions of Shakyamuni, Many Treasures and Superior Practices

1) Shakyamuni Buddha: The Correctness and Appropriateness of the Law

The first point in considering the ceremony of entrustment is, who did the entrusting? The fact that the Law for enlightenment is transferred directly from Shakyamuni—the Buddha of the *saha* world [this world of suffering], also the eternal Buddha who attained enlightenment in the remote past—means that it is the correct teaching that enables those who dwell in this strife-filled *saha* world to free themselves from the sufferings of birth and death.

As described in the "Life Span" chapter of the Lotus Sutra, Shakyamuni is the eternal Buddha at one with the eternal Mystic Law. He is also a Buddha who resides in the reality of the *saha* world and works unceasingly to spread the Law. We can believe and accept, therefore, that the Law transferred by Shakyamuni is the fundamental Law that can liberate all people from the sufferings of birth and death, enabling them to attain Buddhahood. We could say that the transferal of Myoho-renge-kyo by Shakyamuni, as the Buddha who attained enlightenment in the remote past, clearly revealed Myoho-renge-kyo to be the correct, appropriate teaching for leading all people to enlightenment.

2) Many Treasures Buddha: The Universality of the Law

Second, the function of Many Treasures is to attest to the universality of the principles of the Lotus Sutra. According to the sutra, Many Treasures is a Buddha of eons past, who, even after entering nirvana, appears without fail wherever the Lotus Sutra is expounded in order to attest to its veracity (see *The Lotus Sutra*, p. 171). The ceremony of entrustment takes place with Many Treasures Buddha seated beside Shakyamuni Buddha. The presence of Many Treasures, in a sense, demonstrates the universal truth of Myoho-renge-kyo, the heritage that Shakyamuni Buddha entrusted to Bodhisattva Superior Practices.

3) Bodhisattva Superior Practices: An Active Practitioner Who Possesses, Manifests and Propagates the Law

The third component is the existence of those who will actually propagate Myoho-renge-kyo after Shakyamuni's passing. Why was it that the Law had to be entrusted to Bodhisattva Superior Practices? Why was that responsibility not given to the bodhisattvas of the theoretical teaching or the bodhisattvas from other worlds gathered at the Ceremony in the Air? This is an important point regarding who is qualified to propagate the Mystic Law after the Buddha's passing.

The bodhisattvas of the theoretical teaching and the bodhisattvas from other worlds were resplendent in appearance and bearing, justly inspiring awe and reverence in living beings. They were not, however, followers who had received instruction from the Buddha in the remote past, meaning that they were not in possession of the Law originally expounded at that time. They were bodhisattvas who still subscribed to the view that one could first attain enlightenment only after countless eons of arduous Buddhist practice—that one could only achieve Buddhahood by eliminating the earthly desires of the nine worlds.[1] These bodhisattvas were passed over for the entrustment of the Law because they did not embody the principle of "the mutual possession of the Ten Worlds".[2] Simply put, these bodhisattvas may have been endowed with various outstanding physical and spiritual characteristics and enjoyed widespread veneration, but they could not function as leaders capable of awakening people to their Buddha nature and leading them to enlightenment. In this respect, there is a huge difference between the fundamental view of attaining Buddhahood held by the Bodhisattvas of the Earth and that held by the bodhisattvas of the theoretical teaching or the bodhisattvas from other worlds.

The fundamental Law for attaining Buddhahood is originally inherent in life itself. Therefore, its existence can only be communicated to others through personal interaction and efforts to awaken them to their inner Buddha nature.

In addition, the teaching of the Lotus Sutra relates that Superior Practices is a bodhisattva who has been thoroughly trained as a disciple of Shakyamuni from the remote past and consequently is in possession of the Law originally expounded at that time. Only when Myoho-renge-kyo is spread by the Bodhisattvas of the Earth, with the struggle of Bodhisattva Superior Practices leading the way, does it become the ultimate teaching that can liberate all people from the sufferings of birth and death.

Thus, in the transmission of the heritage in the Lotus Sutra's Ceremony in the Air, we have the three components: 1) the Law's correctness and appropriateness; 2) the Law's universality; and 3) an active practitioner. The heritage transmitted in this context constitutes the ultimate Law of life and death that can cure the sufferings of all humankind.

Awakening People to the Mystic Truth Inherent in Their Lives

Next, Nichiren Daishonin says that the five characters of Myoho-renge-kyo entrusted to Bodhisattva Superior Practices by Shakyamuni and Many Treasures constitute a heritage unbroken since the infinite past (see WND-1, 216). This may be taken as a clarification of the significance of Bodhisattva Superior Practices carrying on the heritage of the Law. First, a "heritage unbroken since the infinite past" implies that the life of Bodhisattva Superior Practices is originally endowed with Myoho-renge-kyo, the eternal Mystic Law.

At the start of "On Attaining Buddhahood in This Lifetime," Nichiren writes, "This truth [the mystic truth that is originally inherent in all living beings] is Myoho-renge-kyo" (WND-1, 3). All living beings are fundamentally entities of Myoho-renge-kyo, which is the originally inherent truth. But, owing to innate darkness or ignorance, ordinary people of the Latter Day of the Law are deluded and unaware of the truth of their lives. Because of this ignorance, they cannot overcome the sufferings of birth and death.

The power that enables us to manifest life's inherent mystic truth is the power of wisdom.

It is precisely by believing in the fundamental power of our lives and manifesting the mystic truth inherent within us that we can surmount these sufferings. And it is the noble mission of Bodhisattvas of the Earth, with Bodhisattva Superior Practices at the lead, to teach, reveal and unlock the Mystic Law—the Law inherent in life and the fundamental source of all power—for those thus deluded.

The "Emerging from the Earth" chapter of the Lotus Sutra says that before the Bodhisattvas of the Earth made their appearance as the earth split open, they "[dwelled] in the world of empty space underneath the saha world" (LS, 213). Just what is the "empty space underneath the saha world"? The Great Teacher T'ien-t'ai of China describes it as being in the "utmost depth of the essential nature of phenomena and the ultimate of profound Buddhist principles" ("The Unanimous Declaration by the Buddhas of the Three Existences regarding the Classification of the Teachings and Which Are to Be Abandoned and Which Upheld," WND-2, 843). Very simply, it means that the Bodhisattvas of the Earth dwelled in a state at one with Myoho-renge-kyo—the mystic truth inherent in all life—and emerged from that place into the actual world.

A "heritage unbroken since the infinite past" thus indicates that Bodhisattva Superior Practices is always in a state at one with the eternal Mystic Law. This is what enables him to manifest the mystic truth inherent in people's lives and open the way for all to free themselves from the sufferings of birth and death.

When we take a look at this unbroken heritage from the infinite past on an even profounder and also more practical level, crucial characteristics of Bodhisattva Superior Practices and the Bodhisattvas of the Earth come clearly to the fore. First, in terms of the practical significance of this heritage, the fact that Bodhisattva Superior Practices excels in the power of wisdom to manifest the Mystic Law in his life means that he can do so at will at any time. Second, the fact that he excels in the power of practice to propagate the Law means that he can spread it in even the most evil, defiled age. These two points are considered vital in terms of bringing the heritage of the ultimate Law of life and death to flow in the people's lives in this *saha* world.

The Power of the Heart To Manifest the Mystic Law

Next, let us confirm the fact that Bodhisattva Superior Practices excels in the power to manifest Myoho-renge-kyo. The power that enables us to manifest life's inherent mystic truth is the power of wisdom to break through darkness or ignorance and is ultimately the same as the Buddha's enlightenment. Of the bodhisattvas at the Ceremony in the Air, only Bodhisattva Superior Practices, whose mission is to take the lead in manifesting the Law, is endowed with this supreme power of wisdom. His name is Superior Practices precisely because of his incomparable excellence in practice. The countless Bodhisattvas of the Earth who follow him can acquire the same wisdom he possesses through the principle of "substituting faith for wisdom." In this sense, the Bodhisattvas of the Earth also excel in the power of faith. When we reconsider the Bodhisattvas of the Earth from the standpoint of the power of wisdom and the power of faith—from the standpoint of the power of the heart—their true nature becomes clearer.

The teaching of the Lotus Sutra indicates that the Bodhisattvas of the Earth have been disciples of Shakyamuni since the remote past of his original enlightenment, and that they have been rigorously trained since that time, having learned, awakened to and devoted themselves to spreading the Law to which the Buddha had become enlightened.

In a discussion of these characteristics of the Bodhisattvas of the Earth in "The Object of Devotion for Observing the Mind," Nichiren Daishonin cites such great Buddhist teachers of China as T'ien-t'ai, Miao-lo and Tao-hsien as follows (WND-1, 371–72):

> [The Buddha said of the Bodhisattvas of the Earth,] "These are my disciples, destined to propagate my Law."
>
> (T'ien-t'ai, *The Words and Phrases of the Lotus Sutra*)

> The children propagate the Law of the father, and this benefits the world.
>
> (Miao-lo, *The Annotations on "The Words and Phrases of the Lotus Sutra"*)

> The Law embodied therein [in the Lotus Sutra] is the Law that was realized countless kalpas in the past, and therefore it was entrusted to persons who had been the Buddha's disciples from countless kalpas in the past.
>
> (Tao-hsien, *The Supplement to "The Words and Phrases of the Lotus Sutra"*)

Based on this, Nichiren states that the bodhisattvas of the provisional and theoretical teachings were not in possession of the supreme Law, so they could not possibly appear and propagate it in the Latter Day (see WND-1, 372). Of course, in this context, being in possession of the supreme Law does not simply mean inherently possessing the mystic truth in one's life. Rather, we can interpret it to mean excelling in the power of the heart to break through darkness or ignorance and to manifest the mystic truth. This is a vital requirement for revealing the mystic truth in one's life and teaching others, no matter how evil the age. And it is only in the efforts of such individuals that the heritage of the ultimate Law of life and death flows.

Hence, in another of his writings, in a discussion of what sets the Bodhisattvas of the

Earth apart from other exemplary bodhisattvas of the theoretical teachings and other worlds, such as Wonderful Sound, Manjushri and Medicine King, Nichiren cites the fact that the Bodhisattvas of the Earth are the "ones who had thoroughly forged their resolve" ("General Stone Tiger," WND-1, 953).

The Power of Practice To Spread the Mystic Law

In addition to excelling in the power of the heart to manifest the Mystic Law, another characteristic of the Bodhisattvas of the Earth is their excelling in the power of practice to spread the Mystic Law. At the core of this power of practice lies a vow for *kosen-rufu*, which is the key to propagating the Law in this *saha* world after the Buddha's passing.

In the "Supernatural Powers" chapter of the Lotus Sutra, the Bodhisattvas of the Earth, led by Superior Practices, vow to propagate the Law in an age when the Buddha is no longer present. This vow becomes the driving force behind the power of practice directed toward spreading the teaching in such a troubled, defiled age. In a world rife with evil, the darkness or ignorance shrouding people's lives is deep and pervasive, and those who seek to spread the Mystic Law are sure to encounter great obstacles and persecution. The power to turn back and overcome the polluted current of such an age lies in a solid vow to propagate the Law.

The "Emerging from the Earth" chapter of the Lotus Sutra explains that the Bodhisattvas of the Earth possess the power of practice with which to boldly shoulder the task of propagation in an evil age. They overflow with the vigor that enables them to blaze new frontiers. The sutra describes the characteristic features of these bodhisattvas as "firm in their intent and thought" (corresponding to an unshakable vow), as "[having] the power of great perseverance" (corresponding to the strength to endure hardships) and as "clever at difficult questions and answers" (corresponding to the power of *shakubuku* and the power of speech) (see LS, 216 and 223).

Ultimately, it is only through the power of the heart and the power of practice that the Law of life, Myoho-renge-kyo, can be transmitted to all humankind. The heritage entrusted to and carried on by the Bodhisattvas of the Earth is the "heritage of faith," which Nichiren emphasizes in this writing (WND-1, 218).

The SGI Is a Gathering of Honorable, Courageous Bodhisattvas of the Earth

The second Soka Gakkai president, Josei Toda, often used to call out to our members in the early days of our movement: "Bodhisattvas of the Earth! Let's do it!" "My fellow Bodhisattvas of the Earth! Let's rise into action!"

A member from those days later said, humorously: "When President Toda used to address us as Bodhisattvas of the Earth, at first I didn't think he was talking to us. In all honesty, the idea that we who had so many worries on account of poverty and illness, and who were constantly having family quarrels, were Bodhisattvas of the Earth just didn't seem to add up. I always thought to myself, 'The day will surely come when such outstanding people take faith.'" Humor aside, this may well have been how many members felt. But those who took on the challenges presented by their karma and valiantly forged ahead in the struggle for *kosen-rufu* were honorable, courageous Bodhisattvas of the Earth. This is an indisputable fact that history has proven.

First and foremost, President Toda was himself a leader of the Bodhisattvas of the Earth. While in prison, he gained the profound realization that he was a Bodhisattva of the Earth. After his release, he stood up alone in the desolate ruins of postwar Japan and brought forth a legion of fellow Bodhisattvas of the Earth numbering 750,000 households.

President Toda waged a spiritual struggle to awaken in each person's heart that he or she was a Bodhisattva of the Earth. Citing Nichiren Daishonin's writings, he repeatedly taught that Soka Gakkai members occupy the position of great bodhisattvas, far surpassing even the founders of other Buddhist schools. Mr. Toda wrote: "How can we explain our being granted such an exalted station? It is because in the past we were present at the assembly together with Bodhisattva Superior Practices as Bodhisattvas of the Earth; and because now, as children of the original Buddha [Nichiren Daishonin], we are exerting ourselves in the practice of *shakubuku* of the Latter Day of the Law. We who have such a lofty station must ensure that we never fall into the same state of life as those who have no belief, erroneous belief or inferior belief. At the same time, we must base ourselves on a state of compassion and never look down on such individuals."

The whole purpose of the heritage of the Law is for all people to attain Buddhahood.

President Toda urged us to manifest the power of the heart—that is, to awaken as Bodhisattvas of the Earth and bring forth the spirit of compassion to help all people achieve happiness. All those who stood up in response to his impassioned cry fought as emissaries of the Buddha in the reality of the defiled age of the Latter Day, when slander and abuse abound. And every one of them dramatically transformed his or her life.

In other words, when we awaken to our mission as Bodhisattvas of the Earth to help others revitalize their lives on the most fundamental level, we savor unsurpassed joy. We feel a sense of deep fulfillment that our lives are expanding and growing.

Whenever we threw ourselves into our struggles as disciples of President Toda, the power of practice, the inherent power of Bodhisattvas of the Earth and the power to battle evil would surge forth within us with incredible force, enabling us to break the chains of destiny for ourselves and help others do the same.

We changed from people who sought help into people who helped others. Countless dramas of people changing their lives through faith rippled throughout the land, leading to vast new numbers of Bodhisattvas of the Earth appearing. And all of them went on to achieve strong, secure lives, as they overcame the sufferings of birth and death, and devoted themselves to constructing eternal happiness. And the emergence of Bodhisattvas of the Earth has now spread throughout the world.

What can we say unequivocally of the Soka Gakkai's brilliant history, in light of Buddhism's history as a whole? First, that *kosen-rufu*—the widespread propagation of the Law—means calling forth the Bodhisattvas of the Earth in great numbers throughout the world in the Latter Day and, through their struggle, leading countless people to enlightenment. And second, that this is the ultimate purpose of the transmission of the heritage in the Ceremony in the Air.

The whole purpose of the heritage of the Law is for all people to attain Buddhahood. That is the reason for the Ceremony in the Air and for the entrustment of the five characters of Myoho-renge-kyo from Shakyamuni to Bodhisattva Superior Practices. In the Latter Day, it was the original Buddha, Nichiren Daishonin, who, in terms of his behavior, performed the role of Bodhisattva Superior Practices in opening the flow of the heritage of the Law to all people.

In other words, as we see in the Ceremony of the Air, being entrusted with the heritage proves the legitimacy of the person who exerts practical efforts to lead people to enlightenment through the power of the Mystic Law. At the same time, the legitimate heritage is carried on in the process of the supreme Law that Shakyamuni entrusted to Bodhisattva Superior Practices being propagated in the Latter Day, when Superior Practices and his fellow Bodhisattvas of the Earth appear and embark on a struggle to spread Myoho-renge-kyo—first among the people of Japan and then to all humankind.

Nichiren writes: "Bodhisattva Superior Practices received the water of the wisdom of the Mystic Law from the Thus Come One Shakyamuni and causes it to flow into the wasteland of the people's lives in the evil world of the latter age. This is the function of wisdom" ("The Essentials for Attaining Buddhahood," WND-1, 746–47). The key to carrying on the heritage of the Law is faith. Only through faith can we draw forth the power of the heart and the power of practice of Bodhisattvas of the Earth. Only when we have faith does the heritage come into being. Without faith, there is no heritage.

The Soka Gakkai is a gathering of Bodhisattvas of the Earth that was founded by Tsunesaburo Makiguchi and Josei Toda, mentor and disciple, and accords with the Buddha's decree. Its history is one of spreading the Mystic Law throughout the world based on the heritage of faith. Because of the great struggles of the Soka Gakkai's first three presidents, Bodhisattvas of the Earth have now appeared all over the globe. This global transmission of the heritage of faith means that the heritage of the ultimate Law of life and death has now spread throughout the world. I firmly believe that this is the true purpose of the heritage being transferred from Shakyamuni Buddha to Bodhisattva Superior Practices in the Ceremony in the Air.

1. Illusions, defilements, impurities, earthly passions or, simply, desires. A generic term for all the workings of life that cause one psychological and physical suffering and impede the quest for enlightenment, including desires and illusions in the general sense.

2. A principle formulated by T'ien-t'ai on the basis of the Lotus Sutra stating that each of the Ten Worlds possesses the potential for all ten within itself.

KEY POINTS

The Ultimate Law of Life and Death

This is a declaration that the supreme teaching enabling people to fundamentally overcome the sufferings of birth and death is none other than Myoho-renge-kyo (the Mystic Law). As the basis for this claim, Nichiren makes two principal points in this writing.

First, he shows the legitimacy of the heritage of the Lotus Sutra, which is seen in the Buddhas Shakyamuni and Many Treasures entrusting Myoho-renge-kyo to Bodhisattva Superior Practices, the leader of the Bodhisattvas of the Earth.

Second, Nichiren considers why Myoho-renge-kyo is the supreme teaching for surmounting the sufferings of birth and death. All birth and death, all occurring phenomena, represent transitions or instances of emergence and extinction, which are part of the rhythm of the great Law of the universe itself. We need to reappraise the meaning of birth and death in the context of human beings from this all-encompassing perspective of existence. (p. 12)

The Power of the Heart

Of the bodhisattvas at the Ceremony in the Air, only Bodhisattva Superior Practices, whose mission is to take the lead in manifesting the Law, is endowed with this supreme power of wisdom. His name is Superior Practices precisely because of his incomparable excellence in practice. The countless Bodhisattvas of the Earth who follow him can acquire the same wisdom he possesses through the principle of "substituting faith for wisdom." In this sense, the Bodhisattvas of the Earth also excel in the power of faith. When we reconsider the Bodhisattvas of the Earth from the standpoint of the power of wisdom and the power of faith—from the standpoint of the power of the heart—their true nature becomes clearer. (p. 16)

Spreading the Mystic Law

In addition to excelling in the power of the heart to manifest the Mystic Law, another characteristic of the Bodhisattvas of the Earth is their excelling in the power of practice to spread the Mystic Law. At the core of this power of practice lies a vow for *kosen-rufu*, which is the key to propagating the Law in this *saha* world after the Buddha's passing.

In the "Supernatural Powers" chapter of the Lotus Sutra, the Bodhisattvas of the Earth, led by Superior Practices, vow to propagate the Law in an age when the Buddha is no longer present. This vow becomes the driving force behind the power of practice directed toward spreading the teaching in such a troubled, defiled age. In a world rife with evil, the darkness or ignorance shrouding people's lives is deep and pervasive, and those who seek to spread the Mystic Law are sure to encounter great obstacles and persecution. The power to turn back and overcome the polluted current of such an age lies in a solid vow to propagate the Law. (p. 17)

DIALOGUE AND REFLECTION

1) "Whenever we threw ourselves into our struggles as disciples of President Toda, the power of practice, the inherent power of Bodhisattvas of the Earth and the power to battle evil would surge forth within us with incredible force, enabling us to break the chains of destiny for ourselves and help others do the same. We changed from people who sought help into people who helped others" (p. 18). How has helping others in their practice affected your life?

2) "The Soka Gakkai is a gathering of Bodhisattvas of the Earth that was founded by Tsunesaburo Makiguchi and Josei Toda, mentor and disciple, and accords with the Buddha's decree. Because of the great struggles of the Soka Gakkai's first three presidents, Bodhisattvas of the Earth have now appeared all over the globe" (p. 19). What have you learned from the three founding presidents of the Soka Gakkai?

The Heritage of the ULTIMATE LAW *of* LIFE

SGI PRESIDENT IKEDA'S STUDY LECTURE SERIES

This is a series of lectures by SGI President Daisaku Ikeda on "The Heritage of the Ultimate Law of Life." Nichiren Daishonin states: "Shakyamuni Buddha who attained enlightenment countless kalpas ago, the Lotus Sutra that leads all people to Buddhahood, and we ordinary human beings are in no way different or separate from one another. To chant Myoho-renge-kyo with this realization is to inherit the ultimate Law of life and death."

[3]

Awakening to the Inherent Nature of Life and Death

Gaining True Hope and Freedom

In the previous installment, I discussed Nichiren Daishonin's statement that Myoho-renge-kyo—the heritage passed on from the Buddhas Shakyamuni and Many Treasures[1] to Bodhisattva Superior Practices[2] during the Ceremony in the Air in the Lotus Sutra—is the "ultimate Law of life and death" (*The Writings of Nichiren Daishonin*, vol. 1, p. 216).[3]

In the passage we will be studying this time, Nichiren goes on to explain the profound relationship between "life and death" and "Myoho-renge-kyo." This section can be read as an expression of the inner realization of Nichiren Daishonin, of Bodhisattva Superior Practices, whose life—as I mentioned last time—has in truth, throughout the infinite past, never been separated from Myoho-renge-kyo. This following section clarifies the theoretical grounds for the designation of Myoho-renge-kyo as the "ultimate Law of life and death."

Life and Death Are Part of the Inherent Rhythm of the Mystic Law

> ***Myo* represents death, and *ho*, life. Living beings that pass through the two phases of life and death are the entities of the Ten Worlds, or the entities of Myoho-renge-kyo [literally, "or the lotus of the entity"].**
>
> **T'ien-t'ai says that one should understand that living beings and their environments, and the causes and effects at work within them, are all the Law of *renge* (the lotus).[4] Here "living beings and their**

environments" means the phenomena of life and death. Thus, it is clear that, where life and death exist, cause and effect, or the Law of the lotus, is at work.

The Great Teacher Dengyo states, "The two phases of life and death are the wonderful workings of one mind. The two ways of existence and nonexistence are the true functions of an inherently enlightened mind."[5] No phenomena—either heaven or earth, yin or yang,[6] the sun or the moon, the five planets,[7] or any of the worlds from hell to Buddhahood—are free from the two phases of life and death. Life and death are simply the two functions of Myoho-renge-kyo. In his *Great Concentration and Insight,* T'ien-t'ai says, "Arising is the arising of the essential nature of the Law, and extinction is the extinction of that nature." Shakyamuni and Many Treasures, the two Buddhas, are also the two phases of life and death. (WND-1, 216)

First, Nichiren Daishonin explains that *myo* (mystic) represents death, and *ho* (law), life. This means that the Mystic Law itself embodies the "two phases of life and death," or life in its totality. Put another way, life and death are inherent and integral parts of the Mystic Law, the fundamental Law of the universe. Indeed, they constitute its innate rhythm.

Based on the concept of dependent origination,[8] Buddhism holds that all things exist together in mutual interdependence and that nothing exists in isolation. Living beings, phenomena and their various causes and conditions arise, change and disappear amid an infinite web of interconnectedness. When we think about it, the fact that the universe is boundlessly interconnected and that the life and death of all individual beings are part of that is something truly wondrous and unfathomable. This is why the Law of the universe is called the Mystic Law.

In "The Heritage of the Ultimate Law of Life," Nichiren draws the distinction that *myo* (mystic) represents death and *ho* (law), life. Because *ho* indicates manifest phenomena, it corresponds to life that is manifested as individual living beings. *Myo,* on the other hand, indicating that which is mysterious or inscrutable, corresponds to death, reflecting the fact that the vast universe into which all life fuses at death is difficult to fathom. But the main point of this statement, I believe, is to show that the life and death of all living beings in the infinite tapestry of the universe are functions of the Mystic Law.

The Metaphor of the Ocean and Waves

The relationship between the Mystic Law and life and death could be described as being similar to a wave appearing on the surface of the ocean and then submerging back into the ocean again, wherein the ocean represents the Mystic Law, and the wave, an individual life or phenomenon. The pattern of waves arising from the ocean and then returning to it corresponds to the cycle of birth and death. It must be noted, however, that individual lives do not get swallowed up upon death in the ocean of the Mystic Law and disappear in the same way that a casual observer may see ordinary waves disappearing into the ocean.

If we consider that there are various currents flowing through the ocean not visible from the surface, the difference between life

Seikyo Press

SGI President Ikeda encourages students graduating from the Tokyo Soka Junior and Senior High Schools at their graduation on March 16, 2007. On this occasion, President Ikeda also received the Excellent Accomplishment Award from the Federation of Artistic and Cultural Organizations of Korea.

and death could be likened to that between surface waves and the undulating currents within the ocean's depths. The life essence of an individual is certainly not extinguished at death. Life and death are simply the undulations of the Mystic Law itself. Undulations within the ocean's depths appear on the surface as waves and then submerge again into the ocean, once more becoming invisible undulations. In the same way, a wave of life that manifests on the surface of the ocean of the Mystic Law will, at death, merge once more with that ocean and continue its unseen undulations. Then, when conditions are right, that life essence will appear again as a new wave.

An Existence Originally Joyful, Pure and Bright

Next, Nichiren Daishonin says: "Living beings that pass through the two phases of life and death are the entities of the Ten Worlds" (WND-1, 216). This contains a very important point. The two aspects of life and death—which make up life in its totality—encompass the Ten Worlds, or ten potential states of life inherent in each individual being. This means that all living beings of the Ten Worlds are entities of the Mystic Law that embodies these two phenomena. Or put another way, the phenomena of life and death, inherent in the Mystic Law, are the true substance of the lives of all beings of the Ten Worlds.

For example, let us look at people born into the lowest of the Ten Worlds, the world of hell. While physically experiencing the world of hell (the physical manifestation corresponding to the aspect of life), they also possess within the capacity to experience the other nine worlds. The phenomena of life and death—representing life in its entirety, which is the Mystic Law—are the true substance of their beings.

This is the original and inherent nature of life and death. While filled with anxiety and confusion about the important questions of life and existence, human beings are racked by the sufferings of aging and death. This is because they fail to realize that their own existence is part of the cycle of "birth and death [that] have always been an innate part of life" (*The Record of the Orally Transmitted Teachings*, p. 174). But when we deeply realize this truth, we are liberated from the illusions and sufferings of birth and death.

Based on his profound awakening in prison, Josei Toda, the second Soka Gakkai president, discussed the inherent nature of our lives from time without beginning and described it as a state of life totally free of the illusions of birth and death: "When we observe our existence, we find that [in the remote past of time without beginning] we lived with total freedom in a brilliant realm of purity and joy. We were all beautiful in spirit and of like mind. We who once dwelled in such a sparkling sphere have now all emerged together in this strife-filled *saha* world.

"Looking back, I feel as though it was only yesterday that we lived in that pure, pleasant realm. How could we possibly forget that brilliant place? How could we forget the friends with whom we joyously passed our lives in absolute freedom? And how could we forget the vows we made together at the assembly where the Lotus Sutra was expounded?

"This *saha* world was also originally inhabited by friends who are all joyful and pure and bright and on good terms with one another. Isn't it, therefore, most pitiful and sad that, having been forced to drink the poisons of greed, anger and jealousy by proponents of the provisional Mahayana, Hinayana and non-Buddhist teachings,[9] we have become like deranged children and have all forgotten the remote past?"[10]

Good friends; joyful, pure and bright; dwelling together harmoniously in freedom; who pledged to strive for the happiness of both themselves and others—this describes our original selves of time without beginning, free of all illusion; this describes the realm of time without beginning.

To recover this original self, this realm of time without beginning, we each need to be aware that our own life is an entity of the Mystic Law. And we have to realize that we ourselves possess the power to break free of the chain of causality that gives rise to illusion and leads to suffering.

The Law of the Lotus, the Law of the Simultaneity of Cause and Effect

Nichiren Daishonin says, "Living beings that pass through the two phases of life and death are the entities of the Ten Worlds, or the entities of Myoho-renge-kyo" (WND-1, 216). In this passage, "entity of Myoho-renge-kyo" literally translates as the "lotus of the entity," or the "embodied lotus" (Jpn *totai renge*),[11] and as such expresses the potential for each of us to regain the infinite power of the Mystic Law and restore our original self.

"Lotus," or *renge*, is a metaphor for the simultaneity of cause and effect. With most plants, the flowers bloom first and then the seeds are formed. But with the lotus, the fruit and flowers appear together. If the flowers are likened to the cause and the fruit to the effect, then the lotus, which flowers and seeds at the same time, symbolizes how cause and effect are simultaneous in the Mystic Law.

All living beings have the potential to experience any of the Ten Worlds. But though it may be relatively easy to find ourselves in any of the other nine worlds, bringing forth and experiencing the highest world of Buddhahood is extremely difficult. Why is this?

On deeply pondering and pursuing this question, Shakyamuni Buddha elucidated the causality for revealing the world of Buddhahood. In other words, he clarified the strict law of cause and effect—or principle of causality—that influences and determines a person's state of life in the here and now.

There are two levels to the principle of causality. The first is that of simple karmic retribution—receiving reward or punishment in accord with one's actions. This way of thinking teaches that making good causes leads to happiness, joy and ease, while making bad causes leads to suffering, pain and misery. The second level goes beyond this former idea to reveal a still more fundamental principle of causality governing all life. Buddhism teaches that when we reveal the supreme world of Buddhahood inherent in our lives, we actualize the highest good and can thereby instantly establish a state of unshakable happiness. In other words, it is possible for us—as living beings of the nine worlds, bound by the causality of the three paths (earthly desires, karma and suffering)[12]—to bring forth the effect or fruit of enlightenment by revealing our innate Buddhahood or Buddha nature.

This deeper level of causality taught in Buddhism differs from ordinary temporal cause and effect, or "general causality." At work here is the principle of the simultaneity of cause and effect, which teaches that through a change in the depths of our own hearts or minds, we can bring forth our inherent Buddhahood, right here and now.

Tapping the Great Life Force of the Universe in Our Own Lives

The cycle of birth, death and rebirth—the cycle of transmigration—is a strict causal law that no one can escape. This causality highlights how each individual is responsible for his or her own life, thereby offering a much greater sense of independence and freedom than the idea that the individual is helplessly at the mercy of an arbitrary destiny or fate bestowed by some transcendent, absolute being. But it ultimately leaves people feeling overwhelmed and oppressed by the massive weight of karma they have accumulated over countless existences.

This is where the causality of the Mystic Law comes in. Based on the principle that living beings possess all of the Ten Worlds, it clarifies how we can break free of the heavy weight of accumulated karma by transforming it at the most fundamental level of life itself. Each of us, regardless of what spiritual state we may presently be in, absolutely possesses in the depths of our lives the powerful state of Buddhahood overflowing with supreme wisdom. When we reveal this inner Buddhahood, we can surmount all obstacles. This is the working of "the Law of the lotus" (WND-1, 216)—the law of the simultaneity of cause and effect.

When we awaken to this reality, we can break through any hardship or adversity and positively open up and transform our destiny. This is how we can attain ultimate, indestructible freedom abounding with supreme autonomy. Also, when we are confident of the infinite power within us, an imperturbable hope is born in our hearts. Thus, when difficulties assail us, no matter how serious, we can see them as challenges through which we can demonstrate the power of the Mystic Law within us, and also as wonderful, sought-for opportunities that we should tackle head-on. When we approach things with this positive attitude and tenaciously triumph over each obstacle, we can develop and elevate our own state of life enormously and construct a truly invincible state of freedom. Myoho-renge-kyo is indeed the supreme teaching, bringing people true hope and inner freedom.

Our first Soka Gakkai president, Tsunesaburo Makiguchi, remarked: "The life force of every one of us without exception is a manifestation of the great life force of the universe. Accordingly, the great Law that is the fountainhead of the life force of all universal phenomena, which manifest as agents of that life force—including human beings, which do the same—is the Mystic Law and, as such, is the essence and the substance encompassing all principles governing life."[13]

When we tap the great fundamental life force of the universe inherent in our lives, we achieve a towering state of being in which we can summon up power as immense as the universe itself.

All Universal Phenomena Are the Workings of Compassion

This towering state of life is certainly not governed by a selfish impulse that seeks only personal happiness. Rather, it gives rise to a spirit of mutual support and encouragement directed toward everyone realizing their full potential, and toward drawing forth and harmonizing each person's individuality. To care for and encourage others is compassion—and compassion is a function that pervades the entire universe.

President Toda used to describe the universe as inherently expressing the workings of compassion. He wrote: "In the first place, the universe in its entirety is the substance of the Buddha, and all phenomena in the universe are the workings of compassion. Therefore, compassion is the inherent nature of the universe. . . .

"Since the universe itself is compassion, that of course means that our daily activities naturally constitute the workings of compassion themselves. Because we lead privileged lives as human beings, we must not descend to the same level as animals or plants. Carrying out more exalted activities is the attitude of those truly dedicated to serving the Buddha. . . .

"As Nichiren Daishonin taught, we must chant daimoku with correct faith, encourage others to do the same and foster still more people whose activities naturally abound with compassion."[14]

When we chant Nam-myoho-renge-kyo with the deep conviction that we are entities of the Mystic Law, the fundamental Law of the universe, we can bring forth the great life force of the Mystic Law, which is infused with wisdom and compassion. And we can use it to break through any painful difficulty or obstacle and establish a state of absolute happiness that nothing can destroy. If we continue on this path, then, when the moment of death finally comes, we will savor a state of tremendous inner peace and contentment that derives from maintaining a correct and steadfast attitude in faith. What this means is cherishing the firm conviction that "my life itself is the Mystic Law" and upholding a correct view of life and death based on the Middle Way,[15] while rejecting the views of annihilation or permanence.[16] Achieving a death of that sort is the supreme and ultimate goal of life. Here, both life and death are filled with joy.

At the moment of death, those who complete their present existence with correct and steadfast faith will embody in the very depths of their being the compassionate workings of the universe, which will undoubtedly lead them to once again stand up and make a great vow and embark on a noble struggle for *kosen-rufu*. For we who practice Nichiren Buddhism, death signals the start of a hope-filled journey to our next existence.

1. The two Buddhas Shakyamuni and Many Treasures, who are seated side by side in the Treasure Tower during the Ceremony in the Air described in the Lotus Sutra. Many Treasures appears in order to attest to the truth of Shakyamuni's preaching.
2. Bodhisattva Superior Practices: Leader of the Bodhisattvas of the Earth, disciples of Shakyamuni since the remote past. Shakyamuni entrusts these bodhisattvas with propagation of the Lotus Sutra after his passing.
3. In "Heritage of the Ultimate Law of Life," Nichiren Daishonin writes: "The ultimate Law of life and death as transmitted from the Buddha to all living beings is Myoho-renge-kyo. The five characters of Myoho-renge-kyo were transferred from Shakyamuni and Many Treasures, the two Buddhas inside the treasure tower, to Bodhisattva Superior Practices, carrying on a heritage unbroken since the infinite past" (WND-1, 216).
4. T'ien-t'ai, *The Profound Meaning of the Lotus Sutra.*
5. Dengyo, *The Essential Doctrines Transmitted Within the Tendai Lotus School.*
6. Yin and yang are two universal principles of ancient Chinese philosophy. Yin is the negative, dark and feminine principle; yang is the positive, bright and masculine principle. Their interaction was thought to determine the destiny of all things.
7. Five planets: Mercury, Venus, Mars, Jupiter and Saturn. In the 13th century, the more distant planets were as yet unknown, and Earth was not known to be among the planets.
8. Dependent origination: Also, dependent causation or conditioned co-arising. A fundamental Buddhist doctrine expressing the interdependence of all things. It teaches that no beings or phenomena exist on their own; they exist or occur because of their relationship with other beings or phenomena. Everything in the world comes into existence in response to causes and conditions. That is, nothing can exist independent of other things or arise in isolation. The doctrine of the twelve-linked chain of causation is a well-known illustration of this idea.
9. Provisional Mahayana, Hinayana and non-Buddhist teachings: Teachings prevalent in Japan at the time, in contrast to teaching of the Lotus Sutra, or true Mahayana, which reveals the ultimate truth of the Buddha's enlightenment.
10. Translated from Japanese. Josei Toda, *Toda Josei zenshu* (The Collected Writings of Josei Toda) (Tokyo: Seikyo Shimbunsha, 1985), vol. 1, p. 342.
11. Lotus of the entity: Also, embodied lotus. A reference in the T'ien-t'ai doctrine to the lotus that is the essence of the Lotus Sutra and also the people who are entities of, or who embody, this essence. Nichiren Daishonin described this essence as Myoho-renge-kyo, or Nam-myoho-renge-kyo. In "The Entity of the Mystic Law," he writes: "The supreme principle [that is the Mystic Law] was originally without a name. When the sage was observing the principle and assigning names to all things, he perceived that there is this wonderful single Law [*myoho*] that simultaneously possesses both cause and effect [*renge*], and he named it *Myoho-renge*" (WND-1, 421). The term "lotus of the entity," or "embodied lotus," is contrasted with the "figurative lotus," or the lotus as a metaphor for the Law. Since the lotus of the entity, or lotus of the Law that simultaneously possesses both cause and effect, is difficult to understand, the lotus plant, which blooms and produces fruit at the same time, is employed as a metaphor.
12. Three paths of earthly desires, karma and suffering: They are called paths because one leads to the other. Earthly desires, which include greed, anger, foolishness, arrogance and doubt, give rise to actions that create evil karma. The effect of this evil karma then manifests itself as suffering. Suffering aggravates earthly desires, leading to further misguided action, which in turn brings on more evil karma and suffering. Trapped in this cycle, people are destined to suffer in the lower states of existence known as the six paths.
13. Translated from Japanese. Tsunesaburo Makiguchi, *Makiguchi Tsunesaburo zenshu* (Collected Writings of Tsunesaburo Makiguchi) (Tokyo: Daisanbunmei-sha, 1987), vol. 10, p. 20.
14. Translated from Japanese. Josei Toda, *Toda Josei zenshu* (Collected Writings of Josei Toda) (Tokyo: Seikyo Shimbunsha, 1983), vol.3, pp. 44–45.
15. The way or path that transcends polar extremes. The Middle Way also indicates the true nature of all things, which cannot be defined by the absolutes of existence or nonexistence.
16. This refers to two erroneous ways of viewing death—two extremes. The view of annihilation is the mistaken attachment to the notion that life begins with birth and ends with death. According to this view, there is only the present life, and death represents a complete cessation of existence both physical and spiritual. The view of eternity is also the mistaken notion that what exists here in the present is permanent and unchanging. This view rejects causality, so that neither practicing good nor practicing evil produces any change in one's condition. Shakyamuni Buddha rejected these two extremes and expounded the Middle Way, which he taught is the true and correct path in life.

KEY POINTS

Life and Death Are Part of the Inherent Rhythm of the Mystic Law

Based on the concept of dependent origination, Buddhism holds that all things exist together in mutual interdependence and that nothing exists in isolation. Living beings, phenomena and their various causes and conditions arise, change and disappear amid an infinite web of interconnectedness. When we think about it, the fact that the universe is boundlessly interconnected and that the life and death of all individual beings are part of that is something truly wondrous and unfathomable. This is why the Law of the universe is called the Mystic Law. (p. 23)

An Existence Originally Joyful, Pure and Bright

Nichiren Daishonin says: "Living beings that pass through the two phases of life and death are the entities of the Ten Worlds" (WND-1, 216). This contains a very important point. The two aspects of life and death—which make up life in its totality—encompass the Ten Worlds, or ten potential states of life inherent in each individual being. This means that all living beings of the Ten Worlds are entities of the Mystic Law that embodies these two phenomena. Or put another way, the phenomena of life and death, inherent in the Mystic Law, are the true substance of the lives of all beings of the Ten Worlds. (p. 24)

All Universal Phenomena Are the Workings of Compassion

When we chant Nam-myoho-renge-kyo with the deep conviction that we are entities of the Mystic Law, the fundamental Law of the universe, we can bring forth the great life force of the Mystic Law, which is infused with wisdom and compassion. And we can use it to break through any painful difficulty or obstacle and establish a state of absolute happiness that nothing can destroy. If we continue on this path, then, when the moment of death finally comes, we will savor a state of tremendous inner peace and contentment that derives from maintaining a correct and steadfast attitude in faith. What this means is cherishing the firm conviction that "my life itself is the Mystic Law" and upholding a correct view of life and death based on the Middle Way, while rejecting the views of annihilation or permanence. Achieving a death of that sort is the supreme and ultimate goal of life. Here, both life and death are filled with joy. (pp. 27–28)

DIALOGUE AND REFLECTION

1) SGI President Ikeda states, "The fact that the universe is boundlessly interconnected and that the life and death of all individual beings are part of that is something truly wondrous and unfathomable" (p. 23). What impact does this Buddhist view of life and death have upon your own fear and anxiety regarding death?

2) "When we tap the great fundamental life force of the universe inherent in our lives, we achieve a towering state of being in which we can summon up power as immense as the universe itself. This towering state of life is certainly not governed by a selfish impulse that seeks only personal happiness" (p. 27). How does this resonate with your efforts for the sake of others through participating in SGI-USA activities?

The Heritage of the ULTIMATE LAW *of* LIFE

SGI PRESIDENT IKEDA'S STUDY LECTURE SERIES

This is a series of lectures by SGI President Daisaku Ikeda on "The Heritage of the Ultimate Law of Life." Nichiren Daishonin states: "Shakyamuni Buddha who attained enlightenment countless kalpas ago, the Lotus Sutra that leads all people to Buddhahood, and we ordinary human beings are in no way different or separate from one another. To chant Myoho-renge-kyo with this realization is to inherit the ultimate Law of life and death."

Life and Death As Functions of Myoho-renge-kyo

A Compassionate and Hope-filled View of Life and Death

Nichiren Buddhism is a teaching that fully and clearly elucidates the means for overcoming the sufferings of birth and death. It is the Lotus Sutra—specifically the "Life Span" (sixteenth) chapter—that clarifies the true nature of birth and death. Further, it is Nichiren Daishonin who, by teaching the essence of the Lotus Sutra in the Latter Day of the Law, opened the way for all people to dispel the darkness of ignorance or illusion that is the basic cause of human suffering and attain eternal happiness over the three existences—past, present and future.

Josei Toda, the second Soka Gakkai president, often remarked, "The ultimate problem that Buddhism must resolve is the problem of death." The great wisdom of Nichiren Buddhism reveals the fundamental means for resolving the problems of both life and death and sets forth the path for elevating the life-state of humankind.

Let us continue our discussion of "The Heritage of the Ultimate Law of Life" and study of the profound principles of Nichiren Buddhism, the great teaching that can lead all humanity to enlightenment.

The Two Phases of Life and Death Indicate Life's Boundless Potential

***Myo* represents death, and *ho*, life. Living beings that pass through the two phases of life and death are the entities of the Ten Worlds, or the entities of Myoho-renge-kyo [literally, "or the lotus of the entity"].**

T'ien-t'ai says that one should understand that living beings and their environments, and the causes and effects at work within them, are all the Law of *renge* (the lotus).[4] Here "living beings and their environments" means the phenomena of life and death. Thus, it is clear that, where life and death exist, cause and effect, or the Law of the lotus, is at work.

The Great Teacher Dengyo states, "The two phases of life and death are the wonderful workings of one mind. The two ways of existence and nonexistence are the true functions of an inherently enlightened mind."[5] No phenomena—either heaven or earth, yin or yang,[6] the sun or the moon, the five planets,[7] or any of the worlds from hell to Buddhahood—are free from the two phases of life and death. Life and death are simply the two functions of Myoho-renge-kyo. In his *Great Concentration and Insight*, T'ien-t'ai says, "Arising is the arising of the essential nature of the Law, and extinction is the extinction of that nature." Shakyamuni and Many Treasures, the two Buddhas, are also the two phases of life and death. (*The Writings of Nichiren Daishonin*, vol. 1, p. 216)

In this writing, Nichiren Daishonin gives a concise outline of the profound principles that explain why Myoho-renge-kyo is the ultimate Law of life and death. In the last installment, I discussed the original and inherent nature of life and death, based on Nichiren's observations in the above passage regarding the relationship between them and the Mystic Law.

Nichiren indicates that these two phases, life and death, form an inherent and integral part of the Mystic Law, the fundamental Law of the universe, and that living beings of the Ten Worlds who pass through these two phases are all entities of that Law. This means that the life and death of those who dwell in this *saha* world[1] are not originally characterized by suffering and delusion but are part of the eternal rhythm of the Mystic Law itself. This is the essence of the Buddha's enlightenment to the true aspect of the threefold world,[2] which is described in the "Life Span" chapter of the Lotus Sutra.[3]

Viewed through the eyes of the Buddha, all living beings of the Ten Worlds inherently possess infinite potential; they are entities of the Mystic Law. The Buddha knows that there are no fundamental delusions or sufferings that cannot be surmounted. But ordinary beings for the most part remain trapped in the cycle of birth and death in the six paths,[4] with the four noble worlds[5] remaining much admired goals and the world of Buddhahood in particular—a state of true victory over the sufferings of birth and death—little more than an unreachable ideal or impossible dream.

The Entity of Myoho-renge-kyo Indicates Life's Transformative Potential

To further clarify the true nature of the life and death of living beings of the Ten Worlds, Nichiren Daishonin next speaks about the "entity of Myoho-renge-kyo," which in this passage literally translates as the "lotus of the entity," or the "embodied lotus."[6] The "embodied lotus" represents the principle that all living beings of the Ten Worlds are entities of the Mystic Law. It means that the lives of all living beings here and now are entities of the mutual possession of the Ten

Worlds and have the potential to manifest the highest world of Buddhahood just as they are.

The lotus, or *renge*, is a metaphor for the simultaneity of cause and effect—the principle that both cause and effect are contained in a single moment of life. In other words, it symbolizes the mutual possession of the Ten Worlds. Regardless of which of the Ten Worlds we may be experiencing at any given moment, we can experience any of the other worlds at the very next. Most important, the lotus is a metaphor for our lives at each single moment simultaneously possessing the cause for and effect of attaining Buddhahood—that is, the nine worlds (the cause) and the world of Buddhahood (the effect).

The lives of all living beings have the potential to manifest the highest world of Buddhahood just as they are.

When viewed in terms of the entity of Myoho-renge-kyo, or "embodied lotus," our lives, which undergo the cycle of birth and death, are neither inherently good nor evil. Based on different causes and conditions, they can undergo a state of delusion or a state of enlightenment. In terms of the Ten Worlds, our lives have the innate potential to embody any of the worlds from hell to Buddhahood; this represents the true nature of our lives.

The Simultaneity of Cause and Effect Is the Foundation of Inner Transformation

Next, to amplify the meaning of the entity of Myoho-renge-kyo, or "embodied lotus," Nichiren Daishonin cites a passage by T'ien-t'ai: "Living beings and their environments, and the causes and effects at work within them, are all the Law of *renge* (the lotus)"[7] (WND-1, 216). Here, "living beings and their environments" refers to life activity itself, which undergoes the two phases of life and death. The relationship among life activity and living beings and their environments is now being studied scientifically as well.

Various causal phenomena occur in living beings, in their environments and also between living beings and their environments. Nichiren says that all these phenomena are simply part of the phases of life and death, which are inherent in the Mystic Law. This means that the various causal phenomena involving living beings and their environments also essentially arise in accord with the "Law of the lotus," the law of the simultaneity of cause and effect. In other words, this law is at work in living beings and their environments. What is the practical implication of this truth? Nichiren teaches that when we change our fundamental attitude or mind-set, we can instantly transform both our lives and our environments.

In the Buddhist teachings expounded prior to the Lotus Sutra, it was taught that living beings were shackled in suffering as retribution for negative causes created in past existences and that they could only hope to change this after carrying out countless eons of Buddhist practice and being reborn in a new, higher state of life in the future. By contrast, Nichiren teaches that a profound change in our attitude or mind-set can instantly transform our lives, without changing who we are. And when we change inside, not only do our lives change, but our environment changes as well.

The "Law of the lotus"—the Mystic Law of the simultaneity of cause and effect—enables us to reveal the infinite potential inherent in our lives and attain a state of complete freedom spanning the three existences—past, present and future.

All Changing Phenomena Are Manifestations of the Phases of Life and Death of the Mystic Law

So far, our discussion of the Mystic Law and the lotus has shown that Myoho-renge-kyo is a great Law that teaches the profound significance of the life and death of living beings. Nichiren Daishonin concludes that all birth and death, and all change, are manifestations of the phases of life and death, which are inherent functions of Myoho-renge-kyo.

First, he cites a passage from a commentary by the Great Teacher Dengyo of Japan, which states: "The two phases of life and death are the wonderful workings of one mind. The two ways of existence and nonexistence are the true functions of an inherently enlightened mind"[8] (WND-1, 216). This is to clarify that all change derives from the one ultimate Law—the Mystic Law of the simultaneity of cause and effect.

"The wonderful workings of one mind" might be more easily understood if explained as the principle of "three thousand realms in a single moment of life."[9] A change in our mind or single life-moment can greatly alter our state of life and open up our world. This is because our lives, as entities of the mutual possession of the Ten Worlds, are endowed with the transformative potential to bring forth any of the three thousand realms, that is, all the potential of the entire universe.

Next, Nichiren writes: "No phenomena—either heaven or earth, yin or yang,[10] the sun or the moon, the five planets,[11] or any of the worlds from hell to Buddhahood—are free from the two phases of life and death" (WND-1, 216). Because Buddhism teaches the principles of "three thousand realms in a single moment of life" and "the mutually inclusive relationship of a single moment of life and all phenomena,"[12] environmental factors such as "heaven or earth," "yin or yang," "the sun or the moon," and "the five planets" are also entities of the Mystic Law that go through the phases of life and death. This is also true of living beings and environments of the Ten Worlds, here indicated by "any of the worlds from hell to Buddhahood."

"Heaven or earth, yin or yang, the sun or the moon, the five planets" expresses the cosmology of the ancient Chinese classics, while "the worlds from hell to Buddhahood" expresses the cosmology of Buddhism originating from its earliest inception in India. The prevalent view of the world and the universe during Nichiren's lifetime was widely influenced by Chinese tradition and philosophy, including the principles and theory of yin and yang and the five elements.[13] This developed through the transmission of the philosophy of yin and yang to Japan, where it metamorphosed into a unique system of belief and practice, and through the transmission of various T'ien-t'ai school commentaries on the Buddhist sutras, which were heavily influenced by Chinese thought. Nichiren's choice of terminology here can be seen as reflecting such a philosophical backdrop.

Nichiren is saying that heaven and earth, as well as the forces of yin and yang that underlie them, along with the sun and moon and the five elements, are ultimately all manifestations of the phases of life and death that are inherent functions of Myoho-renge-kyo. Indeed, this is true of all phenomena, as indicated by the statement: "No phenomena . . . are free from the two phases of life and death" (WND-1, 216).

Our lives, in terms of both our subjective beings and our objective environment, are entities of Myoho-renge-kyo, as are all things in the universe. Hence, T'ien-t'ai states, "Arising is the arising of the essential nature of the Law, and extinction is the extinction of that nature"[14] (WND-1, 216). Here, "essential nature of the Law"—namely, the Dharma nature—means the true nature of all things. This true nature is none other than Myoho-renge-kyo.

The Two Buddhas Shakyamuni and Many Treasures Represent the Two Phases of Life and Death

Next, Nichiren Daishonin writes: "Shakyamuni and Many Treasures, the two Buddhas, are also the two phases of life and death" (WND-1, 216). The Buddhas Shakyamuni and Many Treasures seated side by side in the Treasure Tower during the Ceremony in the Air[15] personify the world of Buddhahood inherent in Myoho-renge-kyo. Like us ordinary beings, they are entities of the Mystic Law and go through the phases of life and death.

In this passage, Shakyamuni represents the lord of teachings whose true identity is revealed in the essential teaching (the second half) of the Lotus Sutra. He is the Buddha who has constantly abided in this *saha* world to continue expounding the Mystic Law after attaining enlightenment in the remote past of numberless major world system dust particle *kalpas.*[16]

In the "Life Span" chapter of the Lotus Sutra, Shakyamuni discloses that though he gained supreme enlightenment in the distant past and is a Buddha who abides constantly in the world without ever entering extinction, he has pretended to enter nirvana as an expedient means to guide living beings to enlightenment. Hence, his statement, "*As an expedient means I appear to enter nirvana*" (*The Lotus Sutra*, p. 229). This indicates how the entity of the Buddha's life, though in essence the eternal Mystic Law, actually undergoes a transition from life to death on the phenomenal level.

As for Many Treasures Buddha, he is an ancient Buddha who attained enlightenment and entered nirvana in the distant past. He appears at the assembly where the Lotus Sutra is preached to attest to the truth of its teachings. His appearance can be said to symbolize an entity of the Mystic Law emerging from the phase of death into life.

In any event, for both Shakyamuni and Many Treasures, life and death are means for teaching and revealing the Mystic Law. Because they employ the phases of life and death inherent to all entities of the Mystic Law, these two Buddhas are also functions of the Mystic Law.

The Life and Death of Living Beings in the World of Buddhahood

The life and death of all living beings are functions of Myoho-renge-kyo. Josei Toda often used to say that when we die, we merge with the universe. The life of the universe itself contains all of the Ten Worlds. It contains the worlds from hell and hunger right through to Buddhahood. When we die, our life essence fuses with one of these worlds in the universe—hell, hungry spirits, bodhisattva, Buddhahood and so forth—corresponding to our own inner state.

While we may say that our life essence fuses or merges with the life of the universe, strictly speaking, it is actually already part of the life of the universe itself; inherently, there is no separation between the two. In a sense, the universe is a great ocean of life, which is in a constant state of flux itself; it is continually moving and changing, performing the rhythm of birth and death.

As we confirmed in the previous installment, on one level, our individual lives can be compared to waves that rise from the surface of the vast ocean of the universe. The rising of each wave is analogous to one's individual birth, while the receding of the wave back into the ocean symbolizes one's death. In death, our life essence is like a current flowing within the ocean's depths; it does not become fixed in one particular place. It pervades the universe and moves in sync with the cosmic rhythm of birth and death.

President Toda used to say that living beings are reborn in response to causes and conditions, taking the body and mind and environment most suited to their particular state of life. In the case of living beings in the world of Buddhahood, they can freely choose the time, place and form in which they wish to be reborn. This is the reality of life and death as functions of Myoho-renge-kyo.

When life and death are viewed in terms of the Mystic Law, there is no need to fear death. Death for living beings in the world of Buddhahood means becoming one with the universe that overflows with the workings of compassion. Then, when we are reborn, embodying the compassion and life force of the universe, we once again take vibrant action and conduct ourselves in the manner of a Buddha—in other words, taking the greatest joy in respecting others and working to lead all people to enlightenment.

When we are alive, we reveal the vast state of Buddhahood in our lives, tapping its immense life force to fulfill our mission in this world. Naturally, chanting Nam-myoho-renge-kyo is the fundamental practice for bringing forth this boundless state of being. And after we die, we merge with the world of Buddhahood in the universe and deeply savor and enjoy the eternity of life. The life and death of living beings in the world of Buddhahood is the most sublime life and death, characterized throughout by great joy.

Nichiren Daishonin clearly states: "[One who acts in accord with the original intention of the Buddhas of the three existences] will . . . without hindrance attain the highest level of rebirth, rebirth in the Land of Tranquil Light. Then in no time one will return to the dream realm of the nine worlds, the realm of birth and death, will cause one's body to pervade the lands of the entire phenomenal realm of the ten directions, and will cause one's mind to enter into the bodies of all sentient beings, encouraging them from within, leading and guiding them from without, inner and outer complimenting one another, causes and conditions functioning in harmony, and in this way will utilize the pity and compassion of one's freely exercised transcendental powers to bestow unhindered benefit upon living beings far and wide" ("The Unanimous Declaration by the Buddhas of the Three Existences regarding the Classification of the Teachings and Which Are to Be Abandoned and Which Upheld," WND-2, 860).

As Nichiren indicates here, living beings who seek to be reborn in order to lead others to happiness can realize a swift rebirth, "freely" and "without hindrance."

By contrast, a view of life and death based on the notion of an ideal world existing somewhere apart from this reality, a place we should aspire to dwell in forever after we die, cannot hope to serve as a force for fundamentally changing the world in which we live. Because if we regard some idealized world as the true world, we end up seeing this *saha* world as a provisional realm.

The view of life and death based on the Mystic Law represents an optimistic and hopeful perspective that can genuinely serve as a powerful force for change while allowing us to enjoy lives of absolute freedom and fulfillment in the real world.

President Toda frequently said, "When we understand the true eternity of life, we can elevate the life-state of all humankind." And he would add that this amounted to leading all people to enlightenment.

The universe is a great ocean of life; it is continually moving and changing, performing the rhythm of birth and death.

What precisely does it mean to "lead all people to enlightenment"? President Toda explained this as follows: "When all people manifest the life-state of Buddhahood, that is to say, when they reveal the supreme value of their character, there will be neither war nor hunger, neither disease nor poverty in the world. Enabling all people to attain enlightenment, elevating the character of all people to something of supreme value—this is what it means to carry out '*the Thus Come One's work*'" (LS, 163).[17]

When Bodhisattvas of the Earth appear throughout the world and people awaken to the eternity of life and to the true, inherent nature of life and death as functions of the Mystic Law, there will be an unprecedented revolution in people's view of life and death. At that time, we can definitely transform the karma of humankind, which has long been led astray by the four sufferings—birth, aging, sickness and death. These sufferings arise from fundamental darkness or ignorance toward life's ultimate truth.

The new challenge before us now is to bring this view of life and death to worldwide prominence and make the 21st century the true starting point for dramatically elevating the life-state of humanity.

1. This world, which is full of suffering. *Saha* means the earth; it derives from a root meaning "to bear" or "to endure." For this reason, in the Chinese versions of Buddhist scriptures, *saha* is rendered as endurance.
2. The world of unenlightened beings who transmigrate within the six paths (from hell through the realm of heavenly beings).
3. The "Life Span" chapter of the Lotus Sutra states: "The Thus Come One perceives the true aspect of the threefold world exactly as it is. There is no ebb or flow of birth and death, and there is no existing in this world and later entering extinction. It is neither substantial nor empty, neither consistent nor diverse. Nor is it what those who dwell in the threefold world perceive it to be. All such things the Thus Come One sees clearly and without error" (LS, 226).
4. The lower of the Ten Worlds, conditions of life that indicate states of delusion or suffering. The realms of the six paths include those of hell, hungry spirits, animals, *asuras,* human beings and heavenly beings.
5. The highest four of the Ten Worlds, regarded as states in which one makes efforts to transcend the uncertainty of the six paths. The realms of the four noble worlds include those of voice-hearers, cause-awakened ones, bodhisattvas and Buddhas.
6. Lotus of the entity: Also, embodied lotus. A reference in the T'ien-t'ai doctrine to the lotus that is the essence of the Lotus Sutra and also the people who are entities of, or who embody, this essence. Nichiren Daishonin described this essence as Myoho-renge-kyo, or Nam-myoho-renge-kyo. In "The Entity of the Mystic Law," he writes: "The supreme principle [that is the Mystic Law] was originally without a name. When the sage was observing the principle and assigning names to all things, he perceived that there is this wonderful single Law [*myoho*] that simultaneously possesses both cause and effect [*renge*], and he named it *Myoho-renge*" (WND-1, 421). The term *lotus of the entity,* or *embodied lotus,* is contrasted with the *figurative lotus,* or the lotus as a metaphor for the Law. Since the lotus of the entity, or lotus of the Law that simultaneously possesses both cause and effect, is difficult to understand, the lotus plant, which blooms and produces fruit at the same time, is employed as a metaphor.
7. T'ien-t'ai, *The Profound Meaning of the Lotus Sutra.*
8. Dengyo, *The Essential Doctrines Transmitted Within the Tendai Lotus Sutra.*
9. "Three thousand realms in a single moment of life": A doctrine developed by the Great Teacher T'ien-t'ai of China based on the Lotus Sutra. The principle that all phenomena are contained within a single moment of life, and that a single moment of life permeates the three thousand realms of existence, or the entire phenomenal world.
10. Yin and yang: Two universal principles of ancient Chinese philosophy. Yin is the negative, dark and feminine principle; yang is the positive, bright and masculine principle. Their interaction was thought to determine the destiny of all things.
11. Five planets: Mercury, Venus, Mars, Jupiter and Saturn. In the 13th century, the more distant planets were as yet unknown, and Earth was not known to be among the planets.
12. The principle of "the mutually inclusive relationship of a single moment of life and all phenomena" refers to the inscrutable relationship that exists between ourselves—our minds or each life-moment—and the universe. It teaches that all phenomena are contained in our life and that our life pervades all phenomena.
13. Five elements: The five elements of ancient Chinese cosmology believed to compose the physical universe. They are metal, wood, water, fire and earth. They also correspond to the five planets: Mercury (water), Venus (metal), Mars (fire), Jupiter (wood) and Saturn (earth).
14. T'ien-t'ai, *Great Concentration and Insight.*
15. The second of the three assemblies described in the Lotus Sutra, in which the Buddha Many Treasures emerges from beneath the earth and is suspended in midair. Shakyamuni, after summoning the Buddhas who are his emanations from the ten directions, stations himself in midair, opens the treasure tower, and enters it, taking a seat beside the Buddha Many Treasures.
16. An incredibly long period of time described in the "Life Span," the 16th chapter of the Lotus Sutra, to indicate how long ago Shakyamuni Buddha originally attained enlightenment.
17. Translated from Japanese. Josei Toda, *Toda Josei zenshu* (Collected Writings of Josei Toda) (Tokyo: Seikyo Shimbunsha, 1981), vol. 1, p. 306.

KEY POINTS

The Entity of Myoho-renge-kyo Indicates Life's Transformative Potential

The lives of all living beings here and now are entities of the mutual possession of the Ten Worlds and have the potential to manifest the highest world of Buddhahood just as they are. (pp. 31–32).

The Simultaneity of Cause and Effect Is the Foundation of Inner Transformation

Various causal phenomena occur in living beings, in their environments and also between living beings and their environments. Nichiren says that all these phenomena are simply part of the phases of life and death, which are inherent in the Mystic Law. This means that the various causal phenomena involving living beings and their environments also essentially arise in accord with the "Law of the lotus," the law of the simultaneity of cause and effect. In other words, this law is at work in living beings and their environments. What is the practical implication of this truth? Nichiren teaches that when we change our fundamental attitude or mind-set, we can instantly transform both our lives and our environments. (p. 32)

All Changing Phenomena Are Manifestations of the Phases of Life and Death of the Mystic Law

Our lives, in terms of both our subjective beings and our objective environment, are entities of Myoho-renge-kyo, as are all things in the universe. Hence, T'ien-t'ai states, "Arising is the arising of the essential nature of the Law, and extinction is the extinction of that nature" (WND-1, 216). Here, "essential nature of the Law"—namely, the Dharma nature—means the true nature of all things. This true nature is none other than Myoho-renge-kyo. (p. 34)

The Life and Death of Living Beings in the World of Buddhahood

While we may say that our life essence fuses or merges with the life of the universe, strictly speaking, it is actually already part of the life of the universe itself; inherently, there is no separation between the two. In a sense, the universe is a great ocean of life, which is in a constant state of flux itself; it is continually moving and changing, performing the rhythm of birth and death. (p. 35)

DIALOGUE AND REFLECTION

1) "Nichiren teaches that a profound change in our attitude or mind-set can instantly transform our lives, without changing who we are" (pp. 32–33). How have you experienced this in your own life?

2) SGI President Ikeda states: "If we regard some idealized world as the true world, we end up seeing this *saha* world as a provisional realm. The view of life and death based on the Mystic Law represents an optimistic and hopeful perspective that can genuinely serve as a powerful force for change while allowing us to enjoy lives of absolute freedom and fulfillment in the real world" (p. 36). How has your faith in Nichiren Buddhism changed your view of the world in which we live?

The Heritage of the ULTIMATE LAW *of* LIFE

SGI PRESIDENT IKEDA'S STUDY LECTURE SERIES

This is a series of lectures by SGI President Daisaku Ikeda on "The Heritage of the Ultimate Law of Life." Nichiren Daishonin states: "Shakyamuni Buddha who attained enlightenment countless kalpas ago, the Lotus Sutra that leads all people to Buddhahood, and we ordinary human beings are in no way different or separate from one another. To chant Myoho-renge-kyo with this realization is to inherit the ultimate Law of life and death."

Embracing Myoho-renge-kyo—Striving To Fulfill the Great Vow for *Kosen-rufu* Is the Key to Birth and Death in the Realm of Buddhahood

From Birth and Death in the Realm of Delusion to Birth and Death in the Realm of Buddhahood

Nam-myoho-renge-kyo is the ultimate Law of life and death; it is the sole teaching that opens the way for ordinary people to transform the cycle of birth and death from being pervaded by delusion to being pervaded by the enlightenment of the Buddha. In "The Heritage of the Ultimate Law of Life," Nichiren Daishonin explains that this transformation hinges on realizing that life and death are inherent functions or aspects of Myoho-renge-kyo—the Mystic Law, or fundamental Law of the universe, which has no beginning or end.

When we embrace faith in the Mystic Law and realize that we have been undergoing birth and death in the realm of delusion, we can then perceive the eternally inherent nature of birth and death. This realization activates the great transformative power of the Mystic Law, of which life and death are integral functions. It is the working of the Buddhist principles of the "simultaneity of cause and effect" and the "mutual possession of the Ten Worlds"; it is "the Law of the lotus" (see *The Writings of Nichiren Daishonin*, vol. 1, p. 216).

In this writing, Nichiren describes the phenomena of life and death that are workings of this inherent Law of the lotus as "life and death as functions of Myoho-renge-kyo" (see WND-1, 216). All things in the universe follow the rhythm of life and death inherent in Myoho-renge-kyo. The arising and extinction of all phenomena, the birth and death of all living things constitute life and death as functions of this Law. Hence, Myoho-renge-kyo is also the source of infinite and unending change.

Unaware of this view of life, unenlightened ordinary beings undergo birth and death in the realm of delusion and experience suffering. Buddhas, on the other hand, realizing that their lives and those of others are functions of Myoho-renge-kyo, have overcome the sufferings that accompany birth and death in the realm of delusion and attained a sublime inner state of peace and tranquility. They undergo birth and death in the realm of Buddhahood throughout past, present and future.

Transforming Birth and Death in the Realm of Delusion and Attaining an Inner State of Peace and Tranquility

I have already spoken at length about the most commonly held deluded views of life and death. These are, of course, represented as two extremes—the "view of annihilation" and the "view of permanence." (See installment 1 of this series on pages 1–10.)

The life and death of all living beings are inherently functions of Myoho-renge-kyo, but when our minds are clouded by ignorance, causing us to become confused and attached to worldly desires, we cannot correctly apprehend this truth and instead cling to deluded views of existence. But in the light of the Buddha wisdom that perceives the true aspect of living beings in the threefold world[1]—as described in "Life Span," the 16th chapter of the Lotus Sutra[2]—the view of life and death held by ordinary people shows itself to be nothing but an illusion.

The sutra states that Buddhas apply their wisdom to preaching the Law in order to awaken living beings who are confused and suffering in the reality of the threefold world to the original and inherent nature of life and death—in other words, the essential nature of existence. For this reason, in the "Life Span" chapter, Shakyamuni reveals that he actually attained enlightenment not in his present lifetime in India but at a time in the inconceivably distant past. The ultimate Buddhist view of life is unveiled as Shakyamuni proceeds to explain that he continually undergoes birth and death in the realm of Buddhahood throughout eternity.

The original and inherent nature of birth and death perceived by the Buddha is none other than birth and death in the realm of Buddhahood, which is explained through the example of Shakyamuni's enlightenment in the remote past. Put another way, Shakyamuni's birth and death in the realm of Buddhahood described in the "Life Span" chapter is one and the same as the original and inherent nature of birth and death of all living beings.

When we undergo the cycle of birth and death in the realm of Buddhahood, both life and death shine with unsurpassed brilliance as functions of Myoho-renge-kyo. During the manifest phase of life, the pure life essence of Buddhahood wells forth within us, serving as a powerful source of strength for combating difficulties; it is the engine for overcoming all hardships and building a victorious life. When we bring forth our innate Buddhahood and valiantly grapple with reality, we forge and polish our lives which, when our mission in this existence is completed, will merge into the Buddhahood of the universe. Not only do we enter a state of limitless joy and vast and unbounded freedom, we also become one with the compassion inherent in the universe. This compassionate impulse of the universe directs us toward embarking on another new vibrant existence

Seikyo Press

SGI President Ikeda greets participants at the 6th Soka Gakkai Headquarters Leaders Meeting commemorating May 3, Soka Gakkai Day and Soka Gakkai Mother's Day, held at the Makiguchi Memorial Hall in Hachioji, Tokyo, April 25, 2007.

in the reality of the threefold world in order to lead those who are suffering to enlightenment. In this way, our lives repeatedly undergo birth and death in the realm of Buddhahood.

When we undergo birth and death in the realm of Buddhahood, the latent phase of death becomes a period of replenishment for our next life, much like a good night's sleep gives us fresh energy and vitality for the new day.

Nichiren Daishonin writes: "When he was alive, he was a Buddha in life, and now he is a Buddha in death. He is a Buddha in both life and death. This is what is meant by that most important doctrine called attaining Buddhahood in one's present form ("Hell Is the Land of Tranquil Light," WND-1, 456). Both in life and death we are Buddhas—this is the meaning of undergoing the cycle of birth and death in the realm of Buddhahood.

The fundamental purpose of the heritage of the ultimate Law of life and death is the awakening of all people to the essential nature of birth and death and enabling them to attain Buddhahood.

Faith for Inheriting the Ultimate Law of Life and Death

"Shakyamuni Buddha who attained enlightenment countless kalpas ago, the Lotus Sutra that leads all people to Buddhahood, and we ordinary human beings are in no way different or separate from one another. To chant Myoho-renge-kyo with this realization is to inherit the ultimate Law of life and death. This is a matter of the utmost importance for Nichiren's disciples and lay supporters, and this is what it means to embrace the Lotus Sutra" (WND-1, 216).

As disciples of Nichiren Daishonin, what is the proper way for us to embrace Nam-myoho-renge-kyo—the ultimate Law of life and death—so that we can undergo the cycle of birth and death in the realm of Buddhahood? Nichiren addresses this question on various levels, clarifying the essential points of faith in the Mystic Law.

The first of these is that our faith must be based on the recognition that birth and death in the realm of Buddhahood is the original and inherent nature of our own existence. Nichiren explains: "Shakyamuni Buddha who attained enlightenment countless kalpas ago, the Lotus Sutra that leads all people to Buddhahood, and we ordinary human beings are in no way different or separate from one another. To chant Myoho-renge-kyo with this realization is to inherit the ultimate Law of life and death" (WND-1, 216).

Nichiren's assertion here of the inherent equality and oneness of all three—Shakyamuni Buddha, the Lotus Sutra and ordinary people—is extremely important.

Also, to awaken ordinary people to the inherent truth of birth and death in the realm of Buddhahood, both the actual example of the Buddha who embodies this truth and the teaching or Law that explains this truth are vital.

Now let's examine each of the three components mentioned in the above passage from Nichiren's letter.

(1) "Shakyamuni Buddha Who Attained Enlightenment Countless Kalpas Ago": An Embodiment of Birth and Death in the Realm of Buddhahood

First, let's look at "Shakyamuni Buddha who attained enlightenment countless kalpas ago." This refers to the Buddha who is the embodiment of birth and death in the realm of Buddhahood. In the "Life Span" chapter, Shakyamuni reveals that since attaining enlightenment in the distant past of numberless major world system dust particle *kalpas*[3] ago, his life has endured throughout and will continue likewise into the eternal future, being ultimately without beginning or end.

The Shakyamuni who attained enlightenment for the first time under the *bodhi* tree in India and the Shakyamuni who attained enlightenment in the remote past differ not only in the length of their life spans but also as to the view of birth and death they each embody. The former is a Buddha who aspires to break free from the cycle of birth and death and attain the eternal realm of nirvana. The latter, however, is a Buddha who eternally undergoes the cycle of birth and death in the realm of Buddhahood in order to teach and convert living beings in the *saha* world (this world in which we endure continual sufferings).

Consequently, although various Buddhas are described in the sutras, it is not until Shakyamuni reveals in the Lotus Sutra that he attained enlightenment in the remote past that the inherent truth of birth and death in the realm of Buddhahood is established. Shakyamuni as the Buddha enlightened since the remote past can therefore be considered the embodiment of this inherent truth.

(2) "The Lotus Sutra That Leads All People to Buddhahood": A Teaching for Realizing Birth and Death in the Realm of Buddhahood

Next, let us look at "the Lotus Sutra that leads all people to Buddhahood." The Lotus Sutra's doctrine of universal enlightenment is usually discussed in contrast to the pre-Lotus Sutra provisional teachings, which deny the capacity for Buddhahood in persons of the two vehicles[4], evil people and women. Of course, discussing the Lotus Sutra's superiority relative to the provisional sutras holds great importance. Here, however, let's consider "the Lotus Sutra that leads all people to Buddhahood" from the perspective of birth and death in the realm of Buddhahood.

It goes without saying that the primary meaning of this phrase is that the doctrine of universal enlightenment is found only in this sutra. At the same time, the Lotus Sutra elucidates the Buddha's original vow—a vow of eternal dedication to the cause of helping all living beings attain Buddhahood—as well as the vow of bodhisattvas who pledge to strive alongside the Buddha for this same cause, carrying out the practice of compassion. This could be said to represent the true significance of the Lotus Sutra, the quintessence of the Mahayana teachings.

In "Expedient Means," the second chapter of the Lotus Sutra, Shakyamuni states that he has fulfilled his vow to make all persons "equal to me, without any distinction between us"[5] (*The Lotus Sutra*, p. 36), and indicates that this vow expresses the wish of all Buddhas.[6] Further, throughout his preaching of "the replacement of three vehicles with the one vehicle"[7] in the theoretical teaching (the first 14 chapters) of the Lotus Sutra, he consistently emphasizes that the persons of the three vehicles—the voice-hearers and cause-awakened ones (persons of the two vehicles), and bodhisattvas—can only hope to attain Buddhahood by earnestly dedicating themselves to this vow.

Why was it that in the provisional Mahayana teachings expounded prior to the Lotus Sutra, Shakyamuni had been so critical of Shariputra and all his other disciples of the two vehicles? One reason was that as they showed signs of physical aging, their spirits had also withered and aged. In their hearts, they had limited themselves, thinking: *We have grown old. This is as far as we can go. Let's be content with what we have.* They had clearly lost their fighting spirit to work for the happiness of those suffering.

It is important to note here that in the Lotus Sutra, the persons of the two vehicles are repeatedly urged to remember the vow they made in former lifetimes. For example, the theoretical teaching states that Buddhas preach the Lotus Sutra in order to remind living beings of their original vow as bodhisattvas in past existences. This is particularly emphasized in "Simile and Parable," the third chapter of the Lotus Sutra; "The Parable of the Phantom City," the seventh chapter; and "Prophecy of Enlightenment for Five Hundred Disciples," the eighth chapter.[8]

The last of these three chapters contains the parable of "The Jewel in the Robe," one of the seven parables of the Lotus Sutra. Its message is that when we recover the aspiration that has been within our lives all along, we return to our original and inherent selves. Accordingly, when Shakyamuni's voice-hearer disciples recall the great aspiration inherent in their lives and realize that, despite their present outward form as voice-hearers, they are at heart bodhisattvas and that this is their true identity, they are filled with joy.

In the essential teaching (the last 14 chapters) of the Lotus Sutra, meanwhile, we see the appearance of the Bodhisattvas of the Earth, who uphold the Mystic Law and are committed to fulfilling their vow to lead all people to enlightenment. Further, Shakyamuni proclaims that he has dedicated himself to this same vow as a Buddha since the remote past and will continue to do so in lifetime after lifetime throughout eternity.

Striving to fulfill the vow to lead all people to enlightenment is a concrete realization of our following the path of birth and death in the realm of Buddhahood. We must awaken to the fact that this noble vow is the very essence of our beings. Forgetting this vow and failing to seek the ultimate truth is a fundamental cause of delusion.

The Lotus Sutra reveals that all people have the potential to attain Buddhahood. In other words, it is a teaching that makes it possible for every individual to fulfill life's true purpose by acting in accord with the compassionate workings of the universe.[9]

As outlined above, "the Lotus Sutra that leads all people to Buddhahood" indicates the Lotus Sutra not only as a teaching of universal enlightenment but also as an appeal to translate the vow for universal enlightenment into action. The Lotus Sutra thus teaches both the principle that all people are Buddhas and also the practice to guide and help awaken them to their inherent Buddhahood.

Taking action so that all may attain enlightenment is the driving force that enables us to actualize birth and death in the realm of Buddhahood. In that sense, "the Lotus Sutra that leads all people to Buddhahood" can also be described as a teaching that enables all people to realize birth and death in the realm of Buddhahood.

"We Ordinary Human Beings": Our Oneness With the Buddha and the Law

"Shakyamuni Buddha who attained enlightenment countless kalpas ago, the Lotus Sutra that leads all people to Buddhahood, and we ordinary human beings are in no way different or separate from one another" (WND-1, 216). What this ultimately means is that all three—our lives, the Buddha and the Law—at their essential level embody birth and death in the realm of Buddhahood.

When we chant Nam-myoho-renge-kyo based on the recognition and profound conviction that we are in no way different or separate from either "Shakyamuni Buddha who attained enlightenment countless kalpas ago" or "the Lotus Sutra that leads all people to enlightenment," we, too, can actualize birth and death in the realm of Buddhahood.

There is no difference or distinction among our lives, the Buddha and the Law. To believe that there is, even in the slightest, is a manifestation of delusion arising from our innate ignorance to life's ultimate truth. Only when we comprehend that we are entities that undergo birth and death in the realm of Buddhahood can we be said to be truly practicing Nichiren Buddhism.

Nichiren Daishonin says we must chant Myoho-renge-kyo with the realization that we are in no way different or separate from the Buddha and the Law (see WND-1, 216). Here, *realization* does not simply mean an intellectual appreciation but rather *belief and understanding*[10]—that is, an understanding based on belief, or a heartfelt acceptance and conviction in the depths of one's life. This is essential.

Such profound inner conviction is forged through efforts to lead others to enlightenment with the spirit of not begrudging one's life. SGI members who have dedicated themselves tirelessly for the sake of *kosen-rufu* with resolute faith have, in the course of their struggles, gained a strong and vibrant belief and understanding. They are dedicating themselves to the mission of spreading Nam-myoho-renge-kyo as Bodhisattvas of the Earth and striving to do their very best. As such, they are already manifesting the vast and expansive life-state of Buddhahood of Nam-myoho-renge-kyo equal in every way to that revealed by "Shakyamuni Buddha who attained enlightenment countless kalpas ago" and "the Lotus Sutra that leads all people to enlightenment." Each individual, as an entity of the Mystic Law, is powerfully manifesting the life-state of Nichiren Daishonin embodied in the Gohonzon and living out his or her life in harmony with the Mystic Law.

When we make our lives one with the Mystic Law in this lifetime, we remain so after death and, on our next rebirth, we will dedicate ourselves once more to fulfilling our mission for the Mystic Law. This is the inherent nature of birth and death in the realm of Buddhahood. And it is the essence of a life that forever strives to manifest the workings of compassion.

Nichiren chanted and propagated Nam-myoho-renge-kyo so that ordinary people could attain this state of life. And when we, his disciples, do likewise, the heritage of the ultimate Law of life and death flows within us, and we can instantly realize birth and death in the realm of Buddhahood.

That is also the purpose of faith in Nichiren Buddhism and why Nichiren says: "This is a matter of the utmost importance for Nichiren's disciples and lay supporters," and "This is what it means to embrace the Lotus Sutra" (WND-1, 216).

What is the fundamental path of faith for a disciple? It is to dedicate oneself to *kosen-rufu*, which is the wish of all Buddhas as well as Nichiren's great desire. It is to dedicate oneself to practicing the spirit of the Lotus Sutra—in other words, making efforts to help guide all people to enlightenment.

The Law that enables us to realize birth and death in the realm of Buddhahood beats vibrantly in such activities. Only then can we be said to "embrace the Lotus Sutra" (WND-1, 216) in the truest sense.

The True Way of "Embracing the Lotus Sutra"

The Lotus Sutra teaches the principle of prolonging one's life through faith.[11] This is because Nam-myoho-renge-kyo, the heart of the Lotus Sutra, enables us to manifest our innate Buddhahood, the source of fundamental life force.

When we chant Nam-myoho-renge-kyo with the same great spirit and great desire for *kosen-rufu* as Nichiren Daishonin, we can experience birth and death in the realm of Buddhahood and tap the fundamental life force that resides within us. The Lotus Sutra (Nam-myoho-renge-kyo) has the power to rejuvenate and revitalize our lives. Through its power, in life, we can grow younger and accumulate good fortune,[12] while in death, we can merge with the vast realm of Buddhahood of the universe as a whole and recharge our vital life force.

We, the members of the SGI striving for *kosen-rufu*, carrying on the spirit of the Lotus Sutra and directly connected to Nichiren, are noble individuals in no way different or separate from "Shakyamuni Buddha who attained enlightenment countless kalpas ago" or "the Lotus Sutra that leads all people to Buddhahood."

Our second Soka Gakkai president, Josei Toda, said: "You could describe the life-state of Buddhahood as that of always being reborn brimming with powerful life force and working to your heart's content for the mission you were born for, of achieving all your desired goals and accumulating indestructible benefits. How much more fortunate it would be, then, if we could enjoy such lives many tens, hundreds, thousands and billions of times? Not desiring such happy lives, but greedily seeking only your own tiny happiness, is truly pitiful."[13]

Because, as practitioners of Nichiren Buddhism, we live our lives in direct accord with the essential way of life of Buddhas, we overflow with innate life force. Because we carry out efforts that embody the workings of compassion of time without beginning, we can remain basically joyful and positive, no matter what happens. And because we, who uphold the Soka spirit of mentor and disciple, follow the path of birth and death in the realm of Buddhahood, our lives are strong and invincible. As SGI members, who possess a sound and undistorted view of life and death, we are people of wisdom and true philosophy, people of courage and genuine commitment.

In our practice of compassion based on the Mystic Law, we find a view of life and death that can serve as a model for all humanity and a pioneering example of ordinary individuals positively transforming the inner realm of their lives.

1. The world of unenlightened beings who transmigrate within the six paths (from hell through the realm of heavenly beings).
2. The "Life Span" chapter of the Lotus Sutra states: "The Thus Come One perceives the true aspect of the threefold world exactly as it is. There is no ebb or flow of birth and death, and there is no existing in this world and later entering extinction. It is neither substantial nor empty, neither consistent nor diverse. Nor is it what those who dwell in the threefold world perceive it to be. All such things the Thus Come One sees clearly and without error" (LS, 226).
3. An incredibly long period of time described in the "Life Span," the 16th chapter of the Lotus Sutra, to indicate how long ago Shakyamuni Buddha originally attained enlightenment.
4. Persons of the two vehicles are voice-hearers (Skt *shravaka*) and cause-awakened ones *(pratyekabuddha).*
5. Shakyamuni states: "*At the start I took a vow, / hoping to make all persons / equal to me, without any distinction between us, / and what I long ago hoped for / has now been fulfilled. / I have converted all living beings / and caused them all to enter the Buddha way*" (LS, 36). He goes on to explain that it is the wish of all Buddhas to guide living beings to attain the same enlightened state of life that they possess.
6. Shakyamuni states: "*The original vow of the Buddhas / was that the Buddha way, which they themselves practice, / should be shared universally among living beings / so that they too may attain this same way*" (LS, 41).
7. Replacement of the three vehicles with the one vehicle: A reference to Shakyamuni's statement in the Lotus Sutra that the three vehicles are not ends in themselves—though other, provisional, sutras teach that they are—but expedient means by which he leads people to the one vehicle of Buddhahood. The three vehicles are the teachings expounded for voice-hearers, cause-awakened ones and bodhisattvas, respectively. The one vehicle of Buddhahood means the teaching that enables all people to attain Buddhahood and corresponds to the Lotus Sutra.
8. In "Simile and Parable," Shakyamuni says: "I want to make you recall to mind the way that you originally vowed to follow" (LS, 51). He explains that he is expounding the Lotus Sutra to cause Shariputra to recollect his original bodhisattva vow from ages past.

   In "The Parable of the Phantom City," hoping to prompt his voice-hearer disciples to recall that they carried out bodhisattva practices with him as their teacher in the near distant past of major world system dust particle *kalpas*, Shakyamuni says: "*Those persons who had heard the Law [at that time] / dwelled here and there in various Buddha lands, / constantly reborn in company with their teachers*" (LS, 140).

   And in "Prophecy of Enlightenment for Five Hundred Disciples," Shakyamuni's voice-hearer disciple Purna thinks to himself: "Only the Buddha, the World-Honored One, is capable of knowing the wish that we have had deep in our hearts from the start" (LS, 144). In "The Wisdom of the Lotus Sutra" lecture series, President Ikeda explains that this original wish is the aspiration or desire for the happiness of oneself and others (see *The Wisdom of the Lotus Sutra*, vol. 2).
9. Josei Toda said: "In the first place, the universe in its entirety is the substance of the Buddha, and all phenomena in the universe are the workings of compassion. Therefore, compassion is the inherent nature of the universe."
10. Nichiren discusses the meaning of "belief and understanding" in *The Record of the Orally Transmitted Teachings* (see OTT, 54–55).
11. This is based on the passage in "Life Span," the 16th chapter of the Lotus Sutra, that reads: "We beg you to cure us and let us live out our lives!" (LS, 228). This is in the section that tells the parable of the outstanding physician, who imparts "good medicine" (a metaphor for Myoho-renge-kyo) to his children who have "drunk poison" (succumbed to delusion) and implore him to cure their illness.
12. Nichiren writes, "You will grow younger, and your good fortune will accumulate" ("The Unity of Husband and Wife," WND-1, 464).
13. Translated from Japanese. Josei Toda, *Toda Josei zenshu.*

KEY POINTS

From Birth and Death in the Realm of Delusion to Birth and Death in the Realm of Buddhahood

When we embrace faith in the Mystic Law and realize that we have been undergoing birth and death in the realm of delusion, we can then perceive the eternally inherent nature of birth and death. This realization activates the great transformative power of the Mystic Law, of which life and death are integral functions. It is the working of the Buddhist principles of the "simultaneity of cause and effect" and the "mutual possession of the Ten Worlds"; it is "the Law of the lotus" (see *The Writings of Nichiren Daishonin*, vol. 1, p. 216).

In this writing, Nichiren describes the phenomena of life and death that are workings of this inherent Law of the lotus as "life and death as functions of Myoho-renge-kyo" (see WND-1, 216). All things in the universe follow the rhythm of life and death inherent in Myoho-renge-kyo. The arising and extinction of all phenomena, the birth and death of all living things constitute life and death as functions of this Law. Hence, Myoho-renge-kyo is also the source of infinite and unending change. (p. 40)

The True Way of "Embracing the Lotus Sutra"

When we chant Nam-myoho-renge-kyo with the same great spirit and great desire for *kosen-rufu* as Nichiren Daishonin, we can experience birth and death in the realm of Buddhahood and tap the fundamental life force that resides within us. The Lotus Sutra (Nam-myoho-renge-kyo) has the power to rejuvenate and revitalize our lives. Through its power, in life, we can grow younger and accumulate good fortune, while in death, we can merge with the vast realm of Buddhahood of the universe as a whole and recharge our vital life force.

We, the members of the SGI striving for *kosen-rufu*, carrying on the spirit of the Lotus Sutra and directly connected to Nichiren, are noble individuals in no way different or separate from "Shakyamuni Buddha who attained enlightenment countless kalpas ago" or "the Lotus Sutra that leads all people to Buddhahood." (p. 46)

DIALOGUE AND REFLECTION

1) "All things in the universe follow the rhythm of life and death inherent in Myoho-renge-kyo. The arising and extinction of all phenomena, the birth and death of all living things constitute life and death as functions of this Law. Hence, Myoho-renge-kyo is also the source of infinite and unending change" (p. 40). As disciples of Nichiren Daishonin, what is the proper way for us to embrace Nam-myoho-renge-kyo—the ultimate Law of life and death—so that we can undergo the cycle of birth and death in the realm of Buddhahood?

2) "There is no difference or distinction among our lives, the Buddha and the Law. To believe that there is, even in the slightest, is a manifestation of delusion arising from our innate ignorance to life's ultimate truth. Only when we comprehend that we are entities that undergo birth and death in the realm of Buddhahood can we be said to be truly practicing Nichiren Buddhism" (p. 45). What are the false beliefs we hold that prevent us from accepting this truth?

The Heritage of the ULTIMATE LAW *of* LIFE

SGI PRESIDENT IKEDA'S STUDY LECTURE SERIES

This is a series of lectures by SGI President Daisaku Ikeda on "The Heritage of the Ultimate Law of Life." Nichiren Daishonin states: "Shakyamuni Buddha who attained enlightenment countless kalpas ago, the Lotus Sutra that leads all people to Buddhahood, and we ordinary human beings are in no way different or separate from one another. To chant Myoho-renge-kyo with this realization is to inherit the ultimate Law of life and death."

The Present Holds the Key to Eternal Victory

The Spirit That Now Is the Last Moment of One's Life Assures a Correct and Steadfast Mind at the Moment of Death

For one who summons up one's faith and chants Nam-myoho-renge-kyo with the profound insight that now is the last moment of one's life, the sutra proclaims: "When the lives of these persons come to an end, they will be received into the hands of a thousand Buddhas, who will free them from all fear and keep them from falling into the evil paths of existence" [*The Lotus Sutra,* p. 322]. How can we possibly hold back our tears at the inexpressible joy of knowing that not just one or two, not just one hundred or two hundred, but as many as a thousand Buddhas will come to greet us with open arms!

Concerning one who disbelieves the Lotus Sutra, because the sutra states, "When his life comes to an end he will enter the Avichi hell"[1] [LS, 74], the wardens of hell will surely come for one and take one away by the hands. How pitiful! The ten kings[2] of the world of the dead will then pass judgment, and the heavenly messengers[3] who have been with one since birth will berate one for one's evil deeds.

Think of those thousand Buddhas extending their hands to all of Nichiren's disciples and lay supporters who chant Nam-myoho-renge-kyo as melons or moonflowers extending their slender vines. (*The Writings of Nichiren Daishonin,* vol. 1, pp. 216–17)

In this writing, Nichiren Daishonin clarifies the most essential point in embracing Myoho-renge-kyo, the ultimate Law of life and death, emphasizing that it lies in practicing with the ultimate spirit of faith that "now is the last moment of one's life" (WND-1, 216). When, with this spirit, we embrace the Mystic Law, we can freely reveal in our lives the true aspect of life and death, which Nichiren explains in this writing as "life and death as functions of Myoho-renge-kyo"[4] (see WND-1, 216). In short, we can transform birth and death in the realm of delusion into birth and death in the realm of Buddhahood.[5] This is because viewing the present moment as our last arises from a deep belief in and understanding of the principle of birth and death in the realm of Buddhahood.

Birth and Death in the Realm of Buddhahood

Citing the Lotus Sutra, Nichiren Daishonin asserts that "one who summons up one's faith and chants Nam-myoho-renge-kyo with the profound insight that now is the last moment of one's life" (WND-1, 216) will savor immense inner peace and tranquillity at death, protected by a thousand Buddhas. This is the meaning of a correct and steadfast mind at the moment of death. In other words, those who strive in faith with the spirit that now is one's last moment are on the path of attaining Buddhahood in this lifetime.

In the preceding passage, which we studied in the last installment, Nichiren explains that the essence of accepting and upholding Myoho-renge-kyo lies in believing and understanding that there is absolutely no difference or separation among "Shakyamuni Buddha who attained enlightenment countless kalpas ago," "the Lotus Sutra that leads all people to Buddhahood" and "we ordinary human beings" (WND-1, 216). He then explains in the passage we are now studying that the crux of this belief and understanding is practicing with the spirit that "now is the last moment of one's life."

To believe and understand that the Buddha, the Law and we ourselves "are in no way different or separate from one another" (WND-1, 216) is to be convinced that our own lives, as entities of Myoho-renge-kyo, are one with the Buddha and undergo the same birth and death as the Buddha—that is, experience birth and death in the realm of Buddhahood. It means living with bright hope and optimism while making the revelation of the inherent Buddhahood in this lifetime our ultimate goal. Accordingly, those committed to practicing as Nichiren teaches will naturally come to have the spirit that now is one's last moment.

The moment of death represents a final accounting of this existence—the outcome of which is strictly decided by how we have lived. Will we meet our last moment with immense satisfaction, filled with deep appreciation and free of all regret? Or will we meet the final curtain of this lifetime overwhelmed by regret and self-reproach? A person's whole life is condensed into that last moment, without any possibility of deception or concealment.

That's why it is crucial to live each moment to the fullest, especially if we want to be able to say: "If I were to die right now, I would have no regret or dissatisfaction. My heart would be serene and tranquil." To strive in faith with the spirit that now is our last moment is to earnestly give our all to the present, determined to have no regrets even if this moment should be our very last.

A Brilliant Departure Toward the Next Existence

From the Buddhist perspective of life and death, the last moment, in addition to being a final accounting of our present existence, is also the point of departure toward our next existence.

I once saw evening fall over the Philippines' Manila Bay, which is said to have one of the most beautiful sunsets in the world. The sun sinking below the horizon dyed the sky a rich crimson and the ocean a shimmering gold. It was truly sublime and majestic, like a great painting. A glorious sunset promises a dazzling sunrise the next day. For us who undergo birth and death in the realm of Buddhahood throughout eternity, the moment we pass from life to death is truly a brilliant departure toward our next existence.

Our last moment could be likened to the summit of a mountain—a moment in which our entire experience of this lifetime is condensed. It is also the most crucial and uncompromising event that determines the course of our next existence. With what state of mind will we greet our final moment? A victorious life free of regret promises a peaceful and tranquil death, while a death imbued with deep satisfaction and fulfillment assures a hope-filled departure toward the next life. Our state of mind at the moment of death—which sums up how we have lived this existence—will become the cause that produces future effects. That is the significance of having a correct and steadfast mind at the moment of death.

To have a correct and steadfast mind at the last moment means maintaining right thought—unwavering faith and conviction in the Mystic Law—without losing serenity or composure even in the face of death. Specifically, it indicates a mind that, on approaching death, feels deep satisfaction at having lived without regret and filled with unsurpassed joy at having embraced the Mystic Law.

Let's clarify the meaning and relationship between the spirit that now is one's last moment and a correct and steadfast mind at the moment of death.

First, the spirit that now is one's last moment means living each moment and each day fully and without regret, deeply aware of the significance of our last moment as a final accounting of this life. In this sense, the wisdom and insight into life possessed by those who strive in faith with this spirit gives them confidence and determination, and further fuels their vibrant hope and tireless actions.

A correct and steadfast mind at the moment of death, meanwhile, is derived as a natural course of striving earnestly in faith day after day, month after month, year after year, with the spirit that now is one's last moment. By doing so, we can forge and polish our lives and elevate our state of mind. We can also feel total confidence and satisfaction about how we have lived, so that when the moment of death comes, we can "make our way to Eagle Peak," as Nichiren Daishonin says, peacefully and without regret, having chanted Nam-myoho-renge-kyo earnestly throughout life. This magnificent state of being is what it means to have a correct and steadfast mind at the moment of death.

Very simply, our continual efforts in faith based on the insight that now is the last moment of life will ensure that we have a correct and steadfast mind at the moment of death. And having a correct and steadfast mind at the moment of death makes it possible for us to depart with complete fulfillment and satisfaction toward the next life.

Living a good life based on the insight that now is the last moment assures us of dying a good death based on a correct and steadfast mind at the final moment. And the final accounting of a good life, which is distinguished by correct and steadfast faith, becomes the starting point of another good life in our next existence.

Both life and death are filled with joy. Joy continues unbroken and unceasing, whether one is moving from life to death, or from death to life.

Those Who Live With the Insight That Now Is One's Last Moment Experience Joy in Both Life and Death

Nichiren Daishonin also talks about what happens after the death of a person who has carried through in faith with the insight that now is the last moment of one's life and succeeded in maintaining a correct and steadfast mind at the moment of death. He writes: "[The Lotus Sutra] proclaims: 'When the lives of these persons come to an end, they will be received into the hands of a thousand Buddhas, who will free them from all fear and keep them from falling into the evil paths of existence' [LS, 322]. How can we possibly hold back our tears at the inexpressible joy of knowing that not just one or two, not just one hundred or two hundred, but as many as a thousand Buddhas will come to greet us with open arms!" (WND-1, 216–17).

Nichiren says that upon death a thousand Buddhas will greet and extend their hands to support and assist those dedicated in faith. In Nichiren's day, belief in the Pure Land (Nembutsu) school of Buddhism was widespread in Japan. People were taught that if they chanted the name of Amida Buddha, then when they died, Amida and the bodhisattvas Perceiver of the World's Sounds and Great Power would come to greet them from the paradise of the Pure Land of Perfect Bliss in the west. This is why Nichiren goes out of his way to emphasize that practitioners of the Lotus Sutra will not simply be greeted by one or two Buddhas, or even one hundred or two hundred Buddhas, but rather will be welcomed by a thousand Buddhas. He likens this picture of a thousand Buddhas extending their hands to the image of melons or moonflowers extending their vines. Contemplating such a wonderful scene, he declares, "How can we possibly hold back our tears at the inexpressible joy!" (WND-1, 216).

Both life and death are filled with joy. Joy continues unbroken and unceasing, whether one is moving from life to death, or from death to life.

At the opposite extreme of the joy of Buddhahood is the hellish state of life of those who reject and slander the Mystic Law. Nichiren writes: "Concerning one who disbelieves the Lotus Sutra, because the sutra states, 'When his life comes to an end he will enter the Avichi hell'[6] [LS, 74], the wardens of hell will surely come for one and take one away by the hands" (WND-1, 217). The Lotus Sutra explains that those who disbelieve and slander the Law will fall into the Avichi hell, or the hell of incessant suffering. Nichiren also says that the ten kings will pass judgment on them, and that the heavenly messengers who have been with them since birth will berate them for their evil deeds (see WND-1, 217). Naturally, the ten kings and heavenly messengers are an expression of the uncompromising and inexorable workings of the law of cause and effect inherent in our lives. In essence, no one can escape the severe reckoning of good and evil in terms of this fundamental law. That is the final accounting of one's life, the end result of the karma one has created over the course of a lifetime.

Regarding birth and death in the Ten Worlds, we can experience birth and death in any of the worlds from hell through Buddhahood. Of course, as entities of the mutual possession of the Ten Worlds, it is possible for us to change our state of life during the course of our present lifetime. But it is inevitable that the predominant state of life of the Ten Worlds we have established as the outcome of this existence will carry over into our next existence. That's why it's vital that we fundamentally transform our state of life while we're still alive.

Deepening our perspective on life and death leads to deepening our own lives. Josei Toda, the second Soka Gakkai president, often said, "In truth, we practice faith for the time of our death." The essence of any religion is found in the way that it views life and death.

The Importance of Accumulating "Treasures of the Heart"

Here, let's clarify some key points to avoid any misunderstanding about what we've discussed so far.

First, when we speak of practicing faith with the spirit that now is the last moment of one's life, certainly it isn't meant as a glorification of death. On the contrary, its true meaning is that we live life to the fullest, with all our might, to the very end. Buddhism is definitely not a teaching of martyrdom that encourages us to recklessly discard our lives or treat them as something of little value. At the same time, we should by no means succumb to the thinking that, since Buddhism views life and death as a cycle and we'll be reborn anyway, it's OK for us to choose death as a means to escape the painful struggles of daily life. To discount the possibility of changing one's karma in this lifetime is to doubt and disbelieve one's boundless potential as a human being.

The second point concerns having a correct and steadfast mind at the moment of death. Some people might worry if someone who has died through accident or illness has actually attained Buddhahood. But it is faith alone that determines whether one has a correct and steadfast mind at the moment of death. Those who dedicated themselves earnestly to faith and gave their all until the very end are definitely on the path of birth and death in the realm of Buddhahood. Whatever form their death takes, they will be sure to have a correct and steadfast mind at their last moment. In light of Nichiren Daishonin's teachings, there is not the slightest doubt that such people, by virtue of the good fortune and benefit they have accumulated through working for *kosen-rufu*, will experience a final moment of great victory on the deepest level of life.

The Nirvana Sutra warns bodhisattvas to fear not the destruction of their bodies but the destruction of their minds, because if their minds are destroyed, they will fall into the three evil paths.[7] In this regard, the sutra cautions, they should be especially aware of evil friends who can destroy their faith.[8]

A life that has been forged in the struggle for *kosen-rufu* is indestructible. Based on the Buddhist principle of the oneness of life and death, those who have accumulated "the treasures of the heart" ("The Three Kinds of Treasure," WND-1, 851) have already cultivated the state of life with which to attain Buddhahood. Through the good fortune and benefit they have gained as a result of persevering in their mission for *kosen-rufu*, they experience a magnificent life and death, setting them on a course where they can forever undergo birth and death in the realm of Buddhahood.

Nichiren Buddhism offers a hope-filled view of life and death that makes it possible for all people to lead lives imbued with eternity, happiness, true self and purity. It enables us to advance and win across past, present and future. We should have strong confidence in this.

"Profound Insight" Means a Deep Inner Awareness

Returning to the start of the quotation we are studying this time, we find the passage "with the profound insight that now is the last moment of one's life" (WND-1, 216). Here, "profound insight" means belief and understanding, or resolute faith. It means realizing deep in our hearts that our own birth and death are inherently birth and death in the realm of Buddhahood. One could say that all who work tirelessly for *kosen-rufu* in the SGI already possess this realization in the depths of their lives.

Precisely because life is eternal, we must exert ourselves wholeheartedly in the present. Taking action based on this deep awareness is what it means to possess "the profound insight that now is the last moment of one's life."

Overcoming Obstacles and Devilish Functions

In our discussion on practicing with the spirit that now is one's last moment and having a correct and steadfast mind at the moment of death, we must not overlook the fact that both are crucial aspects of faith in battling obstacles and devilish functions. Because having a correct and steadfast mind at one's final moment also means overcoming the "devil," or hindrance, of death.

Those who habitually avoid confronting the three obstacles and four devils[9] in their daily lives will be utterly unable to defeat the hindrance of death—the most daunting of all obstacles. The essence of practicing with the spirit that now is one's last moment is to not be beguiled or frightened by the workings of devilish functions. For that reason, we must summon forth the faith, wisdom, courage and life force to confront them. One who has battled and completely triumphed over all devilish functions is a Buddha. Put another way, a Buddha is one who has conquered the most formidable of the four devils—the hindrance of the devil king[10] and the hindrance of death—and has attained a "state of deathlessness" [based on enlightenment to the eternity of life].

At the time of the Tatsunokuchi Persecution, Shijo Kingo was ready to protect

Nichiren Daishonin to the very end, even at the risk of his own life; and yet, as the execution appeared imminent, he cried out tearfully, "These are your last moments" ("The Actions of the Votary of the Lotus Sutra," WND-1, 767). Though probably out of concern for his mentor, Shijo Kingo may have given way to fear at seeing this remorseless attack by devilish functions. Nichiren instantly responded with a powerful lion's roar: "You don't understand! What greater joy could there be?" (WND-1, 767). These words, epitomizing a correct and steadfast mind in the face of imminent death, sum up the supreme essence of the life and death of a Buddha. Nichiren fought head-on against the insidious devilish forces that assailed him, triumphing over the hindrance of death and the hindrance of the devil king. The world of Buddhahood is established in the lives of those who fight with this spirit.

"Strengthen your faith day by day and month after month. Should you slacken in your resolve even a bit, devils will take advantage."

Nichiren urges his disciples struggling amid great persecution: "Strengthen your faith day by day and month after month. Should you slacken in your resolve even a bit, devils will take advantage" ("On Persecutions Befalling the Sage," WND-1, 997). Faith that grows stronger day by day and month after month corresponds to faith based on the spirit that now is the last moment of one's life. Faith of this sort enables us to ward off and defeat devilish functions. The opposite of this is "slackening resolve" and "fear of devilish functions."

As indicated by the passage "they will be received into the hands of a thousand Buddhas" (LS, 322), those who have a correct and steadfast mind at the moment of death will be instantly greeted by innumerable Buddhas, bodhisattvas and heavenly deities—the protective functions of the universe (see WND-1, 216). It is vital that we always remember, though, that this is brought about only as a result of our own efforts in faith to combat evil and realize good. The powerful life force of Buddhahood wells forth in the lives of those who possess such a fighting spirit.

For six decades, I have striven unceasingly for *kosen-rufu* with the resolve that now is the last moment of my life. When I was young, I suffered from poor health and might have died at any time. That is why I fought to support and protect President Toda with that rigorous resolve that now is my last moment. I also rose up and battled single-handedly against the onslaught of obstacles and devilish functions besetting my mentor. Later, based on my conviction that spreading the Buddhist view of the eternity of life is indispensable to the goal of world peace, I summoned all of my courage and intellectual resources and embarked on the task of creating peace around the globe.

Because we of the SGI have striven in faith with the spirit that now is our last moment, the original life force from time without beginning has welled forth within our lives. And I firmly believe that we have built the SGI into the global organization it is today because we have advanced together harmoniously in "the spirit of many in body but one in mind" (WND-1, 217).

Countless SGI members have vigorously scaled the challenges of life and reached the brilliant summit of their final moment with a correct and steadfast mind of faith, having practiced throughout their lifetimes with the spirit that now is one's last moment. The triumph of their great human revolution is actual proof that the heritage of the ultimate Law of life and death flows vibrantly throughout the SGI.

1. Wardens of hell: Demons in Buddhist mythology who torment transgressors who have fallen into hell. They work for King Yama, the king of hell, who is said to judge and determine the rewards and punishments of the dead.
2. Ten kings: Mythological kings described in the Ten Kings Sutra, who are popularly believed to take turns judging the dead from the seventh day after a person's death until the second anniversary. The concept of the ten kings is thought to be Chinese in origin, given that the Ten Kings Sutra is likely to have been written in China. King Yama, the king of hell, is also included among these kings.
3. Heavenly messengers: Gods said to dwell on one's shoulders from the time of birth, recording all of one's acts, good and evil, and reporting them to King Yama, who judges the dead. They represent the law of cause and effect at work in one's life. These heavenly messengers usually refer to the gods Same Birth and Same Name.
4. Life and death as functions of Myoho-renge-kyo: Life and death are originally inherent aspects of Myoho-renge-kyo, which is the fundamental Law pervading the universe and all life. Since Myoho-renge-kyo encompasses the Ten Worlds, all things, as entities of Myoho-renge-kyo, undergo the phases of life and death in the Ten Worlds. Accordingly, by embracing the Mystic Law, we can transform birth and death in the realm of delusion of the nine worlds into birth and death in the realm of Buddhahood.
5. Birth and death in the realm of Buddhahood: To freely undergo the cycle of birth and death based on the realization that our lives are entities of the all-pervasive Law of Myoho-renge-kyo and that life and death are inherent functions of Myoho-renge-kyo. Further, it is to embody the immense compassion and life force inherent in the universe and practice the Buddha way in lifetime after lifetime in order to lead all living beings to enlightenment.
6. The hell of incessant suffering, a state of unending torment.
7. Three evil paths: Realms of suffering into which one falls as a result of evil deeds. They are the worlds of hell, hungry spirits and animals, the lowest three of the six paths.
8. The Nirvana Sutra states: "Have no fear of mad elephants. What you should fear are evil friends! Why? Because a mad elephant can only destroy your body; it cannot destroy your mind. But an evil friend can destroy both body and mind.... Even if you are killed by a mad elephant, you will not fall into the three evil paths. But if you are killed by an evil friend, you are certain to fall into them" ("Reply to Hoshina Goro Taro," WND-1, 159).
9. Three obstacles and four devils: Various obstacles and hindrances to the practice of Buddhism. They are listed in the Nirvana Sutra and Nagarjuna's *The Treatise on the Great Perfection of Wisdom*. The three obstacles are (1) the obstacle of earthly desires, or obstacles arising from the three poisons—greed, anger and foolishness; (2) the obstacle of karma, obstacles due to bad karma created by committing any of the five cardinal sins or ten evil acts; and (3) the obstacle of retribution, obstacles caused by the negative karmic effects of actions in the three evil paths. The four devils are (1) the hindrance of the five components, obstructions caused by one's physical and mental functions; (2) the hindrance of earthly desires, obstructions arising from the three poisons; (3) the hindrance of death, meaning one's own untimely death obstructing one's practice of Buddhism, or the premature death of another practitioner causing one to doubt; and (4) the hindrance of the devil king, who is said to assume various forms or take possession of others in order to cause one to discard one's Buddhist practice. This hindrance is regarded as the most difficult to overcome.
10. Devil king: Also, devil king of the sixth heaven or heavenly devil. The king of devils, who dwells in the highest or the sixth heaven of the world of desire. He is also named Freely Enjoying Things Conjured by Others, the king who makes free use of the fruits of others' efforts for his own pleasure. Served by innumerable minions, he obstructs Buddhist practice and delights in sapping the life force of other beings. One of the four devils.

KEY POINTS

Birth and Death in the Realm of Buddhahood

To believe and understand that the Buddha, the Law and we ourselves "are in no way different or separate from one another" (WND-1, 216) is to be convinced that our own lives, as entities of Myoho-renge-kyo, are one with the Buddha and undergo the same birth and death as the Buddha—that is, experience birth and death in the realm of Buddhahood. It means living with bright hope and optimism while making the revelation of the inherent Buddhahood in this lifetime our ultimate goal. Accordingly, those committed to practicing as Nichiren teaches will naturally come to have the spirit that now is one's last moment. (p. 50)

The Importance of Accumulating "Treasures of the Heart"

A life that has been forged in the struggle for *kosen-rufu* is indestructible. Based on the Buddhist principle of the oneness of life and death, those who have accumulated "the treasures of the heart" (WND-1, 851) have already cultivated the state of life with which to attain Buddhahood. Through the good fortune and benefit they have gained as a result of persevering in their mission for *kosen-rufu*, they experience a magnificent life and death, setting them on a course where they can forever undergo birth and death in the realm of Buddhahood. (p. 54)

Overcoming Obstacles and Devilish Functions

The essence of practicing with the spirit that now is one's last moment is to not be beguiled or frightened by the workings of devilish functions. For that reason, we must summon forth the faith, wisdom, courage and life force to confront them. One who has battled and completely triumphed over all devilish functions is a Buddha. Put another way, a Buddha is one who has conquered the most formidable of the four devils—the hindrance of the devil king and the hindrance of death—and has attained a "state of deathlessness" [based on enlightenment to the eternity of life]. (p. 54)

DIALOGUE AND REFLECTION

1) "A correct and steadfast mind at the moment of death, meanwhile, is derived as a natural course of striving earnestly in faith day after day, month after month, year after year, with the spirit that now is one's last moment" (p. 51). How do you cultivate that correct and steadfast state of mind?

2) "The essence of any religion is found in the way it views life and death" (p. 53). What, then, is the essence of Nichiren Buddhism?

The Heritage of the ULTIMATE LAW *of* LIFE

SGI PRESIDENT IKEDA'S STUDY LECTURE SERIES

This is a series of lectures by SGI President Daisaku Ikeda on "The Heritage of the Ultimate Law of Life." Nichiren Daishonin states: "Shakyamuni Buddha who attained enlightenment countless kalpas ago, the Lotus Sutra that leads all people to Buddhahood, and we ordinary human beings are in no way different or separate from one another. To chant Myoho-renge-kyo with this realization is to inherit the ultimate Law of life and death."

[7]

Maintaining Lifelong Faith—Our Faith in This Lifetime Secures Our Happiness Over the Three Existences

It is rare to be born a human being, and life as a human being, moreover, is hard to sustain (see "The Three Kinds of Treasure," *The Writings of Nichiren Daishonin*, vol. 1, p. 851).[1] From the standpoint of eternity, this existence seems but an instant. My mentor, second Soka Gakkai president Josei Toda, often used to say, "You know, a hundred years from now none of us will be here." Life is limited, and the way that we live it is important. Buddhism teaches that we can build victory for all eternity during this lifetime. This is the purpose of our Buddhist practice. And our success in this endeavor hinges on maintaining our Buddhist practice throughout our lives—in other words, continuing in faith.

In our discussion of "The Heritage of the Ultimate Law of Life" so far, we have looked at some of the vital elements in embracing and upholding faith in the ultimate Law—Myoho-renge-kyo. One of these elements, we saw, is chanting Nam-myoho-renge-kyo with the conviction that we are in no way different from the Buddha and the Law, and that the life and death of each of us are inherent functions of Myoho-renge-kyo, phases that unfold in the world of Buddhahood.[2] This is the principle that Shakyamuni, as the Buddha who attained enlightenment in the remote past, taught through the example of his own life and expounded as the essence of the Lotus Sutra, which leads all people to Buddhahood.

Another key element, we learned, consists of summoning up resolute faith based on the profound insight that now is our last moment, and to practice with this spirit as long as we live in order to have a correct and steadfast mind at the moment of death, the final accounting of this existence.[3]

Both naturally underscore the importance of persevering in our Buddhist practice throughout our lives. If we hope to face death with a correct and steadfast mind, we must continue striving in faith with the spirit that now is our last moment. It is to be noted, however, that in "The Heritage of the Ultimate Law of Life," Nichiren Daishonin explains this importance not only from the limited view of this lifetime but from the broader view of life's eternity over past, present and future. In other words, if we faithfully uphold the Mystic Law throughout our lives and have a correct and steadfast mind at the moment of death, not only this present lifetime but all past and future lifetimes—our lives across the three existences—become one, sharing in "the heritage of the Lotus Sutra" (WND-1, 217). We come to see that our lives and deaths throughout eternity are functions of the Mystic Law, shining with the brilliance of the world of Buddhahood.

Life Throughout the Three Existences—Past, Present and Future

> **My followers are now able to accept and uphold the Lotus Sutra because of the strong ties they formed with it in their past existences. They are certain to obtain the fruit of Buddhahood in the future. The heritage of the Lotus Sutra flows within the lives of those who never forsake it in any lifetime whatsoever—whether in the past, the present, or the future. But those who disbelieve and slander the Lotus Sutra will immediately "destroy all the seeds for becoming a Buddha in this world" [LS, 74]. Because they cut themselves off from the potential to attain enlightenment, they do not share the heritage of the ultimate Law of life and death.** (WND-1, 217)

Nichiren Daishonin says: "My followers are now able to accept and uphold the Lotus Sutra because of the strong ties they formed with it in their past existences. They are certain to obtain the fruit of Buddhahood in the future" (WND-1, 217). It is his unequivocal assertion that our strong connection with the Lotus Sutra in past lifetimes is the cause that has enabled us to embrace the sutra in this lifetime, an act that in turn serves as the cause for our attaining Buddhahood in future existences as well. These words are specifically meant as encouragement for the letter's recipient, Sairen-bo, who was trying to practice the Lotus Sutra while in exile. But they can also be read as an affirmation that, through positively transforming our lives in this existence, we can positively transform the totality of our lives—that is, all lifetimes throughout past, present and future.

In terms of chronological sequence, we can readily appreciate that changes made in this existence will affect our future lifetimes. It may be a little more difficult, however, to grasp that such changes can have an impact on our past lifetimes, too. Also, though we speak of transforming the cycle of birth and death, this doesn't mean putting an end to it. When we embrace the Lotus Sutra in our present existence, we come to deeply appreciate that past rounds of birth and death in the realm of suffering and delusion are like a dream, and that life and death as functions of the Mystic Law—that is, birth and death in the realm of Buddhahood—are the actual

Seikyo Press

SGI President Ikeda shakes hands with Nobel Peace laureate Mikhail S. Gorbachev, on the occasion of their ninth meeting, at the Makiguchi Memorial Hall in Hachioji, Tokyo, June 11, 2007.

awakened reality. This is the true aspect of life clearly perceived by the Buddha.[4]

Human beings usually think of the world of suffering as being their actual reality. But from the standpoint of the original and inherent nature of life and death, this world of suffering is akin to a dream. In his writing titled "The Unanimous Declaration by the Buddhas of the Three Existences," Nichiren describes the birth and death experienced in the nine worlds as a dream realm, and the eternal and unchanging world of Buddhahood as the true, awakened realm. He writes:

> **One should also understand that one's own mind that views the dream realm of birth and death in the nine worlds is no different from the waking mind of the world of Buddhahood, the world that is eternal and unchanging. The place in which one views the dream realm of birth and death in the nine worlds is no different from the place in which one experiences the waking state of the world of Buddhahood, eternal and unchanging. There is no difference in the mind itself, and no difference in the place where all this occurs. But the dreams are all false or empty, while what is experienced in the waking state is all true.** (WND-2, 846)

When we look at our past lifetimes from the truly awakened state of life derived through embracing the Mystic Law in the present, we can recognize that we must have had strong ties with the Lotus Sutra from the past. Having a connection with the Lotus Sutra means that by hearing the teaching that enables all people to attain enlightenment, our innate Buddha nature has been activated. This connection can be either positive or negative, so the "strong ties with the Lotus Sutra" (see WND-1, 217) of which Nichiren speaks in this writing are not limited to a positive relationship. Whether we embrace faith in the Lotus Sutra or reject it, in either instance our Buddha nature is stimulated.

Our connection with the Lotus Sutra in past lifetimes is the cause for us to embrace the sutra in the present, and by continuing to do so until the final moment, we will leave this world with a correct and steadfast mind of faith. This lifetime, therefore, serves as the cause for our attaining the fruit of Buddhahood in subsequent lifetimes, too.

As we have already discussed in previous installments, this future attainment of Buddhahood does not mean dwelling tranquilly in some otherworldly paradise or becoming a transcendent Buddha. It means assuming the form of a Buddha who, amid the cycle of birth and death, embodies the compassionate workings of the universe and forever strives to free living beings from suffering in the reality of the *saha* world. A Buddha continually undergoes the cycle of birth and death throughout past, present and future. This is what Nichiren means by "in any lifetime whatsoever" (WND-1, 217)—which can also be expressed as "life across the three existences."

The Law of Cause and Effect—Everything Ultimately Hinges on the Present

Next, let's look at the Buddhist principle of causality that operates over the three existences—past, present and future. An important point, first, is that in his discussions of causality, Nichiren Daishonin always places primary focus on the present. In "The Opening of the Eyes," he quotes a passage from the Contemplation on the Mind-Ground Sutra on the workings of causality over the three existences:

> **If you want to understand the causes that existed in the past, look at the results as they are manifested in the present. And if you want to understand what results will be manifested in the future, look at the causes that exist in the present.** (WND-1, 279)

I was deeply struck when I first read these words in my youth, because they drove home to me that, when it comes to cause and effect, nothing is more important than the present and our own faith. This sutra passage and Nichiren's related explanation in "The Opening of the Eyes" clarify that the essence of the Buddhist view of causality lies in changing one's present self. We see Nichiren express both unassailable confidence in the ability to transform any negative karma from the past, and boundless hope in the certainty of enjoying immense happiness in future lifetimes, all achieved as a result of his present actions for the sake of the Law (see WND-1, 287).[5]

Nichiren Buddhism enables each of us to establish a solid self in the present so that we can transform past sorrows and misery into inexhaustible hope for the future. The heart of Nichiren's teaching is that no matter what difficulties we may now face, we should earnestly challenge the present with unflagging optimism and the belief that we can change the future.

In any event, our faith, our Buddhist practice, in this existence determines the direction of all of our lifetimes throughout past, present and future, whether they will be pervaded by happiness and compassion or by sorrow and darkness.

Faith means infinite hope. There is not the slightest doubt that we can create the causes for our eternal future happiness in this present lifetime and in this present moment. Because its beneficial powers are difficult to fathom, the Law is called "mystic."

Continued Faith Secures Our Course Over the Three Existences

A vital aspect of our Buddhist practice lies in continuing it throughout our lives. In his "Letter to Niike," Nichiren Daishonin emphasizes the importance of maintaining faith to the very end:

> **Be diligent in developing your faith until the last moment of your life. Otherwise you will have regrets. For example, the journey from Kamakura to Kyoto takes twelve days. If you travel for eleven but stop with only one day remaining, how can you admire the moon over the capital?** (WND-1, 1027)

This is a well-known passage. Though having had the great good fortune to embrace Nichiren Buddhism, if we stop practicing before we reach the end of our lives, we cannot attain the ultimate summit of Buddhahood. Since the flame of Buddhist practice is easily extinguished, Nichiren urges us to remain diligent in developing our faith.

Why is the flame of faith easily extinguished? Because people allow themselves to be defeated by the desire for fame and fortune or by onslaughts of the three obstacles and four devils.[6] Nichiren says: "Strengthen your faith day by day and month after month. Should you slacken in your resolve even a bit, devils will take advantage" ("On Persecutions Befalling the Sage," WND-1, 997). A slackening or wavering in our resolve or faith triggers our fundamental darkness, our negativity. To maintain faith throughout our lives, therefore, rests on our resolve to keep on striving in our Buddhist practice.

Nichiren himself vowed never to retreat or falter on the path of faith. For example, speaking of his resolve immediately before declaring the establishment of his teaching, he says: "I vowed to summon up a powerful and unconquerable desire for the salvation of all beings and never to falter in my efforts" ("The Opening of the Eyes," WND-1, 240). And even while in exile on Sado, he was determined never to abandon his vow, declaring: "I will be the pillar of Japan. I will be the eyes of Japan. I will be the great ship of Japan. This is my vow, and I will never forsake it!" ("The Opening of the Eyes," WND-1, 280–81). Nichiren personally demonstrated with his life the paramount importance of remaining steadfast in faith.

Deepening Our Faith Day By Day

From this perspective, I affirm that all SGI members are certain to enjoy lives of victory based on faith.

In terms of Nichiren Daishonin's view of life and death—the Buddhist view of life's eternity—it is clear that the moment of death is the culmination of our present lifetime. This is because it represents not only the final page of this existence but also the departure toward the next.

Nichiren specifically stresses the importance of "first learning about death" (see "The Importance of the Moment of Death," WND-2, 759).[7] And President Toda often said: "The purpose of our Buddhist practice is for the sake of our final moment."

Therefore, it is a basic premise in Nichiren Buddhism that unceasing faith means faith that grows deeper "day by day and month after month" (WND-1, 997) until the closing page of one's life. Indeed, we need to strongly bear in mind that we must continue to deepen our faith.

Even plants and trees naturally undergo steady, continuous growth. In passing, we might only notice striking events such as when they're in flower, but a person who looks at things with the eyes of a poet or a keen observer may perceive even the subtlest day-to-day changes.

Similarly, our faith should also continue to grow and deepen surely and steadily day after day as we exert ourselves in our daily practice and in SGI activities. Persevering in the two ways of practice and study in the SGI—the organization advancing *kosen-rufu* in exact accord with Nichiren's teachings—continually functions to deepen our faith toward attaining Buddhahood in this lifetime. As Nichiren writes: "If one dyes something repeatedly in indigo, it becomes even bluer than the indigo leaves. The Lotus Sutra is like the indigo, and the strength of one's practice is like the deepening blue" ("Hell Is the Land of Tranquil Light," WND-1, 457). Through our efforts in faith each day, our lives are increasingly imbued with Myoho-renge-kyo.

In more concrete terms, deepening our faith means strengthening our prayer, our conviction in chanting Nam-myoho-renge-kyo, which is a reflection of our life-state. As we continue in our Buddhist practice, our conviction will deepen.

A Life of Self-Realization, Social Contribution and Victory

Faith is something that should continue to deepen over the course of a lifetime. In terms of a lifelong commitment to human development and spiritual growth, let us look at the example found in ancient India. Prior to Shakyamuni's time, it had become customary to view life as divided into four distinct periods. These are known as the four *ashramas*, or stages of life.

The first stage is that of the student (*brahmacari*). This is the period for studying under a teacher to become an educated and well-rounded individual.

The second stage is that of the householder (*grihastha*). This is the period for taking on responsibility in society and family life.

The third stage is that of the retiree (*vanaprastha*). This is the period for detaching oneself from the pursuit of worldly wealth and status, for retiring and focusing on religious practice.

The fourth stage is that of the renunciant (*sannyasi*). This is the period for discarding attachments and embarking on a journey toward spiritual enlightenment and emancipation from the sufferings of birth and death.

In other words, the people of ancient India followed a four-stage path of developing themselves, assuming social and family responsibilities, focusing on religious practice and realizing the ultimate meaning of life. This essentially sums up how they lived their lives.

With a similar lifelong commitment to faith, we of the SGI are today forging ahead with self-realization, social contribution and victory in life as our goals.

The age of the youth division—from teen years onward—is primarily a time for awakening to a purpose in life and polishing oneself. This could be described as the time of "self-discovery and training." Discovering a firm sense of purpose during this period gives powerful impetus to the development of one's talent and potential. The growth of young people with fresh determination is truly awe-inspiring.

I met President Toda when I was 19 and received direct training and instruction from him for close to a decade. This year marks the 60th anniversary of my embracing faith in Nichiren Buddhism. I built the foundations for my entire life during this period of my youth when I struggled alongside my mentor.

Next is the age of the men's and women's divisions—encompassing the period up to retirement. If the age of the future and youth divisions is the period of "self-discovery and training," then this next age could be described as the period of "implementation and actual proof." It is the time to show actual proof of faith—in one's work and personal life, in the community and in society at large. It is the time to thoroughly fulfill our personal mission or social responsibilities, and to fully and freely demonstrate the true power of faith in society.

Next is the age of the Many Treasures Group[8]—the elders in our realm of faith. This is the time for making one's life shine even more brilliantly with the light of faith, aiming for the ultimate goal of revealing Buddhahood in this lifetime. This could be described as the period of maturity and joy. There is no retirement age in faith. Rather, this period of life is the key time for further deepening one's faith and causing it to really shine. The starting point and purpose of Buddhism lies in coming to terms with and overcoming the sufferings of birth, aging, sickness and death. Our challenge in the final chapter of our lives is to personally triumph over these most fundamental issues of human existence and achieve the ultimate goal of our Buddhist practice. President Toda said: "The final part of your life is important. If the last years of your life are happy, then you have won."

The Record of the Orally Transmitted Teachings states: "The words 'four sides' [of the treasure tower] stand for birth, aging, sickness, and death. We use the aspects of birth, aging, sickness, and death to adorn the tower that is our body" (OTT, 90). The Lotus Sutra says that when the treasure tower appeared, all of its four sides emitted a sweet fragrance.[9] Nichiren here explains that these four sides are none other than birth, aging, sickness and death, which adorn our lives with their beautiful fragrance. This interpretation of the four universal sufferings as a life-adorning fragrance is truly profound.

This describes a state of being that is awakened to the original and inherent nature of life and death—life and death as functions of Myoho-renge-kyo—overflowing with the fundamental life force of the universe and pervaded by the limitless joy of birth and death in the realm of Buddhahood. This awareness is the key to regarding birth, aging, sickness and death as a fragrance that adorns the treasure tower of our lives, and to forever enjoy great life force and immense fortune and benefit, imbued with the four virtues of eternity, happiness, true self and purity.

1. Nichiren Daishonin writes: "It is rare to be born a human being. The number of those endowed with human life is as small as the amount of earth one can place on a fingernail. Life as a human being is hard to sustain—as hard as it is for the dew to remain on the grass" ("The Three Kinds of Treasure," WND-1, 851).
2. Nichiren writes: "Shakyamuni Buddha who attained enlightenment countless kalpas ago, the Lotus Sutra that leads all people to Buddhahood, and we ordinary human beings are in no way different or separate from one another. To chant Myoho-renge-kyo with this realization is to inherit the ultimate Law of life and death. This is a matter of the utmost importance for Nichiren's disciples and lay supporters, and this is what it means to embrace the Lotus Sutra" (WND-1, 216).

3. Nichiren writes: "For one who summons up one's faith and chants Nam-myoho-renge-kyo with the profound insight that now is the last moment of one's life, the sutra proclaims: 'When the lives of these persons come to an end, they will be received into the hands of a thousand Buddhas, who will free them from all fear and keep them from falling into the evil paths of existence' [LS, 322]. How can we possibly hold back our tears at the inexpressible joy of knowing that not just one or two, not just one hundred or two hundred, but as many as a thousand Buddhas will come to greet us with open arms!" (WND-1, 216–17).
4. "Life Span," the 16th chapter of the Lotus Sutra, states: "The Thus Come One perceives the true aspect of the threefold world exactly as it is. There is no ebb or flow of birth and death, and there is no existing in this world and later entering extinction. It is neither substantial nor empty, neither consistent nor diverse. Nor is it what those who dwell in the threefold world perceive it to be. All such things the Thus Come One sees clearly and without error" (LS, 226).
5. In "The Opening of the Eyes," Nichiren indicates that the reason he has encountered persecution in this lifetime is to enable him to quickly expiate the offense of slandering the Law in previous existences and attain Buddhahood through the benefit of upholding the Mystic Law. This is called the principle of lessening karmic retribution. He concludes the writing by saying: "For what I have done, I have been condemned to exile, but it is a small suffering to undergo in this present life and not one worth lamenting. In future lives I will enjoy immense happiness, a thought that gives me great joy" (WND-1, 287).
6. Three obstacles and four devils: Various obstacles and hindrances to the practice of Buddhism.
7. Nichiren writes: "Looking back, I have been studying the Buddha's teachings since I was a boy. And I found myself thinking, 'The life of a human being is fleeting. The exhaled breath never waits for the inhaled one. Even dew before the wind is hardly a sufficient metaphor. It is the way of the world that whether one is wise or foolish, old or young, one never knows what will happen to one from one moment to the next. Therefore I should first of all learn about death, and then about other things'" (WND-2, 759).
8. A group for Soka Gakkai members 60 years or older, similar to the SGI-USA's Golden Stage Group.
9. The Lotus Sutra states: "All four sides [of the treasure tower] emitted a fragrance of tamalapatra and sandalwood that pervaded the whole world" (LS, 170).

KEY POINTS

The Broader View of Life's Eternity

If we hope to face death with a correct and steadfast mind, we must continue striving in faith with the spirit that now is our last moment. It is to be noted, however, that in "The Heritage of the Ultimate Law of Life" Nichiren Daishonin explains this importance not only from the limited view of this lifetime but from the broader view of life's eternity over past, present and future. In other words, if we faithfully uphold the Mystic Law throughout our lives and have a correct and steadfast mind at the moment of death, not only this present lifetime but all past and future lifetimes—our life across the three existences—become one, sharing in "the heritage of the Lotus Sutra" (WND-1, 217). We come to see that our lives and deaths throughout eternity are functions of the Mystic Law, shining with the brilliance of the world of Buddhahood. (p. 60)

Earnest Challenge and Unflagging Optimism

Nichiren Buddhism enables each of us to establish a solid self in the present so that we can transform past sorrows and misery into inexhaustible hope for the future. The heart of Nichiren's teaching is that no matter what difficulties we may now face, we should earnestly challenge the present with unflagging optimism and the belief that we can change the future.

In any event, our faith, our Buddhist practice, in this existence determines the direction of all of our lifetimes throughout past, present and future, whether they will be pervaded by happiness and compassion or by sorrow and darkness. (p. 62)

Adorning the Treasure Tower

The Record of the Orally Transmitted Teachings states: "The words 'four sides' [of the treasure tower] stand for birth, aging, sickness, and death. We use the aspects of birth, aging, sickness, and death to adorn the tower that is our body" (OTT, 90). The Lotus Sutra says that when the treasure tower appeared, all of its four sides emitted a sweet fragrance. Nichiren here explains that these four sides are none other than birth, aging, sickness and death, which adorn our lives with their beautiful fragrance. This interpretation of the four universal sufferings as a life-adorning fragrance is truly profound. (p. 65)

DIALOGUE AND REFLECTION

1) How does our practice of Nichiren Buddhism affect the past, present and future?

2) What is meant by the statement that our lives are "adorned" with birth, aging, sickness and death?

The Heritage of the ULTIMATE LAW *of* LIFE

SGI PRESIDENT IKEDA'S STUDY LECTURE SERIES

This is a series of lectures by SGI President Daisaku Ikeda on "The Heritage of the Ultimate Law of Life." Nichiren Daishonin states: "Shakyamuni Buddha who attained enlightenment countless kalpas ago, the Lotus Sutra that leads all people to Buddhahood, and we ordinary human beings are in no way different or separate from one another. To chant Myoho-renge-kyo with this realization is to inherit the ultimate Law of life and death."

[8]

"Many in Body But One in Mind"

The True Heritage of Faith Flows in the Harmonious Community of Practitioners Who Share the Great Vow for Kosen-rufu

Until this point, Nichiren Daishonin had described the characteristics of faith infused with the heritage of the ultimate Law of life and death. To summarize, such faith is marked by: (1) confidence that one will attain Buddhahood in this lifetime; (2) the profound insight that now is the last moment of one's life; and (3) continuing to practice Buddhism as long as one lives.

The heritage of attaining Buddhahood is found in such firm, resolute faith.

Teaching others about faith in the Mystic Law and actualizing a more peaceful world is the object of our movement for *kosen-rufu.* Of vital importance to this endeavor are the harmonious community of practitioners and the mentor-disciple spirit.

The Harmonious Community of Practitioners and the Mentor-Disciple Spirit

All disciples and lay supporters of Nichiren should chant Nam-myoho-renge-kyo with the spirit of many in body but one in mind, transcending all differences among themselves[1] to become as inseparable as fish and the water in which they swim. This spiritual bond is the basis for the universal transmission of the ultimate Law of life and death. Herein lies the true goal of Nichiren's propagation. When you are so united, even the great desire for widespread propagation [kosen-rufu] can be fulfilled. But if any of

Nichiren's disciples disrupt the unity of many in body but one in mind, they would be like warriors who destroy their own castle from within. (*The Writings of Nichiren Daishonin*, vol. 1, p. 217)

The correct flow of the heritage of the ultimate Law of life and death is contingent on the struggle of mentor and disciple to realize widespread propagation. In the Latter Day of the Law[2] this is a battle between the Buddha and devilish functions. Without a harmonious community of practitioners solidly united in purpose and brimming with the spirit of mentor and disciple, we cannot hope to triumph in that endeavor.

In the passage we are studying in this installment, Nichiren Daishonin voices his expectations for all of his disciples, both priest and laity, describing his ideal vision of the mentor-disciple relationship and the harmonious community of practitioners who strive with him to realize *kosen-rufu* in the Latter Day of the Law. In doing so, he urges his followers to transcend all differences among themselves, to become as inseparable as fish and water, and to unite in the spirit of "many in body but one in mind." The heritage of the ultimate Law of life and death, he says, flows in the lives of those who chant Nam-myoho-renge-kyo—a practice for both oneself and others—based on this spirit of equality and unity.

"Transcending All Differences Among Themselves"

Let us first look at the term *differences* in the passage "transcending all differences among themselves." What Nichiren Daishonin specifically means here are feelings of antagonism, discrimination and selfishness that arise from the tendency to see self and others, or diverse phenomena or events, as separate and disconnected—a tendency that obstructs empathy and understanding. The heritage of the Buddha will not exist in such a negative, ego-driven mind-set.

It's too easy for the human heart to succumb to egoism and self-interest when one is tempted by power, prestige or personal profit; strongly attached to status and position; or obsessed with fame and fortune. Faith is ultimately a struggle with our own self-centeredness.

No matter how high a leadership position or what fine-sounding things people may say, if they have lost their faith and are motivated by self-serving ends, they will find it impossible to remain in the pure and harmonious community of practitioners who share the great vow or desire for *kosen-rufu.*

Indeed, in this writing, Nichiren refers to those practitioners who disrupt the unity of "many in body but one in mind" as being "like warriors who destroy their own castle from within" (WND-1, 217). In other words, they are like "worms within the lion's body," destroying the *kosen-rufu* movement from the inside. Hence, he instructs his followers on the importance of "transcending all differences among themselves."

"Become As Inseparable As Fish and the Water in Which They Swim"

In addition, Nichiren Daishonin says that his followers should "become as inseparable as fish and the water in which they swim" (WND-1, 217). This indicates a spirit of harmony and unity. It also implies a spirit of mutual respect, understanding, support and caring regardless of superficial differences in circumstances or position. Simply put, it means getting along together.

When we work together for the same great objective of *kosen-rufu* based on the spirit of mentor and disciple, inspiring, encouraging and supporting one another, we will naturally come into rapport and strive to maintain positive, respectful relations. In dynamic and growing organizations, one often finds that there are good working relationships and rapport among the leaders.

The emperor Liu Pei and his loyal prime minister Chuko K'ung-ming, two of the main protagonists of the Chinese classic *The Romance of the Three Kingdoms,* shared a relationship of profound mutual respect and admiration, described as being "like fish and water."

When we embrace the great vow of the Buddha as our own, chanting Nam-myoho-renge-kyo and undertaking the Buddha's work for the happiness of humanity and the realization of *kosen-rufu,* we can come to appreciate that all our fellow members are people worthy of the greatest respect who, like us, are leading lives of supreme mission. This forms the basis of a vibrant relationship of camaraderie and inspiration that is above antagonism or discrimination.

The Spirit of "Many in Body But One in Mind" and the Heritage of Faith

Furthermore, Nichiren Daishonin stresses the importance of uniting in the spirit of "many in body but one in mind." This is the very foundation of the harmonious community of practitioners. Needless to say, it also encompasses the two preceding points I have just made.

"Many in body"—which can also be translated as "different in body"—means that we each have our own unique personalities, talents and roles to play and so on. In a general sense, "one in mind"—or, "one in heart"—means sharing a common goal or common values. More specifically for us, it means sharing faith in the Mystic Law and the great vow for *kosen-rufu.*

The spirit of "many in body but one in mind" in Buddhism refers to the individual and the group harmonizing based on the Law. It indicates a richly diverse and dynamic community of capable people who inspire one another in their efforts to advance *kosen-rufu.* Nichiren concludes that the heritage of the ultimate Law of life and death flows in the lives of those who chant Nam-myoho-renge-kyo with this spirit.

In this writing and elsewhere, he emphasizes that unity is the key to achieving success and victory in all endeavors,[3] and that unity is indispensable in the struggle for *kosen-rufu* in the Latter Day of the Law—a struggle between the Buddha and devilish functions. He also expresses his firm conviction that as long as he and his followers are united in their commitment for *kosen-rufu,* they can triumph over even the most formidable obstacles.[4]

Chanting With a Shared Commitment

The spirit of "many in body but one in mind," in a sense, represents the ultimate manifestation of the "strategy of the Lotus Sutra,"[5] which is chanting Nam-myoho-renge-kyo to the Gohonzon—specifically, chanting with a shared commitment for *kosen-rufu.*

No plans or strategies for *kosen-rufu* will succeed without such shared commitment in chanting. Strong practice based on such unity will also give rise to tremendous momentum. So even should there appear individuals who seek to disrupt the unity of our movement, their negative influence will be rebuffed by everyone's focused spirit.

"One in mind," or shared commitment, also refers to the great vow for *kosen-rufu*—the great vow of the Buddha who seeks to lead all people to enlightenment and also the great vow of the mentor. "One in mind" means making this great vow our own and working toward its actualization. The essence of this shared commitment can be found in chanting Nam-myoho-renge-kyo inspired by the wish for *kosen-rufu,* and this unity in chanting pulses vitally in the Soka Gakkai.

Uniting in the spirt of "many in body but one in mind" means all of us aligning our hearts with the great vow of the Buddha and the spirit of the mentor.

A Rhythm of Perfect Victory

When we advance in the united spirit of "many in body but one in mind" based on chanting for the realization of *kosen-rufu,* we generate a powerful forward impetus and the energy to secure victory. Everyone who shares in this spirit can work together harmoniously and feel joy even in the midst of difficult struggles. Unity of purpose holds the key to creating such a rhythm of victory, a rhythm of dynamic activity.

In other words, the "rhythm of the Mystic Law" emerges when all unite their hearts with the heart of the Buddha, with the great vow for *kosen-rufu.* Because everyone's life resonates with the Buddha's lofty spirit, it leads to growth, development, joy and victory. It also gives rise to an indestructible bastion of creative talent, happiness and peace, where people are linked together by deep bonds far surpassing ordinary ties of friendship.

Uniting in the spirit of "many in body but one in mind" means all of us aligning our hearts with the great vow of the Buddha and the spirit of the mentor. In that respect, the oneness of mentor and disciple is the essence of this united spirit in faith.

In this writing, Nichiren Daishonin goes on to clarify the crucial point that the true goal of his propagation lies in ensuring that his followers embody the spirit of "many in body but one in mind." For only a community of practitioners united in this way can succeed to the Buddha's heritage and develop an enduring movement, based on the oneness of mentor and disciple, to ensure that this heritage continues to be widely transmitted into the future.

Nichiren realized that, after his passing, for there to be a solidly united gathering of followers in which his spirit lived on would mean that people of future generations who had never personally met him could still embrace faith and practice as his disciples. They would share the same commitment for *kosen-rufu* and thus permit the heritage of faith for attaining Buddhahood to flow on indefinitely. Therefore, he writes, when his followers are united in the spirit of "many in body but one in mind," "even the great desire for widespread propagation [*kosen-rufu*] can be fulfilled" (WND-1, 217). It is a declaration that the Buddha's great desire or vow for *kosen-rufu* will be passed on without interruption and *kosen-rufu* will certainly be achieved as long as there is a unified gathering of practitioners who uphold the Mystic Law. Unity is the most crucial ingredient in fulfilling this great aspiration.

In the Soka Gakkai, the struggles of first president Tsunesaburo Makiguchi and second president Josei Toda were dedicated to building a strong united organization pulsing with the rhythm of perfect victory. I, too, have devoted my life to carrying on and completing this mission, and today we have realized a solidly united, harmonious community of practitioners, serving as the foundation for worldwide *kosen-rufu.*

My dearest wish now is that the youth who are our successors will fully inherit this noble rhythm of victory driven by the unity of "many in body but one in mind."

The Meaning of "One in Mind"

Toward that end, I'll affirm the meaning of several points regarding the concept of "one in mind," or unity of purpose, which is the key to victory.

(1) The Great Vow for Kosen-rufu

First, "one in mind," or unity of purpose, refers to the great desire or vow for *kosen-rufu.*

In the midst of the Atsuhara Persecution,[6] Nichiren Daishonin wrote to his youthful disciple Nanjo Tokimitsu[7]: "My wish is that all my disciples make a great vow" ("The Dragon Gate," WND-1, 1003). This is a passionate call to his followers to dedicate their lives to the cause of *kosen-rufu.*

The great vow to realize *kosen-rufu* is also the very heart of the mentor-disciple spirit shared by Mr. Makiguchi, Mr. Toda and me. We have inherited this vow through directly connecting our lives to Nichiren Daishonin. All three of us have given ourselves to its actualization with tireless dedication and ungrudging effort. This is truly the essence of the spirit of "many in body but one in mind."

"One in mind" also means the spirit to steadfastly battle destructive forces that seek to obstruct and harm our noble movement. During the years, there have occasionally been individuals in our organization who forgot all about faith, forsook our shared commitment to *kosen-rufu* and succumbed to the desire for fame and fortune. Motivated by self-interest, these individuals tried to disrupt the harmonious community of practitioners, which is a grave offense in Buddhism. It is important that we take a fearless stand against such destructive actions. This is the essence of the Lotus Sutra, and it is also the Soka Gakkai spirit.

(2) Respecting Our Fellow Practitioners

Next is the point that this oneness of mind, or unity of purpose, must be built on genuine respect for our fellow practitioners.

The spirit of *kosen-rufu* taught in the Lotus Sutra rests on the profound belief that all people possess the Buddha nature and thus the potential to attain Buddhahood. A community of practitioners harmoniously united for the sake of *kosen-rufu* will naturally reflect this philosophy of the Lotus Sutra in its own spirit and actions.

Bodhisattva Never Disparaging[8] undertook the practice of bowing in reverence to all those he encountered, based on his belief that everyone has the Buddha nature and can attain enlightenment through faith in the Lotus Sutra. He also bowed in respect to those who did not uphold the sutra.

It goes without saying that our fellow members who embrace the Gohonzon and strive for *kosen-rufu* will all definitely attain Buddhahood, and we should therefore accord them the utmost respect. As "Encouragements of the Bodhisattva Universal Worthy," the 28th chapter of the Lotus Sutra, says regarding those who embrace its teachings, "You should rise and greet him from afar, showing him the same respect you would a Buddha" (*The Lotus Sutra*, p. 324).

The unity of "many in body but one in mind" symbolizes a bond based on the Buddhist philosophy of respect for all people. "One in mind" therefore implies a spirit of mutual respect among fellow practitioners.

(3) Faith Grounded in the Shared Commitment of Mentor and Disciple

Third, "one in mind" simply means faith grounded in the shared commitment of mentor and disciple. The essence of the spirit of "many in body but one in mind" is found in this faith, which means attuning our hearts with the great vow for *kosen-rufu*—the profound desire of the Buddha and of all true leaders of *kosen-rufu*.

Nikko Shonin,[9] Nichiren Daishonin's disciple and direct successor, remained true to his mentor's spirit throughout his life and built a harmonious community of practitioners directly connected to Nichiren. In contrast, the five senior priests,[10] fearing persecution by the authorities and forgetting the spirit of mentor and disciple, strayed from the correct path of *kosen-rufu*.

Turning against one's mentor is the epitome of disrupting the unity of "many in body but one in mind."

"Soka Gakkai Buddha"

As long as the fundamental spirit of striving for *kosen-rufu* demonstrated by the first three presidents pulses vitally in our organization and everyone is united in the spirit of "many in body but one in mind," the Soka Gakkai will forever possess the great life force of the Buddha who seeks to lead all people to enlightenment.

This vibrant force shines with the great light of compassion that breaks through the darkness of people's suffering and imparts courage and hope. It resounds with the lion's roar that vanquishes injustice and steadfastly champions truth. And it inspires immense confidence in all people that they can transform their karma and realize happiness for both themselves and others.

Endowed with this power of the Buddha, the Soka Gakkai towers as a community of practitioners solidly united in purpose, a great and indestructible bastion of the shared commitment of mentor and disciple that will surmount even the fiercest onslaughts of "the three obstacles and four devils." Therefore, President Toda predicted that in the sutras of the future, the Soka Gakkai's name would be recorded as "Soka Gakkai Buddha." The unified gathering of the Soka Gakkai, directly connected to Nichiren and working to make *kosen-rufu* a reality, is itself a Buddha. This was my mentor's unshakable conviction.

President Toda often said, "The Soka Gakkai organization is more precious than my own life." I have sought to protect and nurture this harmonious community of practitioners, which is carrying out the Buddha's will and decree, as if it were President Toda's life itself. Making the unity of "many in body, one in mind" the organization's guiding credo, I have done my very best to develop the Soka Gakkai and advance *kosen-rufu.*

Let us continue exerting ourselves wholeheartedly in faith and taking sincere action to create unity in diversity—many in body but one in mind—and thereby further expand our harmonious community of practitioners, built by the first three presidents through the shared commitment of mentor and disciple. For this itself is the path of *kosen-rufu* and is a sure step toward world peace.

1. The passage "transcending all differences among themselves" could be rendered literally as "without any thought of self or other, this or that." This is not a denial of individuality, but rather urges the bridging of the gaps between people that arise from self-centeredness.
2. Latter Day of the Law: A 10,000-year period in which Shakyamuni's teachings are said to fall into confusion and lose the power to lead people to enlightenment.
3. Nichiren writes: "If the spirit of many in body but one in mind prevails among the people, they will achieve all their goals, whereas if one in body but different in mind, they can achieve nothing remarkable. The more than three thousand volumes of Confucian and Taoist literature are filled with examples . . . . Even an individual at cross purposes with himself is certain to end in failure. Yet a hundred or even a thousand people can definitely attain their goal, if they are of one mind" ("Many in Body, One in Mind," WND-1, 618).
4. Nichiren writes: "Although Nichiren and his followers are few, because they are different in body, but united in mind, they will definitely accomplish their great mission of widely propagating the Lotus Sutra. Though evils may be numerous, they cannot prevail over a single great truth, just as many raging fires are quenched by a single shower of rain. This principle also holds true with Nichiren and his followers" (WND-1, 618).
5. The strategy of the Lotus Sutra means battling hardships and difficulties based on chanting Nam-myoho-renge-kyo to the Gohonzon. In "The Strategy of the Lotus Sutra," Nichiren says: "Employ the strategy of the Lotus Sutra before any other" (WND-1, 1001).
6. Atsuhara Persecution: A series of threats and acts of violence against Nichiren Daishonin's followers in Atsuhara Village, in Fuji District of Suruga Province (part of present-day Shizuoka Prefecture), during a period of three years, beginning in earnest in 1278. The persecution culminated with Hei no Saemon, the deputy chief of the Office of Military and Police Affairs, ordering the execution of three of Nichiren's followers—the brothers Jinshiro, Yagoro and Yarokuro—who steadfastly refused to recant their faith.
7. Nanjo Tokimitsu (1259–1332): A staunch follower of Nichiren Daishonin and the steward of Ueno Village in Fuji District of Suruga Province (part of present-day Shizuoka Prefecture). During the Atsuhara Persecution, Tokimitsu used his influence to protect his fellow believers, sheltering some in his home. Nichiren honored him for his courage and tireless efforts by calling him "Ueno the Worthy," though he was only about 20 at the time.
8. Bodhisattva Never Disparaging: A bodhisattva described in "Bodhisattva Never Disparaging," the 20th chapter of the Lotus Sutra. This bodhisattva—Shakyamuni in a previous lifetime—would bow to everyone he met and say: "I have profound reverence for you, I would never dare treat you with disparagement or arrogance. Why? Because you are all practicing the bodhisattva way and are certain to attain Buddhahood" (LS, 266–67). But he was attacked by arrogant people, who beat him with sticks and staves and threw stones at him. The sutra explains that his practice of bowing to others' Buddha nature became the cause for him to attain Buddhahood.
9. Nikko Shonin (1246–1333): Nichiren Daishonin's disciple and the only one of the six senior priests who remained true to Nichiren's spirit. He became Nichiren's disciple at a young age, serving him devotedly and even accompanying him into exile on Sado Island. When Nichiren retired to Mount Minobu, Nikko devoted his energies to propagating activities in Suruga Province (part of present-day Shizuoka Prefecture) and surrounding areas. After Nichiren's passing, the other senior priests gradually began to distance themselves from their mentor's teachings. As a result, Nikko determined to part ways with them. He settled in Suruga's Fuji District, where he dedicated the rest of his life to protecting and propagating Nichiren's teaching and to raising disciples.
10. Five senior priests: Five of the six senior priests, excluding Nikko, designated by Nichiren shortly before his death as his principal disciples. These five later betrayed their mentor's teaching.

KEY POINTS

A Spirit of Harmony

Nichiren Daishonin says that his followers should "become as inseparable as fish and the water in which they swim" (WND-1, 217). This indicates a spirit of harmony and unity. It also implies a spirit of mutual respect, understanding, support and caring regardless of superficial differences in circumstances or position. Simply put, it means getting along together.

When we work together for the same great objective of *kosen-rufu* based on the spirit of mentor and disciple, inspiring, encouraging and supporting one another, we will naturally come into rapport and strive to maintain positive, respectful relations. (pp. 69–70)

A Shared Commitment for *Kosen-Rufu*

The spirit of "many in body but one in mind," in a sense, represents the ultimate manifestation of the "strategy of the Lotus Sutra," which is chanting Nam-myoho-renge-kyo to the Gohonzon—specifically, chanting with a shared commitment for *kosen-rufu.*

No plans or strategies for *kosen-rufu* will succeed without such shared commitment in chanting. Strong practice based on such unity will also give rise to tremendous momentum. So even should there appear individuals who seek to disrupt the unity of our movement, their negative influence will be rebuffed by everyone's focused spirit.

"One in mind," or shared commitment, also refers to the great vow for *kosen-rufu*—the great vow of the Buddha who seeks to lead all people to enlightenment and also the great vow of the mentor. "One in mind" means making this great vow our own and working toward its actualization. The essence of this shared commitment can be found in chanting Nam-myoho-renge-kyo inspired by the wish for *kosen-rufu,* and this unity in chanting pulses vitally in the Soka Gakkai. (pp. 70–71)

Respect for One's Fellow Members

Bodhisattva Never Disparaging undertook the practice of bowing in reverence to all those he encountered, based on his belief that everyone has the Buddha nature and can attain enlightenment through faith in the Lotus Sutra. He also bowed in respect to those who did not uphold the sutra.

It goes without saying that our fellow members who embrace the Gohonzon and strive for *kosen-rufu* will all definitely attain Buddhahood, and we should therefore accord them the utmost respect. As the "Encouragements of the Bodhisattva Universal Worthy," the 28th chapter of the Lotus Sutra, says regarding those who embrace its teachings, "You should rise and greet him from afar, showing him the same respect you would a Buddha" (LS, 324). (p. 73)

DIALOGUE AND REFLECTION

1) Nichiren Daishonin says that his followers should "become as inseparable as fish and the water in which they swim" (WND-1, 217). Why is unity so important in Nichiren Buddhism?

2) *The Lotus Sutra* states, "You should rise and greet him from afar, showing him the same respect you would a Buddha" (LS, 324). Do you show your fellow SGI-USA members this degree of respect? What are different ways to show your respect?

Lectures on *The* HERITAGE *of the* ULTIMATE LAW *of* LIFE

SGI PRESIDENT IKEDA'S STUDY LECTURE SERIES

(9)

THE ONENESS OF MENTOR AND DISCIPLE

The Eternal Bond of Mentor and Disciple Who Dedicate Their Lives to the Great Vow for Kosen-rufu

Lecture

Buddhism is a teaching conveyed through the mentor-disciple relationship. The oneness, or shared commitment, of mentor and disciple forms the essence of Buddhist practice. If we forget the mentor-disciple relationship, we cannot attain Buddhahood. Nor can we achieve eternal happiness or realize *kosen-rufu*. It is through the bond of mentor and disciple that the Law is transmitted. Buddhism is the Law of life; and the Law of life cannot be transmitted through words or concepts alone.

The heritage of the ultimate Law of life and death flows in the lives of those who strive for *kosen-rufu* based on the path of mentor and disciple. Please remember that without the mentor-disciple relationship, the flow of this heritage will be cut off.

The Wish of the Mentor Is the Great Wish for *Kosen-rufu*

Nichiren has been trying to awaken all the people of Japan to faith in the Lotus Sutra so that they too can share the heritage and attain Buddhahood. But instead they have persecuted me in various ways and finally had me banished to this island [of Sado]. You [Sairen-bo] have followed Nichiren, however, and met with suffering as a result. It pains me deeply to think of

your anguish. Gold can be neither burned by fire nor corroded or swept away by water, but iron is vulnerable to both. A worthy person is like gold, a fool like iron. You are like pure gold because you embrace the "gold" of the Lotus Sutra. The sutra states, "Just as among all the mountains, Mount Sumeru is foremost, so this Lotus Sutra is likewise" (*The Lotus Sutra*, p. 286]. It also states, "The good fortune you gain thereby . . . cannot be burned by fire or washed away by water" (LS, 287–88).

It must be ties of karma from the distant past that have destined you to become my disciple at a time like this. Shakyamuni and Many Treasures certainly realized this truth. The sutra's statement, "Those persons who had heard the Law / dwelled here and there in various Buddha lands, / constantly reborn in company with their teachers" (LS, 140), cannot be false in any way. (*The Writings of Nichiren Daishonin*, vol. 1, p. 217)

At the beginning of the section we are studying in this installment, Nichiren Daishonin reveals the spirit of the mentor in the mentor-disciple relationship in Buddhism. He writes, "Nichiren has been trying to awaken all the people of Japan to faith in the Lotus Sutra so that they too can share the heritage and attain Buddhahood" (WND-1, 217). This passage can be read as expressing the fundamental spirit of the Buddha of the Latter Day, which pervades Nichiren's life of momentous struggle for *kosen-rufu.*

This desire to enable all people to equally share in the heritage of attaining Buddhahood is itself the spirit of the Lotus Sutra, and also the great wish, or vow, of the Buddha described in the sutra.

The Lotus Sutra is permeated by the Buddha's great vow to enable all people to attain Buddhahood. Shakyamuni teaches that a person who inherits and carries on this vow is a genuine bodhisattva and true disciple of the Buddha. He also calls on his followers to widely propagate the Law throughout the world after his passing, stressing the importance of winning in the struggle against negative forces that seek to obstruct the flow of *kosen-rufu.*[1]

Accordingly, the great vow of the Buddha and the wish of the mentor—for the enlightenment of all people and the happiness of self and others—are none other than the great vow, or wish, for *kosen-rufu* itself.

During the Tatsunokuchi Persecution and Sado Exile, there were those among Nichiren's disciples who, failing to understand this spirit of the mentor, ignorantly slandered him and abandoned their faith. Adversity invariably separates the genuine from the false. In the midst of this great wave of persecution, Nichiren taught the vital

SGI President and Mrs. Ikeda enjoy a warm exchange with jazz artists Herbie Hancock and Wayne Shorter, Tokyo, October 13, 2007.

Seikyo Press

importance of the mentor-disciple relationship and inspired true disciples who shared his powerful commitment to stand up. He engaged in a struggle to rebuild his community of followers after repression by state authorities had resulted in "999 out of 1,000 people who gave up their faith" ("Reply to Niiama," WND-1, 469).

Even on Sado, there appeared a steady stream of people who decided to follow Nichiren after observing at close hand his integrity and dauntless struggle as a votary of the Lotus Sutra. They were disciples of "pure gold" who joined Nichiren knowing full well that he was an exile. One of these people was the Tendai priest and fellow exile Sairen-bo.

The True Heritage of Faith Is Open to All People

When considering Nichiren Daishonin's wish to enable all people to share the heritage for attaining Buddhahood, the most crucial point is that the heritage of Buddhism is open to all. This universally accessible nature of the heritage is so important that it simply cannot be emphasized too strongly. When it is correctly understood, Buddhism can serve as a humanistic and universal religion; when it is not, Buddhism can become narrow and authoritarian, deviating from the original spirit of the Buddha.

Since this writing is a reply concerning the heritage of the ultimate Law of life and death, we can surmise that its recipient, Sairen-bo, may have questioned the way the heritage was understood in the Japanese Tendai school of the day. In another writing by Nichiren, titled "Establishing the Correct Method of Contemplation," we learn that high-ranking priests of the Tendai school cloaked the transmission of the heritage in mystery, used it as a means to enhance their own or their school's authority, or treated it as something to be bought and sold for large sums of money. In this way, the transmission of the heritage itself had become a source of corruption and decadence.[2]

Next, Nichiren says, "But instead they have persecuted me in various ways and finally had me banished to this island [of Sado]" (WND-1, 217). Referring here to his own struggles during the past 20 years, Nichiren indicates that the endeavor of *kosen-rufu* is one of overcoming an unending series of great obstacles. The spirit of the mentor in the mentor-disciple relationship in Buddhism, as I mentioned earlier, is the great wish for *kosen-rufu*. Here, we can also see Nichiren's willingness to undergo repeated persecution for his cause as the essence of the mentor's conduct, which is taking action without begrudging one's life.

The sutra states that if one propagates the correct teaching in the evil age of the Latter Day of the Law when people's lives are defiled by the five impurities, one is certain to encounter great, even life-threatening, persecution. However, as indicated by the statement, "I rejoiced, saying that I had long expected it to come to this," Nichiren relished obstacles, confronting them head-on and calmly triumphing over them ("The Actions of the Votary of the Lotus Sutra," WND-1, 764). His whole life was characterized by a dauntless spirit. The simple manner in which he says, "But instead they have persecuted me in various ways and finally had me banished to this island," are a reflection of his serene state of being, which derived from living based on the Law and not begrudging his life. It was a state of being overflowing with the heart of the lion king, unswayed by even the harshest persecution.

A Person of "Pure Gold" Upholds the Lotus Sutra Even in the Face of Great Obstacles

Thus in this writing, Nichiren Daishonin clarifies that the spirit and conduct of the mentor in the struggle for *kosen-rufu* in the Latter Day of the Law consist of the following: the "great vow for *kosen-rufu*" to enable all people to attain enlightenment and the "selfless action" to triumph over one great obstacle after another.

Nichiren then observes, "You [Sairen-bo] have followed Nichiren, however, and met with suffering as a result" (WND-1, 217). This fact, Nichiren says, qualifies Sairen-bo as a person of "pure gold." In praising Sairen-bo for being such a dedicated disciple, Nichiren teaches that the all-important heritage in Buddhism flows in the lives of those who practice in the same spirit as the mentor.

Nothing is known as to the specific persecutions that befell Sairen-bo. But Nichiren's disciples on Sado obviously suffered various kinds of harassment and discrimination. It is not difficult to imagine that among the villainous individuals who sought to kill Nichiren, there were those who also attacked his followers.

GREAT VOW

Nichiren Daishonin in several letters emphasizes the importance of his disciples making a great vow (see "The Dragon Gate," WND-1, 1003). The Lotus Sutra reads, "We beg that the merit gained through these gifts / may be spread far and wide to everyone, / so that we and other living beings / all together may attain the Buddha way" (LS, 130). That, in essence, is the vow: to practice for oneself and others, and to spread the Lotus Sutra throughout the world.

It's important to note that what is often translated into English as *vow* can also be read as a pledge to fulfill a wish or desire. One who fully and consistently lives to fulfill this desire or vow, no matter what opposition might arise, is called a Buddha. Regarding this, SGI President Ikeda comments: "'I want to become happy and for everyone else to become happy too.' This is the original mind, the pure wish, functioning in the depths of life since time without beginning. Those who totally embrace this spirit are Buddhas. Because it is the Buddha's all-encompassing wish, it is the 'great vow'" (*Lectures on the "Expedient Means" and "Life Span" Chapters of the Lotus Sutra,* vol. 3, p. 177).

The vow of the disciple, of a bodhisattva, is not an imposed obligation. It is freely declared and joyously put into action. *Nam* can be read as dedication or devotion. The vow, or wish, to awaken Buddhahood in ourselves and others is something we renew every time we chant Nam-myoho-renge-kyo.

Bodhisattvas are said to make four universal vows: (1) to save innumerable living beings, (2) to eradicate countless earthly desires, (3) to master immeasurable Buddhist teachings and (4) to attain supreme enlightenment.

In his writing "The Differences between Hinayana and Mahayana," Nichiren says: "Again, the persons known as bodhisattvas in all cases take the so-called four universal vows, the first of which reads, 'Living beings are numberless: I vow to save them.' If this vow is not fulfilled, then it is impossible to fulfill the fourth vow, which reads, 'Enlightenment is supreme: I vow to attain it'" (WND-2, 471).

In describing the hardships faced by Abutsu-bo and his wife, the lay nun Sen-nichi, also his followers on Sado, Nichiren writes: "Every single steward and Nembutsu believer worthy of the name kept strict watch on my hut day and night, determined to prevent anyone from communicating with me. Never in any lifetime will I forget how in those circumstances you [the lay nun Sennichi], with Abutsu-bo carrying a wooden container of food on his back, came in the night again and again to bring me aid . . . [Because of your support for me,] you were driven from your land, fined, and had your house taken from you" ("The Sutra of True Requital," WND-1, 933).

With regard to Sairen-bo encountering persecution on account of his having become Nichiren's disciple, Nichiren writes, "It pains me deeply to think of your anguish" (WND-1, 217). And he lauds Sairen-bo as a person of "pure gold" because the latter persisted in following Nichiren through thick and thin, without being defeated by difficulties along the way.

Further, Nichiren clearly indicates that Sairen-bo is a person of "pure gold" because he embraces the " 'gold' of the

THE "FORMER AFFAIRS OF THE BODHISATTVA MEDICINE KING"

From the 23rd chapter of the Lotus Sutra

"This sutra can save all living beings. This sutra can cause all living beings to free themselves from suffering and anguish. This sutra can bring great benefits to all living beings and fulfill their desires, as a clear cool pond can satisfy all those who are thirsty. It is like a fire to one who is cold, a robe to one who is naked, like a band of merchants finding a leader, a child finding its mother, someone finding a ship in which to cross the water, a sick man finding a doctor, someone in darkness finding a lamp, the poor finding riches, the people finding a ruler, a traveling merchant finding his way to the sea. It is like a torch that banishes darkness. Such is this Lotus Sutra. It can cause living beings to cast off all distress, all sickness and pain. It can unloose all the bonds of birth and death" (LS, 286).

Lotus Sutra" (WND-1, 217). Embracing the Lotus Sutra specifically means internalizing the great vow of the mentor who has dedicated his life as a votary of the Lotus Sutra and, even in times of adversity, maintaining the same resolute and selfless faith as the mentor.

In other words, a person of "pure gold" is another name for a person of selfless dedication to the Law. Such people are to be exalted, as Nichiren indicates, "If the Law that one embraces is supreme, then the person who embraces it must accordingly be foremost among all others" ("Questions and Answers about Embracing the Lotus Sutra," WND-1, 61).

Those who base themselves on the highest principles or truth will not be deceived by surface phenomena or swayed by anything. They are always able to discern the underlying essence. By contrast, foolish people who lack solid guiding principles will always be confused and readily defeated by hardships or obstacles. They base themselves on their own foolish minds.

Sairen-bo most certainly had a deep recognition that the Lotus Sutra was the Buddha's highest teaching. Moreover, his unwavering resolve and readiness to follow Nichiren made him a disciple of "pure gold."

Sairen-bo was profoundly inspired on Sado by witnessing a true votary who practiced the Lotus Sutra—the "king of sutras"—in exact accord with its teaching and spirit, and strove selflessly to lead all people to enlightenment. This is expressed in Sairen-bo's own words, which Nichiren shares, "In your letter you mention that you became a disciple of mine and pledged to follow me at the beginning of the second month, and that from now on, though you may not measure up to others, you would be most pleased and honored if I would continue to count you among my disciples" ("Reply to Sairen-bo," WND-1, 309).

Sairen-bo no doubt immediately and correctly grasped that advancing together with a true votary of the Lotus Sutra is the essence and ultimate meaning of embracing the Lotus Sutra. That is probably why he unhesitatingly chose the course of enduring persecution together with Nichiren.

Nichiren next cites two passages from the "Former Affairs of the Bodhisattva Medicine King" chapter of the Lotus Sutra. This is to illustrate the true life-state of those who embrace the Lotus Sutra.

The first passage concerns the Lotus Sutra, or the Law, which they embrace, "Just as among all the mountains, Mount Sumeru is foremost, so this Lotus Sutra is likewise" (LS, 286). Just as Mount Sumeru towers at the center of the world, so the Lotus Sutra is the supreme and unsurpassed Law.

The second passage concerns the indomitable state of life attained by those who embrace the Law, "The good fortune you gain thereby . . . cannot be burned by fire or washed away by water" (LS, 287–88). Because those who embrace the Mystic Law can bring forth the infinite power of Buddhahood within their lives, they can triumph over all, without being defeated by hardship or suffering.

To embrace the Lotus Sutra is to feel deep joy in living as a person of wisdom, a person of "pure gold." Such vibrant pride and self-worth give rise to the strength, courage and wisdom to endure and overcome all obstacles.

The Eternal Karmic Ties of Mentor and Disciple

Nichiren Daishonin also tells Sairen-bo of the profound karmic ties they share as mentor and disciple, "It must be ties of karma from the distant past that have destined you to become my disciple at a time like this" (WND-1, 217). Nichiren indicates that this mysterious bond can perhaps only be fathomed by the Buddhas Shakyamuni and Many Treasures.

Further, he explains that the profound karmic ties shared by mentor and disciple who uphold the Lotus Sutra are an indisputable truth, citing a passage from "The Parable of the Phantom City" chapter, "Those persons who had heard the Law dwelled here and there in various Buddha lands, constantly reborn in company with their teachers" (LS, 140). This passage reveals the depth of the mentor-disciple bond.

To give a brief explanation of its meaning, since the distant time of major world system dust particle *kalpas* in the past, Shakyamuni's voice-hearer disciples had constantly been born in various Buddha lands with Shakyamuni as their mentor and carried out bodhisattva practice together.

The important point here is that Shakyamuni's voice-hearer disciples in the Lotus Sutra were actually bodhisattvas who had undertaken bodhisattva practice in past lifetimes. Through these words of the Buddha, the voice-hearers remember that they originally possessed the life-state of bodhisattvas. The Lotus Sutra reveals that since the immeasurable past, the voice-hearers have possessed the "wish that we have had deep in our hearts from the start" (LS, 144). That is, the wish to attain supreme enlightenment and free all living beings from suffering. Therefore, the voice-hearers, by recalling their great wish from the distant past, discover and awaken to their identity as living beings who have carried out the same bodhisattva practice as their teacher, Shakyamuni.

This passage indeed describes the eternal relationship of mentor and disciple who strive together to realize the most profound aspiration of human beings and of all life—the enlightenment and happiness of both self and others. A true mentor in Buddhism is one who enables

TRANSMISSION OF BUDDHIST TEACHINGS

The transmission of Buddhist teachings, since the very beginning, has been a matter of person-to-person learning, especially in the earliest days before the teachings were written down. Thus, there has always been an emphasis on the relationship of teachers and their disciples.

The way that this relationship manifests, however, differs greatly among the various forms of Buddhism. Often, the teacher was looked upon as the possessor of a supernatural power, or a secret endowment of Buddhist teachings unattainable by practice and study alone.

In the Lotus Sutra, however, the relationship is one of equality of teacher and student, as clarified in such statements as: "Shariputra, you should know that at the start I took a vow, / hoping to make all persons / equal to me, without any distinction between us, and what I long ago hoped for / has now been fulfilled" (LS, 36) and "At all times, for all things / I preach the Law equally; / as I would for a single person, / that same way I do for numerous persons" (LS, 103).

In Nichiren Daishonin's time, the heritage of a Buddhist school's doctrines was most often something transmitted through ceremony and ritual, as if it were a supernatural essence rather than a philosophy for living. Nichiren wrote "The Heritage of the Ultimate Law of Life" to overturn this misconception and to clarify that in his teachings, as with the Lotus Sutra, there was no secret doctrine, no mystical transmission, and that the teacher and the student were one. This point is made particularly clear when he states, "Shakyamuni Buddha who attained enlightenment countless kalpas ago, the Lotus Sutra that leads all people to Buddhahood, and we ordinary human beings are in no way different or separate from one another" (WND-1, 216).

us to remember this aspiration. True disciples, meanwhile, are ones who follow the mentor's teaching, who never forget that this most profound aspiration is in fact their own, and who—convinced from the bottom of their hearts that this is so—launch into action in accord with the mentor's instructions.

The most profound mentor-disciple relationship is that of mentor and disciple who struggle together for *kosen-rufu.* Their lives are linked on the deepest level. The eternal world of Buddhahood exists in the depths of their lives. Both mentor and disciple then dwell in the immense life-state of the "palace of the ninth consciousness,[3] the unchanging reality that reigns over all of life's functions" ("The Real Aspect of the Gohonzon," WND-1, 832).

"Those Persons Who Had Heard the Law Dwelled Here and There in Various Buddha Lands, Constantly Reborn in Company With Their Teachers"

At the third memorial (second anniversary) in November 1946, for his mentor, Tsunesaburo Makiguchi, second Soka Gakkai president Josei Toda said: "In your vast and boundless compassion, you let me accompany you even to prison. As a result, I could read with my entire being the passage from the Lotus Sutra, 'Those persons who had heard the Law dwelled here and there in various Buddha lands, constantly reborn in company with their teachers' [LS, 140]. The benefit of this was coming to know my former existence as a Bodhisattva of the Earth and to absorb with my very life even a small degree of the sutra's meaning. Could there be any greater happiness than this?"[4]

This captures the essence of the mentor-disciple relationship in Buddhism.

In those early days of our organization, there were many other Soka Gakkai leaders who proclaimed to be disciples of President Makiguchi. But once the wartime persecution of the Soka Gakkai affected them personally and led to their imprisonment, they did a complete turnaround and recanted their faith. Showing gross ingratitude, there were even some who openly turned against President Makiguchi, cursing at the mentor to whom they were so deeply indebted. The human heart can be frightening.

Only Mr. Toda, President Makiguchi's true disciple, was unwavering in his awareness of the profound and noble bond of mentor and disciple, speaking with gratitude of President Makiguchi's "vast and boundless compassion."

This lofty mentor-disciple relationship is the vital spirit of the Soka Gakkai. If this spirit lives on, our movement will continue to develop eternally. The mentor-disciple spirit of the first three presidents is key to securing the foundations of the *kosen-rufu* movement for the future.

Mr. Toda states that by going to prison with his mentor, he was able to realize his former existence as a Bodhisattva of the Earth and the sutra's meaning. He found the key in the sutra passage concerning being reborn in lifetime after lifetime with one's mentor.

Both mentor and disciple dedicate their lives eternally to bodhisattva practice—this point is crucial to understanding the Lotus Sutra's essence. Once in a lecture open to all members, President Toda explained: "When I said: 'I'm going to go and be reborn in the country of Japan when it's in a state of ruin. Why don't you all come with me?' you all replied, 'OK, let's go!' 'Yes, why not!' And as a result, we all appeared in this world. . . .

"The sutra says that wherever they may be, practitioners of the sutra are sure to be born together with their mentor in various Buddha lands. This is certainly not a lie. It means that mentor and disciple are always born together. In light of these words of Nichiren, I feel tremendous gratitude to all of you. We were born together in this world as a result of a promise we made in the past."[5]

In another writing, Nichiren Daishonin says, "I wonder if you and I have not been pledged to each other as teacher and disciple from countless kalpas in the past" ("Reply to Sairen-bo," WND-1, 309). Mentor and disciple share karmic ties that extend over past, present and future. When we strive with all our might for *kosen-rufu,* we can sense this profound connection.

It is the first three presidents of the Soka Gakkai who have revived in the present age an active and engaged mentor-disciple spirit—the essence of Nichiren Buddhism. It would be no exaggeration to say that were it not for the appearance of the Soka Gakkai, the spirit of mentor and disciple of the Lotus Sutra and Nichiren Buddhism would have all but disappeared.

The Mentor-Disciple Relationship Is the Essence of the Lotus Sutra

So why is the mentor-disciple relationship valued so highly in Buddhism? Let me reconfirm the Buddhist significance of this relationship.

In general terms, a mentor is someone who teaches one enhanced skills or technical expertise, deeper knowledge, a loftier way of life, a more fulfilling state of mind and so forth. People look up to someone as a mentor when that person helps them in some way to improve or develop themselves.

In the Buddhist teaching of the Lotus Sutra, the teacher Shakyamuni Buddha, based on his awakening to the Law, strove together with his disciples to enable them to achieve their highest potential as human beings. This Law was none other than the Mystic Law, which the Buddha's disciples could not perceive on their own. Their awareness was clouded by fundamental darkness, and they had no conception of the Law. Therefore, even if they were given theoretical explanations of the Law or told to practice to overcome sufferings, the life-state of Buddhahood could not be conveyed to them through such words alone. Rather, it was through being inspired by coming into contact with the Buddha's character, along with these words of instruction, that they awakened to the Law within their lives. This is how the Law was communicated to them.

And this is why the mentor-disciple relationship holds so much importance in Buddhism. The Law is conveyed through the life-to-life bonds of the mentor-disciple relationship. Based on this Law, it is possible for us to achieve our human revolution.

This also explains why Nichiren Daishonin refers to the deep mentor-disciple bond between himself and Sairen-bo in this writing on the transmission of the heritage of the ultimate Law of life and death.

It follows that Buddhism does not set forth the mentor as a mystical or transcendent superhuman being. Nichiren states, "Outside of the attainment of Buddhahood, there is no 'secret' and no 'transcendental powers'" (*The Record of the Orally Transmitted Teachings*, p. 125). As this passage suggests, the supreme and only mystery in Buddhism is the ability of human beings to attain Buddhahood in their present form. Moreover, the secret and transcendental powers for attaining Buddhahood are something that can be manifested in the lives of all people.

What, then, were the disciples to do after their teacher Shakyamuni Buddha had passed away? Did it mean that, without the Buddha there to teach the Law through his own example, Buddhism could not be transmitted in a true sense? The Lotus Sutra directly addresses these questions.

The sutra teaches that the core of Shakyamuni's being is nothing other than the "vow of the Buddha." Shakyamuni explains, "At the start I took a vow, / hoping to make all persons / equal to me, without any distinction between us" (LS, 36). That is, the vow to enable all people to attain the same state of enlightenment as he had.

In the theoretical teaching (the first 14 chapters) of the Lotus Sutra, the voice-hearers awaken to the fact that they, too, have originally dedicated their lives to the same great vow as the Buddha. This clarifies that Shakyamuni and his voice-hearer disciples are committed to the same fundamental wish.

The essential teaching (the last 14 chapters) of the sutra reveals the true identity of Shakyamuni as the Buddha who has continued to preach the Law—

THE NINE CONSCIOUSNESSES

The early Buddhist philosophy of India postulated six kinds of discernment, also known as six consciousnesses. Later Indian scholars such as Vasubandhu and Asanga, fifth-century pioneers of Mahayana Buddhist thought, recognized a seventh and an eighth level of consciousnesses (Skt *vijnana* or discernment). Based on their insights, the sixth-century Buddhist translator and scholar Paramatha postulated a ninth level of consciousness, and the idea of nine consciousnesses came to be adopted by various Chinese Buddhist schools, including the T'ien-t'ai school.

The first five of the nine consciousnesses correspond to the five empirical senses: sight, hearing, smell, taste and touch. The sixth, mind-consciousness, is formed from the correlation of sensory information, to create an understanding of the physical environment. The seventh, *mano*-consciousness, is an inner-directed awareness. It is through the seventh consciousness that understanding of and attachment to the concept of self derive. The eighth consciousness, *alaya*, is a consciousness that stores past causes from this life and previous lives. In Chinese, it was rendered as "storehouse consciousness." The ninth is the *amala*-consciousness, which is free from any karmic defilement. According to Nichiren Daishonin, "The body is the palace of the ninth consciousness, the unchanging reality that reigns over all of life's functions" ("The Real Aspect of the Gohonzon," WND-1, 832). In Nichiren's view, there is no fundamental distinction between the physical reality of life and its true nature as the essential Law of the universe, Myoho-renge-kyo. He also states, "The words of a wise man of old also teach that 'you should base your mind on the ninth consciousness, and carry out your practice in the six consciousnesses'" ("Hell Is the Land of Tranquil Light," WND-1, 458). In other words, our Buddhist practice involves tapping into our ninth consciousness—our innate Buddha nature—and allowing its wisdom and life force to illuminate all levels of consciousness. We then engage our six consciousnesses (our senses and thoughts), thus illuminated, as we take action in the real world for own happiness and that of others.

teaching and converting living beings in the *saha* world based on this vow—ever since attaining enlightenment in the inconceivably distant past. This is the "Buddha of actual attainment in the remote past" expounded in the "Life Span" chapter. In addition, the essential teaching clarifies that the bodhisattvas who share the mentor's commitment—those who after the Buddha's passing pledge to carry on the Buddha's vow and devote themselves to the Buddha's work of leading all living beings to happiness—are the Bodhisattvas of the Earth.

The Lotus Sutra from beginning to end teaches the oneness, or shared commitment, of mentor and disciple. Looking over the history of Buddhism, the deification of Shakyamuni began when his disciples forgot to strive with the same commitment he had. If Shakyamuni who attained enlightenment in the remote past is turned into a transcendent, superhuman being, then the mentor-disciple relationship cannot function. The point is that when the Buddha's disciples fail to emulate his spirit and conduct, the Buddha merely becomes an object of veneration or worship. The Buddha therefore can no longer serve as a model for others' human revolution.

The Lotus Sutra reveals that a vow lies at the core of Shakyamuni Buddha's character. It further clarifies that the Law is transmitted to disciples who make that vow their own and strive in the same spirit. This paves the way for conveying the life-state of the Buddha to living beings even in the age after his passing.

Especially important in achieving the great vow for *kosen-rufu* is the willingness to take action without begrudging one's life. The "Life Span" chapter of the Lotus Sutra says that even after his passing, Shakyamuni will appear where there are practitioners striving in faith with the spirit of "single-mindedly desiring to see the Buddha, not hesitating even if it costs them their lives" (LS, 230).

Even after Shakyamuni's death, the life-state of the Buddha can be conveyed to those who take action based on the great vow for *kosen-rufu* and the spirit of selfless dedication, which constitute the core of the Buddha's life.

Nichiren set forth Nam-myoho-renge-kyo as the means for manifesting our innate Buddhahood. He revealed that the great vow for *kosen-rufu* and selfless dedication are the key to Buddhist practice in the evil age of the Latter Day of the Law. By doing so, he secured the transmission of the heritage for attaining Buddhahood.

Everything rests on the fundamental power inherent in the mentor-disciple relationship. Nichiren's true disciple and direct successor, Nikko Shonin, says: "In the teaching of Nichiren, one attains Buddhahood by correctly following the path of mentor and disciple. If one veers from the path of mentor

STUDY GUIDE

A summary of key points from SGI President Ikeda's lecture

The shared commitment of mentor and disciple forms the essence of Buddhist practice. The great vow of the mentor for the enlightenment of all people and the happiness of self and others is the vow, or wish, for *kosen-rufu*. This is the spirit of the Lotus Sutra.

Nichiren compares his disciple Sairen-bo to "pure gold" because he maintained pure faith and dedication even in the face of persecution. Sairen-bo emulated the model set by his mentor, Nichiren, in remaining unperturbed by harsh opposition.

Those who lack solid guiding principles are easily swayed in times of adversity, while those with a firm grounding in faith and wisdom can face and withstand any hardship. Because of the strength of the mentor and disciple's shared vow for *kosen-rufu*, they can triumph over the severe obstacles that arise when fighting for the enlightenment of all people.

Shakyamuni, awakened to the Mystic Law, endeavored to teach his disciples the truth to which he'd become enlightened. Theoretical explanations of the Law are insufficient to overcome the fundamental darkness that clouds people's understanding of their own Buddha nature. The disciples had to observe, become inspired by and emulate the Buddha's behavior, and when their observation was supported by Shakyamuni's instruction, the disciples were awakened.

When disciples failed to share Shakyamuni's vow and failed to emulate his behavior as a human being, they began to treat him as a god. This represented a breakdown in the mentor and disciple relationship, causing the decline of Buddhism. If Shakyamuni had attained enlightenment as a superhuman being, there would be no way for ordinary people to emulate his conduct or to attain the state he'd attained. The deification of a Buddha reduces that Buddha to an external object of veneration and does not enable the disciples to reach their true potential.

The Lotus Sutra describes the "vow of the Buddha" as follows: "At the start I took a vow, / hoping to make all persons / equal to me, without any distinction between us" (LS, 36).

The great vow for the happiness of all people requires unhesitating willingness to dedicate one's life, as Nichiren did. He fulfilled this vow in the Latter Day of the Law and established the practice of chanting Nam-myoho-renge-kyo to enable people to reveal their innate Buddhahood.

While other Buddhist schools viewed their "heritage" as being passed on through elaborate formalities or secret rituals, the heritage of Nichiren Buddhism exists in the shared vow and action of mentor and disciple, and is open to all people.

Through the actions of the three founding Soka Gakkai presidents, the SGI continues in the shared commitment of mentor and disciple, spreading Nam-myoho-renge-kyo throughout the globe.

and disciple, then even if one upholds the Lotus Sutra, one will fall into the hell of incessant suffering."[6]

In the present age, it is the first three Soka Gakkai presidents who awakened to the great vow for *kosen-rufu*, the vow of the Buddha, and have striven with the spirit of not begrudging their lives.

As the disciple of Mr. Makiguchi and Mr. Toda, I have won in successive momentous struggles against the three powerful enemies.[7] I have created a history of absolute victory as a disciple. I can proudly report to Mr. Toda that I have won on all fronts. I have no regrets whatsoever.

Mr. Makiguchi and Mr. Toda. Mr. Toda and me. Through the actions of its first three presidents, the Soka Gakkai has forged the path of shared commitment of mentor and disciple, the essence of Buddhism. Because the mentors and disciples of Soka have been victorious, we have made worldwide *kosen-rufu*—the decree of the Lotus Sutra and the wish of Nichiren—a reality.

"If teacher and disciple are of different minds," writes Nichiren, "they will never accomplish anything" ("Flowering and Bearing Grain," WND-1, 909). But when mentor and disciple are united, they can achieve even the loftiest goals. The mentor-disciple bond is an unparalleled force for victory.

[Supplemental materials provided by the SGI-USA Study Department.]

1. In the "Former Affairs of the Bodhisattva Medicine King" chapter of the Lotus Sutra, Shakyamuni says: "After I have passed into extinction, in the last five hundred year period you must spread it [this teaching] abroad widely throughout Jambudvipa [the entire world] and never allow it to be cut off, nor must you allow evil devils, the devils' people, heavenly beings, dragons, yakshas or kumbhanda demons to seize the advantage!" (LS, 288)
2. Nichiren Daishonin writes: "The scholars of the Tendai school at the present time have forgotten about the heritage of T'ien-tai's teaching that was secretly preserved in the stone tower storehouse. Because of this, they have ceased the custom of passing on the heritage of T'ien-t'ai's secret Law, and instead describe themselves as embracing the heritage of the threefold contemplation in a single mind. Trusting to their own ideas, they fashion a document describing that heritage, put it in a brocade bag and hang it around their neck, or hide it away in a box and sell it for a high price. As a result, the erroneous teachings of theirs have come to be propagated everywhere throughout the country, and the true doctrine of Buddhism taught by T'ien-t'ai has become obliterated and lost. . . . T'ien-t'ai's original intentions have in this way been forgotten and the wonderful Law of Shakyamuni Buddha demoted" ("Establishing the Correct Method of Contemplation," WND-2, 518).
3. The ninth, or *amala-*, consciousness is the Buddha nature, or the fundamental purifying force, that is free from all karmic impediments.
4. Translated from Japanese. Josei Toda, *Toda Josei zenshu* (Collected Writings of Josei Toda) (Tokyo: Seikyo Shimbunsha, 1983), vol. 3, p. 386.
5. Translated from Japanese. Josei Toda, *Toda Josei zenshu*, vol. 7, p. 472.
6. Translated from Japanese. *Fuji Nikko Shonin shoden* (Detailed Biography of Nikko Shonin) (Tokyo: Seikyo Shimbunsha, 1974), vol. 2, p. 261.
7. Three powerful enemies: The verse section of the "Encouraging Devotion" chapter of the Lotus Sutra describes the people who will persecute a person who spreads the Lotus Sutra in the evil age after Shakyamuni's passing. In his *Annotations on "The Words and Phrases of the Lotus Sutra,"* the Great Teacher Miao-lo of China describes these people as belonging to three categories: arrogant lay people, arrogant monks and nuns, and arrogant false sages (*see* LS, 193–94).

Lectures on
The HERITAGE *of the* ULTIMATE LAW *of* LIFE

SGI PRESIDENT IKEDA'S STUDY LECTURE SERIES

(10)

THE CLUSTER OF BLESSINGS BROUGHT BY THE BODHISATTVAS OF THE EARTH

The Practice of the Buddha's True Disciples To Awaken All People to the Power of the Mystic Law Inherent in Life

Lecture

Revitalizing all people from the very depths of their lives, changing the world into a true realm of happiness and peace—these are the fundamental objectives of the Lotus Sutra. And those who strive throughout their lives with a personal commitment to realize these goals are Bodhisattvas of the Earth.

In the defiled age of the Latter Day of the Law, the Bodhisattvas of the Earth impart the light of hope to those who are suffering, tirelessly reaching out to each individual with compassion and courage until fresh life force wells forth. With an unwavering belief in the potential for good that resides in each person, they persevere in conducting sincere dialogue and never cease in their efforts to awaken others' Buddha nature. Because the Bodhisattvas of the Earth themselves embody the power of the Mystic Law, they are able to press on tenaciously with their noble work amid the great sea of humanity and, through the brilliance of their character and integrity, awaken the Buddha nature of others. The Lotus Sutra proclaims that countless such genuine practitioners are sure to appear in the Latter Day of the Law.

The Bodhisattvas of the Earth are experts in the art of life who help people transform themselves on the most fundamental level and gain true inner happiness. Their wisdom and actions are based on the profound philosophy that both they and others possess the Buddha nature. This belief enables them to overcome self-centeredness and negative karma, and bring the power of compassion inherent in the universe to flow forth abundantly. This is the source of their shining and infinitely inspiring character as well as their unceasing efforts to lead others to enlightenment.

This is the true reason for the transmission of the heritage of the ultimate Law of life and death—to enable all people to attain Buddhahood. If someone misses this key point, then however much they might read the Lotus Sutra, they effectively shut themselves off from the heritage of attaining Buddhahood. Therefore, only when one has a deep inner awareness that one is a Bodhisattva of the Earth—a protagonist in the effort to enable all people to attain enlightenment and stands up with the mentor in faith to carry out this mission—can one be said to have truly internalized the teachings of the Lotus Sutra.

The crux of the heritage of the ultimate Law of life and death can be found in the practice of mentor and disciple demonstrated by the Bodhisattvas of the Earth, who are led by Bodhisattva Superior Practices. In this and the next installment, we will look at passages in which Nichiren Daishonin discusses the profound meaning behind this.

Practice Is the Lifeline of Buddhism

How admirable that you have asked about the transmission of the ultimate Law of life and death! I have never heard of anyone who has asked such a question. I have answered in complete detail in this letter, so please take it deeply to heart. The important point is to carry out your practice confident that Nam-myoho-renge-kyo alone is the heritage that was transferred from Shakyamuni and Many Treasures to Bodhisattva Superior Practices.

The function of fire is to burn and give light. The function of water is to wash away filth. The winds blow away dust and breathe life into plants, animals, and human beings. The earth produces the grasses and trees, and heaven provides nourishing moisture. The five characters of Myoho-renge-kyo are also like that. They are the cluster of blessings brought by the Bodhisattvas of the Earth, disciples of the Buddha in his true identity. The Lotus Sutra says that Bodhisattva Superior Practices will appear now, in the Latter Day of the Law, to propagate this teaching, but has this happened? Whether or not Bodhisattva Superior Practices has appeared in this world, Nichiren has already made a start in

THE LATTER DAY OF THE LAW

The Latter Day of the Law, also known as the age of Decadent Law or Final Law, is the last of the three periods following the death of Shakyamuni Buddha. In the first period, the Former Day, the teaching, practice and proof of Shakyamuni's Buddhism were present, and it is said that numerous people attained enlightenment. The second period, the Middle Day, is also known as the age of Semblance to the Law. During this time, the teachings of Shakyamuni became formalized, and the emphasis was on the meditative practices of such philosophers as Nagarjuna and T'ien-t'ai. Very few people attained enlightenment. The third age, the Latter Day of the Law, is defined in the Great Collections Sutra as an "age of quarrels and disputes," in which Shakyamuni's teachings are "obscured and lost."

These sorts of predictions led to a deep sense of foreboding in Asian society around the time of Nichiren Daishonin. Many Buddhist leaders responded by emphasizing teachings that this world is a place devoid of hope and to be despised, and that one should aspire for rebirth in a pure realm after death.

The Lotus Sutra, however, looks at the Latter Day as a time when the other Buddhist teachings, which were preached as expedients to lead people to awaken to the ultimate Law or truth, have lost their power to save people. It is a time when this ultimate Law, inherent in the essential teaching of the Lotus Sutra, will prevail. The Lotus Sutra teaches that this is the age in which the Bodhisattvas of the Earth will successfully propagate the essential teaching, leading people away from misery and toward enlightenment. It also teaches that this world itself equates to the pure land. Therefore, the Lotus Sutra represented a message of hope amid the gloomy spiritual atmosphere of the times known as the Latter Day of the Law.

Opinions as to the beginning, ending and length of these periods vary, depending on the source. The view of Nichiren Buddhism is that the Latter Day of the Law represents the modern period, from around the time of Nichiren onward. Nichiren, as the votary of the Lotus Sutra, brought the essential teaching of Nam-myoho-renge-kyo to the people of his day, and the SGI has spread this teaching throughout the world. (See *The Soka Gakkai Dictionary of Buddhism*.)

propagating this teaching. (***The Writings of Nichiren Daishonin*, vol. 1, pp. 217–18**)

In Buddhism, practicing the teachings based on the relationship of mentor and disciple is essential.

Many bodhisattvas appear in the Lotus Sutra. However, only the Bodhisattvas of the Earth are the true disciples of Shakyamuni Buddha as he is depicted in the essential teaching of the Lotus Sutra. There, Shakyamuni is revealed as the eternal Buddha, having attained enlightenment in the infinite past. The leader of the Bodhisattvas of the Earth is Bodhisattva Superior Practices. The Lotus Sutra was transmitted from Shakyamuni to Superior Practices (as the representative of all the Bodhisattvas of the Earth)—namely, from the teacher embodying the eternal state of Buddhahood to his genuine disciples.

In the passage above, Nichiren Daishonin begins by praising Sairen-bo's seeking spirit, saying: "How admirable that you have asked about the transmission of the ultimate Law of life and death! I have never heard of anyone who has asked such a question" (WND-1, 217). Then, he recommends the practice of chanting and spreading Nam-myoho-renge-kyo, stating: "The important point is to carry out your practice confident that Nam-myoho-renge-kyo alone is the heritage that was transferred from Shakyamuni and Many Treasures to Bodhisattva Superior Practices."

In this passage, Nichiren specifically addresses Sairen-bo's question from the standpoint of practice. He clarifies that the key to inheriting the ultimate Law of life and death lies in spreading Nam-myoho-renge-kyo following the example of Bodhisattva Superior Practices. Nichiren underlines the necessity for disciples to practice in the same spirit as Bodhisattva Superior Practices.

Next, by drawing parallels with the functions of the five elements of earth, water, fire, wind and space,[1] Nichiren outlines the power of Nam-myoho-renge-kyo. Disciples manifest this power when they practice with the same dedicated spirit as Bodhisattva Superior Practices. These functions represent the power of compassion inherent in the universe, which was believed to be composed of the five elements.

The functions of the five elements, he says, are the functions of Myoho-renge-kyo as well as "the cluster of blessings brought by the Bodhisattvas of the Earth, disciples of the Buddha in his true identity" (WND-1, 218). Through the wondrous workings inherent in life itself, these bodhisattvas propagate Myoho-renge-kyo and benefit people.

Nichiren goes on to allude that he himself is Bodhisattva Superior Practices, the first to carry out these practices and manifest the power of Nam-myoho-renge-kyo. By doing so, he is urging Sairen-bo to practice Nam-myoho-renge-kyo in the same spirit as himself and in accord with his teachings.

Practice is the lifeline of Buddhism. A religion that lacks practice becomes nothing but an intellectual pastime.

Nichiren indicates that in order to partake of the heritage for attaining Buddhahood, it is essential to practice Nam-myoho-renge-kyo—the Law entrusted to Bodhisattva Superior Practices. There is no such heritage outside of this. On the basis of this point alone, it is abundantly clear just how much the Nichiren Shoshu priesthood has deviated from Nichiren Buddhism by teaching a mystical transmission of the heritage and demanding blind obedience based thereupon.

The Beneficial Workings of the Bodhisattvas of the Earth and the Functions of the Five Elements

Just what does it mean to practice Nam-myoho-renge-kyo in accord with Nichiren Daishonin's teachings? To clarify this, Nichiren refers to the functions of the five elements. Let us look at them one by one.

"The function of fire is to burn and give light"—fire burns things and produces light which illuminates. "The function of water is to wash away filth"—water cleanses and purifies. "The winds blow away dust and breathe life into plants, animals, and human beings"—wind clears away dust. The additional statement that it "breathes life into plants, animals, and human beings" was no doubt added because wind was viewed as an animating force by the ancients. "The earth produces the grasses and trees"—grasses and trees grow and thrive in the earth; this indicates the function of nurturing life. And finally, "Heaven provides nourishing moisture"—heaven, meaning the sky, causes rain to fall, nourishing and sustaining all things.

"Heaven," mentioned last, corresponds to "space" in the five elements. Nichiren here refers to the inherent functions of nature represented by the five elements that compose the universe.

After indicating the innate value-creative functions of the five elements, Nichiren says: "The five characters of Myoho-renge-kyo are also like that. They are the cluster of blessings brought by the Bodhisattvas of the Earth, disciples of the Buddha in his true identity" (WND-1, 218). He is declaring that the functions of the five elements are themselves the functions of the five characters of Myoho-renge-kyo and that they constitute the blessings, or the beneficial workings, of the Bodhisattvas of the Earth.

In other words, the compassionate workings inherent in the universe itself are the essence of the functions of Myoho-renge-kyo, and the Bodhisattvas of the Earth benefit others by means of these inherent functions of the Mystic Law.

From Nichiren's words, we can conclude that the true nature of the benefit of the Bodhisattvas of the Earth is to enable people to substantively express, in their own character and behavior, the compassionate functions that are innate in life.

In *The Record of the Orally Transmitted Teachings*, after identifying the functions of the four elements of earth, water, fire and wind,[2] Nichiren explains that these are the blessings, or beneficial workings, of the four bodhisattvas who are the leaders of the Bodhisattvas of the Earth (see OTT, 118). According to this passage as well as the commentary of Nichikan and other writings, when the functions of the four bodhisattvas are correlated to the four elements, Superior Practices corresponds to fire, Pure Practices to water, Boundless Practices to wind and Firmly Established Practices to earth. These functions of the four bodhisattvas are themselves the functions of Myoho-renge-kyo.

The Mystic Law has the power to burn away earthly desires that give rise to suffering, to illuminate the darkness of ignorance in people's lives and to dispel the clouds of karma. This aspect is symbolized by Bodhisattva Superior Practices. The Mystic Law also has the power to bring forth the pure life-state of Buddhahood unsullied by the evils and impurities of the world; this is represented by Bodhisattva Pure Practices. Bodhisattva Boundless Practices symbolizes the power to sweep away all delusions and worries and establish a brilliant state of absolute freedom that is never deadlocked. Bodhisattva Firmly Established Practices represents the power to sweep away the sufferings caused by earthly desires and eliminate the illusions of birth and death, and to nurture all things with abundant life force, unperturbed by any obstacle.

Therefore, Nichiren, citing a passage from Tao-hsien's *Supplement to "The Words and Phrases of the Lotus Sutra,"*[5] correlates the four bodhisattvas with the four virtues of eternity, happiness, true self and purity (see OTT, 118).[3] Thus the practices of the four bodhisattvas, the universal practices of the Bodhisattvas of the Earth, transcend the four sufferings of birth, aging, sickness and death and manifest the four virtues of eternity, happiness, true self and purity.

Also, citing *The Supplement to "The Words and Phrases"*—Nichiren describes the life-state embodied in each of the names of the four bodhisattvas. When all of these spiritual characteristics or enlightened attributes are combined, they comprise an unsurpassed state of being in which "the sufferings of birth and death are nirvana" and "earthly desires are enlightenment."[4] For reference, I'd like to discuss this particular passage from *The Supplement to "The Words and Phrases"* indicating the four bodhisattvas' relationship to birth and death: "There are times when a single person possesses all four of these principles [namely, the four virtues of eternity, happiness, true self and purity]. To transcend the two types of death [birth and death in the six paths and birth and death in the higher

BODHISATTVAS OF THE EARTH

"At this time the Bodhisattvas of the Earth appear in the world for the first time solely to bring the medicine of the five characters of Myoho-renge-kyo to the ignorant people of the Latter Day" ("The Object of Devotion for Observing the Mind," WND-1, 375).

"Nichiren alone took the lead in carrying out the task of the Bodhisattvas of the Earth. He may even be one of them. If Nichiren is to be counted among the Bodhisattvas of the Earth, then so must his disciples and lay supporters" ("The True Aspect of All Phenomena," WND-1, 385).

"There should be no discrimination among those who propagate the five characters of Myoho-renge-kyo in the Latter Day of the Law, be they men or women. Were they not Bodhisattvas of the Earth, they could not chant the daimoku. At first only Nichiren chanted Nam-myoho-renge-kyo, but then two, three, and a hundred followed, chanting and teaching others. Propagation will unfold this way in the future as well. Does this not signify 'emerging from the earth'?" ("The True Aspect of All Phenomena," WND-1, 385).

"These bodhisattvas are possessors of the essential or original Law. The original Law is Nam-myoho-renge-kyo. This daimoku, Nam-myoho-renge-kyo, is something that is without exception possessed by the bodhisattvas who emerge from the earth, but it is not possessed by the bodhisattvas of the theoretical teaching, those who were taught and converted by the Buddha in his transient status. From the substance of this original Law is derived the function that is propagated as the practice of concentration and insight, and is called the principle of three thousand realms in a single moment of life. In effect, all the explanations given by great and ordinary teachers are directed toward the propagation of this function of the Wonderful Law" (*The Record of the Orally Transmitted Teachings*, p. 119).

realms] is known as Superior Practices. To go beyond the two opposing views that life is cut off after one existence or that it is eternally the same is called Boundless Practices. Because one overcomes the five categories of illusions and entanglements,[5] that state is designated Pure Practices. And because one is as perfect in virtue as [the Buddha who attained enlightenment under] the bodhi tree, that state is named Firmly Established Practices" (OTT, 118).

"Two types of death" here specifically refers to the "transmigration with differences and limitations"[6] that living beings in the six paths undergo and the "transmigration with change and advance"[7] that people of the two vehicles (voice-hearers and cause-awakened ones) and bodhisattvas undergo. "Transcending the two types of death" means moving beyond these two forms of transmigration and instead repeating the cycle of birth and death in the realm of Buddhahood,[8] which we have already discussed at length earlier in this series. Put another way, this is the state of being in which both life and death are filled with joy, in which one undergoes the cycle of birth and death with a real and profound sense of life's eternity. The Bodhisattvas of the Earth can reside in this truly autonomous state of life because they live in accord with the eternal Mystic Law.

Next, "to go beyond the two opposing views" indicates a state of life that is free of attachment to life or fear of death, transcending the mistaken views of existence characterized by the views of annihilation and permanence.[9] "Overcoming the five categories of illusions and entanglements" means freeing oneself of the five types of abiding earthly desires that cause living beings in the threefold world to become attached to life. And "[being] as perfect in virtue as [the Buddha who attained enlightenment under] the bodhi tree" means basing oneself on the complete and perfect life-state of the Buddha's enlightenment.

In short, these characteristics express the transformative functions within people's own lives, which underlie the principles of "earthly desires are enlightenment" and "the sufferings of birth and death are nirvana." Indeed, the word "practices" in the names of the four bodhisattvas alludes to efforts that are directed toward inner transformation.

The Life-State of "Bodhisattva-Buddhas"

In "The Heritage of the Ultimate Law of Life," Nichiren refers to "the cluster of blessings brought by the Bodhisattvas of the Earth, disciples of the Buddha in his true identity" (WND-1, 218).

"Disciples of the Buddha in his true identity" means disciples instructed by Shakyamuni as the Buddha enlightened since the remote past described in the "Life Span of the Thus Come One"

THE LEADERS OF THE BODHISATTVAS OF THE EARTH (CHART)

Nichiren Daishonin ascribes various traits to the four leaders of the Bodhisattvas of the Earth. These symbolic traits are important, as they represent traits inherent in us all. Also, the four leaders appear on the Gohonzon.

(See *The Soka Gakkai Dictionary of Buddhism* and *The Record of the Orally Transmitted Teachings*.)

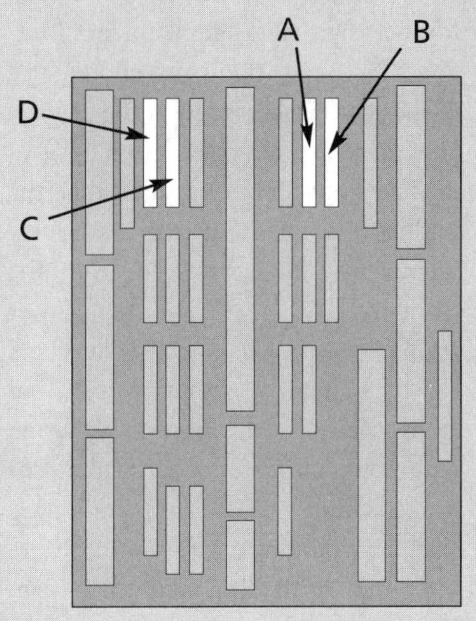

Name	Virtue	Merits	Element	Position on Gohonzon
Superior Practices	True Self	To transcend the two types of birth and death (in the six paths and higher realms).	Fire (which burns)	*Namu Jogyo Bosatsu* (Skt *Vishishtacharitra*). (position A)
Boundless Practices	Eternity	To go beyond the two opposing views that life is cut off after one existence or that it is eternally the same.	Wind (which blows away dust)	*Namu Muhengyo Bosatsu* (Skt *Anantacharitra*). (position B)
Pure Practices	Purity	Overcoming the five categories of illusions and entanglements.	Water (which purifies)	*Namu Jyogyo Bosatsu* (Skt *Vishuddhacharitra*). (position C)
Firmly Established Practices	Happiness	To be as perfect in virtue as Shakyamuni under the bodhi tree.	Earth (which nourishes plants and trees)	*Namu Anryugyo Bosatsu* (Skt *Supratishthitachari-tra*). (position D)

chapter of the Lotus Sutra. Because the Bodhisattvas of the Earth possess as their inner enlightenment the eternal Mystic Law that is one with that Buddha, they can stand up alone and propagate that Law even in the evil age after Shakyamuni's passing.

The Lotus Sutra explains that the Bodhisattvas of the Earth are bodhisattvas who have emerged from the world of truth that lies in the lower region beneath the earth.[10] The Great Teacher T'ien-t'ai says this world of truth means "the depths of the Dharma nature, the ultimate region of the profound source" (OTT, 119), indicating that the Bodhisattvas of the Earth are enlightened to the ultimate truth. Nevertheless, these bodhisattvas persist in carrying out bodhisattva practice—that is, they continually strive in an evil age to transform their own lives and the lives of others with the goal of achieving *kosen-rufu.* But in terms of their inner enlightenment, they already possess the life-state of Buddhahood that is awakened to the Mystic Law. As such, they could be called "bodhisattva-Buddhas." Nichiren revealed and spread Nam-myoho-renge-kyo in order to make it possible for all people to achieve this state of life. By deeply believing in Nam-myoho-renge-kyo and practicing exactly as Nichiren teaches, any person can attain the life-state of a "bodhisattva-Buddha."

Nichiren states: "Thus we may say that the bodhisattvas who emerge from the earth are the bodhisattvas of the essential teaching. The word 'essential' or 'original' represents the merits [blessings] handed down from the past of numberless major world system dust particle kalpas ago, the merits [blessings] that are without beginning and without end.

"These bodhisattvas are possessors of the essential or original Law. The original Law is Nam-myoho-renge-kyo" (OTT, 119).

The Bodhisattvas of the Earth who practice Nam-myoho-renge-kyo already possess the Mystic Law. Since that is the case, they can propagate the Mystic Law through one-on-one, life-to-life interaction—reaching out to the Buddha nature of others with their own Buddhahood.

No matter what karma others may be struggling with, one can only really lead them to enlightenment by awakening them to the fact that the power to break through that karma already exists within their lives. Only Bodhisattvas of the Earth possessing the essential or original Law are able to bring about this awakening.

In the Latter Day of the Law, there is utterly no possibility that salvation will come "from above," that is to say, by the grace of a transcendent Buddha who descends from the heavens. People can only become aware of the infinite power existing within their own lives by encountering Bodhisattvas of the Earth who have emerged from the lower region that is the world of truth, in other words, "from below."

A Global Gathering of Bodhisattvas of the Earth

The Soka Gakkai has revived this bodhisattva practice in the modern age through its practice of Nichiren Buddhism.

Soka Gakkai founding president, Tsunesaburo Makiguchi, once remarked: "We must clearly distinguish between believers and practitioners. While there is no dispute about the fact that someone who believes [in the Mystic Law] will have their prayers answered and realize benefit, this alone does not constitute bodhisattva practice. There is no such thing as a self-centered Buddha who simply accumulates personal benefit and does not work for the well-being of others. Unless we carry out bodhisattva practice, we cannot attain Buddhahood."[11]

Mr. Makiguchi understood that bodhisattva practice is the heart of Nichiren Buddhism, and he embodied it in his own actions. This practice was missing from the Nichiren Shoshu priesthood of the day. Mr. Makiguchi recognized that the power of Buddhism can only be demonstrated through the actual proof of faith shown by practitioners in their daily lives. He also keenly perceived that Buddhist salvation was not about the Buddha saving people by means of his resplendent appearance,[12] but rather about people bringing forth their own inner potential through personally challenging themselves in bodhisattva practice and inspiring others to do the same.

Mr. Makiguchi's staunch disciple, Josei Toda, who accompanied him to prison, had a spiritual awakening in his prison cell to his original identity as a Bodhisattva of the Earth. After his release from prison, he went on to call forth 750,000 courageous Bodhisattvas of the Earth; and it is they who built the foundations of the Soka Gakkai.

Indeed, the members of the Soka Gakkai alone have persevered in the practice of chanting and spreading Nam-myoho-renge-kyo with a profound awareness of their mission as Bodhisattvas of the Earth. As Nichiren Daishonin writes, "Were they not Bodhisattvas of the Earth, they could not chant the daimoku" ("The True Aspect of All Phenomena," WND-1, 385).

Today, countless intrepid bodhisattvas have emerged from "the great earth of the Dharma nature"[13] in 190 countries and territories around the world in order to realize *kosen-rufu*. The emergence of the Bodhisattvas of the Earth as expounded in the Lotus Sutra is being reenacted in the present age by none other than the SGI.

Bodhisattvas of the Earth are unhindered by such distinctions as nationality, culture or race. In fact, our global network of Bodhisattvas of the Earth is today forging deep mutual understanding and sympathy transcending differences of ideology, creed and religion. All people are equal, and everyone is worthy of respect. When we awaken to the incredible power that lies within us, we can change our world.

The solidarity of awakened people

can help others realize their highest potential and thus make the world a better place. We have now entered an age when our gathering of Bodhisattvas of the Earth is attracting praise far and wide. The time has come when people everywhere are earnestly seeking the egalitarian and humanistic "Buddhism of the people" of Nichiren Daishonin.

Based on the mentor-disciple spirit of Soka, let us now show the world the real "power of the people" that is the hallmark of the Bodhisattvas of the Earth.

[Supplemental materials provided by the SGI-USA Study Department.]

1. Five elements: According to ancient Indian belief, the five constituents of all things in the universe. They are earth, water, fire, wind and space. Space is interpreted as integrating and harmonizing the other four elements.
2. Four elements: earth, water, fire and wind. Each corresponds to a quality of matter: earth to solidity, water to moisture, fire to heat and wind to motion. Their respective functions correspond to four intrinsic functions of the universe itself: to sustain and preserve, to gather and contain, to mature, and to cause growth. Disharmony among the four elements in the human body was said to cause illness.
3. Tao-hsien: An eighth-century priest of the T'ien-t'ai school in China. Said to have been a disciple of Miao-lo, he wrote *The Supplement to "The Words and Phrases of the Lotus Sutra,"* a commentary on both T'ien-t'ai's *Words and Phrases of the Lotus Sutra* and Miao-lo's *Annotations on "The Words and Phrases of the Lotus Sutra."*
4. "The sufferings of birth and death are nirvana" means that the Buddha's enlightened life-state of true peace and tranquillity (nirvana) manifests in the lives of ordinary people who undergo the sufferings of birth and death. "Earthly desires are enlightenment" means that the wisdom for awakening to the ultimate truth for attaining Buddhahood manifests in the lives of ordinary people who are ruled by earthly desires.
5. The five categories of illusions and entanglements: Also, the five types of abiding earthly desires. Five types of earthly desires found in living beings transmigrating through the six paths of the threefold world, which consists of the world of desire, the world of form and the world of formlessness. They represent a further subdivision of the three illusions of perception, thought and ignorance: (1) illusions of perception of the threefold world (the abiding earthly desires arising from seeing things as they seem, not as they really are); (2) illusions of thought of the world of desire (the abiding earthly desires in the world of desire); (3) illusions of thought of the world of form (the abiding earthly desires in the world of form); (4) illusions of thought of the world of formlessness (the abiding earthly desires in the world of formlessness); and (5) illusions of ignorance of the threefold world (the abiding earthly desires arising from ignorance in the threefold world).
6. Transmigration with differences and limitations: The transmigration of unenlightened beings among the six paths. In this cycle of rebirth, living beings are said to be born with limited life spans and in different forms according to their karma.
7. Transmigration with change and advance: The transmigration that voice-hearers, cause-awakened ones and bodhisattvas undergo on the way to emancipation. It refers to becoming free from transmigration in the realm of delusion, and advancing to higher stages of practice until one attains emancipation.
8. Birth and death in the realm of Buddhahood: To freely undergo the cycle of birth and death based on the realization that our lives are entities of the all-pervasive Law of Myoho-renge-kyo, and that life and death are inherent functions of Myoho-renge-kyo. Further, it is to embody the immense compassion and life force inherent in the universe and practice the Buddha way in lifetime after lifetime in order to lead all living beings to enlightenment.
9. This refers to two erroneous ways of viewing death—two extremes. The view of annihilation is the mistaken attachment to the notion that life begins with birth and ends with death. According to this view, there is only the present life, and death represents a complete cessation of existence both physical and spiritual. The view of permanence is also the mistaken notion that what exists here in the present is permanent and unchanging. This view rejects causality, so that neither practicing good nor practicing evil produces any change in one's condition.
10. The Lotus Sutra states: "The bodies of these bodhisattvas were all golden in hue, with the thirty-two features and an immeasurable brightness. Previously they had all been dwelling in the world of empty space underneath the saha world" (LS, 213).
11. Translated from Japanese. Tsunesaburo Makiguchi, *Makiguchi Tsunesaburo zenshu* (Collected Works of Tsunesaburo Makiguchi) (Tokyo: Daisanbunmei-sha, 1987), vol. 10, p. 151.
12. This refers to the remarkable characteristics, such as the thirty-two features, attributed to Buddhas and bodhisattvas.
13. Nichiren Daishonin says: "Concerning the passage 'Unsoiled by worldly things like the lotus flower in the water, they emerge from the earth' [*see* LS, 222]. '[Unsoiled by] worldly things' means being completely unsullied by such things as greed, just as the lotus flower born in the water is not stained by mud. The lotus flower is a metaphor for the bodhisattvas who emerge from the earth. 'Earth' means the great earth of the Dharma nature, or enlightenment. In other words, the votary of the Lotus Sutra is like the lotus flower that is unsullied by the muddy water" (*Gosho zenshu*, p. 833).

STUDY GUIDE

A summary of key points from SGI President Ikeda's lecture

The Bodhisattvas of the Earth depicted in the Lotus Sutra are people who, in the defiled age of the Latter Day of the Law, impart the light of hope to those who are suffering. These bodhisattvas tirelessly reach out to each individual, with compassion and courage, until fresh life force wells forth from their life. Disciples of Shakyamuni Buddha and practitioners of the essential teaching of the Lotus Sutra in the Latter Day of the Law, through the practice of the Mystic Law, are determined to awaken all people to their inherent Buddhahood.

Their belief in the greatness of all people allows them to overcome self-centeredness. Barriers such as race, culture and nationality are not hindrances to the Bodhisattvas of the Earth.

Those who seek to practice the Lotus Sutra only for themselves are not Bodhisattvas of the Earth and will be unable to receive the heritage of the ultimate Law.

Nichiren Daishonin alluded that he was fulfilling the mission of Bodhisattva Superior Practices, one of the four leaders of the Bodhisattvas of the Earth. He states, "Whether or not Bodhisattva Superior Practices has appeared in this world, Nichiren has already made a start in propagating this teaching" (WND-1, 218). Nichiren was the first person to declare and spread Nam-myoho-renge-kyo during the Latter Day of the Law.

The Bodhisattvas of the Earth practice the Lotus Sutra by chanting Nam-myoho-renge-kyo and sharing that teaching with other people. This is an active practice and not a merely academic and intellectual exercise. This point is stressed by the fact that all four leaders of the Bodhisattvas of the Earth have "practices" in their name.

The benefits of the practices of the four leaders can be manifested in the life of every person who chants and spreads the Mystic Law. In "The Heritage of the Ultimate Law of Life," Nichiren Daishonin likens these benefits to the functions of the four elements, each one a metaphor for a way to overcome delusion (see chart on page 101).

The "Earth" from which the Bodhisattvas emerge is, according to T'ien-t'ai, the world of truth, the depths of the Dharma nature innate in life. Because they emerge from this essential truth, though they function as Bodhisattvas, they are Buddhas. Nichiren refers to them as "possessors of the essential or original Law."

The members of the SGI, who chant Nam-myoho-renge-kyo and spread the essential teaching throughout the world, are clearly Bodhisattvas of the Earth.

Lectures on
The HERITAGE *of the* ULTIMATE LAW *of* LIFE

SGI PRESIDENT IKEDA'S STUDY LECTURE SERIES

(11)

BODHISATTVA SUPERIOR PRACTICES

Pioneering the Way for Human Victory by Unlocking the Highest Potential of All People

How admirable that you have asked about the transmission of the ultimate Law of life and death! I have never heard of anyone who has asked such a question. I have answered in complete detail in this letter, so please take it deeply to heart. The important point is to carry out your practice confident that Nam-myoho-renge-kyo alone is the heritage that was transferred from Shakyamuni and Many Treasures to Bodhisattva Superior Practices.

The function of fire is to burn and give light. The function of water is to wash away filth. The winds blow away dust and breathe life into plants, animals, and human beings. The earth produces the grasses and trees, and heaven provides nourishing moisture. The five characters of Myoho-renge-kyo are also like that. They are the cluster of blessings brought by the Bodhisattvas of the Earth, disciples of the Buddha in his true identity. The Lotus Sutra says that Bodhisattva Superior Practices will appear now, in the Latter Day of the Law, to propagate this teaching, but has this happened? Whether or not Bodhisattva Superior Practices has appeared in this world, Nichiren has already made a start in propagating this teaching. (*The Writings of Nichiren Daishonin*, vol. 1, pp. 217–18)

Lecture

Inner joy and vitality are indispensable to realizing happiness for ourselves and others and to construct an alliance of people dedicated to the cause of good. We can only deeply inspire others through our own lives, and we can only spur them to embark on inner change through our actions and conduct as people undertaking this same challenge.

How can we break through the closed, hardened shell of a person's life in the Latter Day of the Law, which as a result of karma and self-absorption often resembles an inhospitable frozen wasteland? And how can we activate people's Buddha nature and awaken them on a fundamental level so that they can transform their lives? This is the endless challenge of our Buddhist practice. And that is why we ourselves must be active and engaged Buddhists who continue to work on our own inner transformation.

In the Lotus Sutra, the Bodhisattvas of the Earth[1]—the countless bodhisattvas who emerge dynamically from the earth when the ground trembles and splits open—come forward to take on this mission. And Bodhisattva Superior Practices is their leader.

The Significance of the Transmission From Shakyamuni and Many Treasures to Bodhisattva Superior Practices

Nichiren Daishonin clarifies the practice for receiving the heritage of the ultimate Law of life and death, saying, "The important point is to carry out your practice confident that Nam-myoho-renge-kyo alone is the heritage that was transferred from Shakyamuni and Many Treasures to Bodhisattva Superior Practices" (WND-1, 217). In terms of the ceremony of entrustment, or transmission,[2] that took place during the Ceremony in the Air in the Lotus Sutra, this passage can be read as an exhortation to practice with the firm belief that Nam-myoho-renge-kyo is the great Law that was passed on to Superior Practices by Shakyamuni and Many Treasures.

Based on this view, in the last installment I focused on the importance of practicing the Buddha's teaching as taught by Bodhisattva Superior Practices and of maintaining the shared commitment of mentor and disciple with Bodhisattva Superior Practices as the mentor.

Nichiren states: "The Lotus Sutra says that Bodhisattva Superior Practices will appear now, in the Latter Day of the Law, to propagate this teaching, but has this happened? Whether or not Bodhisattva Superior Practices has appeared in this world, Nichiren has already made a start in propagating this teaching" (WND-1, 218).

Here, Nichiren is effectively affirming that he himself is Bodhisattva Superior Practices, who vowed to appear in the Latter Day of the Law. Therefore, the heritage of the ultimate Law of life and death flows in the lives of those who practice as Nichiren teaches and with the same commitment as he has.

Nichiren concludes in this writing that we should practice Nam-myoho-

Seikyo Press

SGI President Ikeda presents Chinese Ambassador to Japan Cui Tiankai (left) with a Chinese poem he composed with his wish of Sino-Japanese friendship, November 19, 2007.

renge-kyo as the Law that was entrusted to Superior Practices by Shakyamuni and Many Treasures. But a deeper interpretation can also be given to his emphasis of this point—namely, that this entrustment signifies a major transition from the Buddha of true effect to the Buddha of true cause and, by extension, from the Buddhism of true effect to the Buddhism of true cause.

In short, it is not simply a transfer of the Law from Buddha to bodhisattva, but rather a radical change in the very framework of the Buddhist teachings and in the person who serves as the teacher, or—to use Buddhist terminology—"the lord of teachings." When considered in this light, the profound significance of Nam-myoho-renge-kyo, as the Law entrusted to Superior Practices, becomes clear.

From the Buddha of True Effect to the Buddha of True Cause

Let us look briefly at the meaning of true cause and true effect. In the "Life Span" chapter of the Lotus Sutra, Shakyamuni reveals that he has "in fact attained Buddhahood"[3] in the remote past. True cause refers to the practice he undertook at that time to realize that goal, while true effect refers to the enlightened state of Buddhahood he achieved as a result. That is the literal meaning of these concepts.

The "Life Span" chapter further indicates that the Buddha who "in fact attained enlightenment" in the remote past is actually the true identity, the essential nature, of all Buddhas. This Buddha has continuously appeared ever since that time in the *saha* world and various other lands, as either a bodhisattva or Buddha, to instruct living beings. Based on this explanation, the concept of true cause and true effect describes the fundamental causality through which all Buddhas attain enlightenment.

In that respect, the designation "true effect" refers to the Buddha—and the teachings—that reveal the ultimate effect of attaining Buddhahood. All the teachings attributed to Shakyamuni fall into the category of the Buddhism of true effect, which reveals the fundamental effect of the Buddha's attainment of enlightenment in the remote past.

The Buddha and the teachings of true effect expound a supreme state of existence that, in a sense, transcends what is attainable by human beings. Because this is beyond ordinary comprehension, the Buddha and the teachings of true effect ultimately have no meaning for ordinary people except as metaphors.

Referring to the essence of the Buddha and the teachings of true effect, Nichiren Daishonin states in "The Gift of Rice" that they teach that the clarity of the Buddha's mind is like the moon and the purity of the Buddha's mind is like a flower (see WND-1, 1126).[4] With this simple illustration, he indicates that they are merely figurative.

In contrast, the designation of "true cause" refers to the Buddha and the teachings that reveal the supreme and fundamental cause for attaining enlightenment. Since the cause lies on the side of the practitioners, the teachings of true cause are those that expound the ultimate causality for attaining Buddhahood in a way that is relevant to the lives of ordinary people.

Bodhisattva Superior Practices, having received the heritage of the Law from Shakyamuni and Many Treasures, is a bodhisattva who appears in this actual *saha* world as an ordinary human being. In order to realize the Lotus Sutra's ideal of universal enlightenment, it is necessary for him to not only practice the ultimate Law of cause and effect for attaining Buddhahood but also to embody it in his own life as a human being, and to then convey it to others in the Latter Day.

The Buddhism of true cause is predicated on ordinary people embodying the ultimate Law of cause and effect for attaining Buddhahood in their lives, just as they are. Both cause and effect reside within us. The Buddhism of true cause describes this as "the Mystic Law of the simultaneity of cause and effect."

Nichiren states: "Shakyamuni Buddha, who has attained perfect enlightenment,[5] is our own flesh and blood. His practices and the resulting virtues are our bones and marrow" ("The Object of Devotion for Observing the Mind," WND-1, 365). When we firmly establish in our lives the merit of practice and the benefit of Buddhahood, we can manifest within us the life-state of the Buddha of perfect enlightenment.

PRACTICE FOR ONESELF AND OTHERS

The Japanese term *jigyo-keta* translates into English as "practice for oneself and others." *Jigyo*, literally "self-practice," refers to the Buddhist practice for personal benefit and the accumulation of wisdom. *Keta*, literally, "changing others," means instructing and converting others so that they will embrace Buddhist teachings. It means to practice Buddhism in order to benefit others. While it can be considered a general term for the Buddhist spirit of altruism, it should be noted that sharing Buddhism with another person and helping that person carry out their practice is the ultimate intent of Nichiren Buddhism. This practice also ultimately enriches oneself.

Practice for oneself and others should not be considered two distinct practices, but rather two aspects of a bodhisattva's complete practice. Nichiren indicated that the correct practice of Nam-myoho-renge-kyo includes both practice for oneself and practice for others.

The Buddhism of true cause expounds the Buddha and the teaching in terms of people's actual practice. In "The Gift of Rice," Nichiren says, "It is the teaching that the moon itself is mind, and the flower itself is mind" (WND-1, 1126). This means that actual phenomena such as the moon or flowers themselves embody the mind of the Buddha.

Consequently, in light of the fact that Bodhisattva Superior Practices embodies the Mystic Law and spreads the Buddhism of true cause in the *saha* world, it follows that Shakyamuni and Many Treasures represent the Buddhas of true effect, while Bodhisattva Superior Practices represents the Buddha of true cause.

Furthermore, for ordinary people who are striving to attain the Way, the Buddhism of true effect, symbolized by the Buddhas Shakyamuni and Many Treasures, is a teaching that only inspires awe, the goal of enlightenment seeming like some unreachable object high in the heavens. In contrast, the Buddhism of true cause is a teaching accessible to all that inspires people to propagate the Mystic Law of the simultaneity of cause and effect that Bodhisattva Superior Practices took the lead in embodying in his own life.

In the Buddhism of true effect, true cause and true effect are taught as being distinct and separate, while in the Buddhism of true cause, true cause and true effect are taught as being present simultaneously in the Mystic Law. Therefore, even though the same terms may be used in both teachings, they are fundamentally different.

The Mystic Law of the simultaneity of cause and effect is the true seed of Buddhahood. It can be said that Shakyamuni originally became a Buddha by awakening to the existence of this seed and embodying the cause and effect for attaining enlightenment in his life. However, many of the teachings that are ascribed to Shakyamuni do not mention the seed of Buddhahood itself and only remain within the realm of the Buddhism of true effect.

The crux of the Lotus Sutra lies in its explanation of the entrustment, or transmission, of the heritage of the Law from Shakyamuni and Many Treasures to Bodhisattva Superior Practices. The very fact that the Lotus Sutra depicts this transfer of the Law signals that a fundamental shift in emphasis in the teaching from true effect to true cause will be essential at a future time if the Lotus Sutra ideal and Buddha vow of universal enlightenment is to be realized.

The Essence of the Buddhism of True Cause—A Struggle Against Devilish Functions

The substance of the entrustment in the Lotus Sutra lies in its signaling a change in the teacher and in the teachings, with the focus moving from true effect to true cause.

The statement, "Whether or not Bodhisattva Superior Practices has appeared in this world, Nichiren has already made a start in propagating this teaching" (WND-1, 218), is a declaration that Nichiren Daishonin is the teacher of true cause who will accomplish this great transition in Buddhism.

Throughout his life, Nichiren held fast to his vow to enable all people to attain enlightenment and to realize a society where all can live in peace and happiness. These are the aspirations of the Lotus Sutra. He infused his faith in the Lotus Sutra into the practice of chanting Nam-myoho-renge-kyo, which he taught to others without sparing his voice. And he was persecuted by corrupt priests and secular authorities who could not understand the true meaning of the Lotus Sutra. Yet while encountering momentous obstacles like those described in the Lotus Sutra, he persevered unflaggingly in his struggle without begrudging his life, triumphing over all.

Through these struggles as a human being residing in the *saha* world, he solidly established in his life the merit of practice and the benefit of Buddhahood, and came to manifest the life-state of the Buddha of perfect enlightenment, the embodiment of the Mystic Law of the simultaneity of cause and effect. I am referring to Nichiren casting off his transient status and revealing his true identity as the Buddha of the Latter Day of the

THE TREASURE TOWER

The treasure tower, as depicted in the 11th chapter of the Lotus Sutra, is a massive and lavishly decorated stupa that emerges from the earth. The tower houses Many Treasures, a Buddha from a distant land called Treasure Purity, who arrives to hear Shakyamuni preach the Lotus Sutra and attest to its veracity. It is adorned with seven kinds of gems, which Nichiren Daishonin interprets as symbolizing the seven treasures, or elements of Buddhist practice; namely, hearing the correct teaching, believing it, keeping the precepts, engaging in meditation, practicing assiduously, renouncing one's attachments and reflecting on oneself (see "On the Treasure Tower," WND-1, 299).

Nichiren in his writings interprets the treasure tower in several interrelated ways, equating it with the Law of Myoho-renge-kyo, with the Gohonzon, or object of devotion, and with one's life itself. For example, he tells a disciple: "Abutsu-bo is therefore the treasure tower itself, and the treasure tower is Abutsu-bo himself. No other knowledge is purposeful" (WND-1, 299).

Because a person's innate Buddhahood, Nam-myoho-renge-kyo and the Law reflected in the Gohonzon are essentially one, the treasure tower refers equally to all three aspects.

Law[6] at the time of the Tatsunokuchi Persecution (1271).

In "Aspiration for the Buddha Land," which he wrote on Sado Island a short time later, Nichiren says: "The secret Law that is the one great reason the Buddhas make their advent will be spread for the first time in this country. How could Nichiren not be the one who will do this?" (WND-1, 213). He also declares, "The Law has already appeared" (WND-1, 214), and goes on to cite the sutra's prediction of the appearance of Bodhisattva Superior Practices.

Nichiren inscribed the Gohonzon, the object of devotion, by embodying in the form of a mandala the true cause and true effect that he manifested in his life. And he also established Nam-myoho-renge-kyo of the Three Great Secret Laws[7] as the practical means by which all people could achieve genuine, lasting happiness, which is the fundamental aim of the Lotus Sutra.

Nichiren's deep conviction as to his identity as Bodhisattva Superior Practices is evident from statements he makes in various writings. For example, in "The Teaching, Practice, and Proof," he says: "Who among our contemporaries, what school of Buddhism, is actually propagating the object of devotion and the sanctuary of the essential teaching? Not a single person carried out this task during the 2,220 years and more following the Buddha's passing.... Superior Practices, the leader of the Bodhisattvas of the Earth, has already made his advent in this world, so the great Law, the essence of the Lotus Sutra that was entrusted to him, will spread without fail" (WND-1, 482).

This passage vividly conveys Nichiren's towering state of life. It is as if he is saying: "I alone uphold the banner of the Mystic Law and have brought to life the spirit of the Lotus Sutra. No one can refute this fact. It is an unprecedented event in the history of Buddhism."

In "The Heritage of the Ultimate Law of Life," too, Nichiren's words resound with his awareness as the teacher of the Latter Day who inherited the Law passed on from Shakyamuni and Many Treasures and opened the way for its widespread propagation. He also calls on his disciples to share his spirit and advance on the same path. It is by carrying on Nichiren's teachings and helping others become happy that we can actualize the great path of universal enlightenment that is the goal of Nichiren Buddhism.

Nichiren is the Buddha of the Latter Day of the Law who established the Buddhism of the people, a teaching open to all. He proved the power of the Buddhist Law through his own lifelong efforts as a "bodhisattva-Buddha," as an ordinary human being.

In the period before his exile to Sado, while encountering harsh persecution as a votary of the Lotus Sutra, he maintained a victorious spirit. He battled the three powerful enemies[8] and surmounted the three obstacles and four devils; he set an example of one person resolutely triumphing over the hindrances of death and the devil king [i.e., near execution and life-threatening persecution by the ruling authorities].[9] This was what he did at Tatsunokuchi when he discarded his transient status and revealed his true identity.

Nichiren stated: "I survived even the Tatsunokuchi Persecution and emerged safely from other great persecutions. By now, the devil king must be thoroughly discouraged"[10] (*Gosho zenshu*, p. 843). This is truly a declaration of one person's lofty and heroic spiritual victory over all manner of devilish functions.

Nichiren Buddhism is based on the mentor-disciple relationship, teaching disciples to persevere in life with the same strength and fortitude as the mentor. Nichiren left behind his example so that all people, by living with the same spirit he did, could lead triumphant lives.

In one sense, human beings are weak and vulnerable, and find it extremely difficult to break through the darkness of their innate ignorance. But they also have the capacity for infinite nobility

THE THREE GREAT SECRET LAWS

The core principles of Nichiren Daishonin's teaching are the object of devotion of the essential teaching, the *daimoku* (Nam-myoho-renge-kyo) of the essential teaching and the sanctuary of the essential teaching. Here, "essential teaching" refers to the teaching of Nam-myoho-renge-kyo and not to the essential teaching, or the latter fourteen chapters, of the Lotus Sutra.

The Three Great Secret Laws represent Nichiren's embodiment of the Mystic Law, to which he was enlightened and manifested fully in his life, in a form that all people can practice and thereby gain access to that Law within their own lives.

He associated the Three Great Secret Laws with the three types of learning set forth in Buddhism—precepts, meditation and wisdom.

Specifically, the object of devotion corresponds to meditation, the sanctuary (Jpn *kaidan*, literally, precepts platform) to precepts and the *daimoku* to wisdom. Because embracing this object of devotion called the Gohonzon is the only precept in Nichiren's teaching, the place where the Gohonzon is enshrined corresponds to the place where one vows to observe the Buddhist precepts—the ordination platform, or sanctuary, of the essential teaching. The *daimoku* of the essential teaching indicates the invocation or chanting of Nam-myoho-renge-kyo with faith in the object of devotion; it includes chanting for oneself and teaching it to others. They are called "secret" because they are teachings that had never previously been revealed. They were hidden in the subtext, or in the depths of the lines, of the Lotus Sutra until Nichiren, through his vow and practice, revealed them for the sake of the happiness of all humankind.

(Adapted from *The Soka Gakkai Dictionary of Buddhism*)

when they believe in the fundamental power inherent in their own lives and the lives of others. When people come into contact with the victorious life of a great champion like Nichiren, they can discover their own limitless potential.

Victory can take many forms, but there is surely no greater victory than breaking through the darkness of innate ignorance, bringing forth the life-state of Buddhahood and producing an infinite number of successors who can carry on the noble cause of *kosen-rufu*. In view of the scale of the victory he achieved, Nichiren is the fundamental teacher of the Latter Day of the Law. Most important, because he opened the path for all people to reveal their inherent Buddhahood by chanting Nam-myoho-renge-kyo and established a truly humanistic religious philosophy, we regard him as a teacher of humankind.

The Great Path of a Humanistic Religion

Buddhism is originally a teaching that restores the dignity of human life. Moreover, it extols the sanctity of all life, not just human beings.

Immediately after defeating the devilish functions that assailed him and attaining enlightenment, Shakyamuni realized a perfectly serene and peaceful state of mind like the sun shining tranquilly in the heavens. And he set out to expound his teachings so that all people could unlock within them this same boundless and joyous state of life.

The Lotus Sutra, deeply infused with this essence, is a teaching of revitalization that celebrates the limitless potential of human beings. This is the original message of Buddhism.

Nichiren Daishonin distilled the essence of the sutra in the single Law of Nam-myoho-renge-kyo and established it as a teaching that is open to all people. And the Soka Gakkai has energetically extended this great, joyous path of humanistic religion throughout the world.

The genuine practice of Buddhism from the times of Shakyamuni and Nichiren lives on in the practice of mentor and disciple in the Soka Gakkai. This practice is comprised of efforts based on a stand-alone spirit (the spirit to act based on a sense of full personal responsibility in the struggle for *kosen-rufu*).

By committing ourselves to the great vow for *kosen-rufu*, we can manifest our own inherently enlightened life-state. And by taking action with an ungrudging spirit, we can free people from suffering and help them revitalize their lives. These awakened people in turn, through the power of dialogue, can inspire still others, giving them fresh courage and conviction. The stand-alone practice of the first three presidents—united by the bonds of mentor and disciple—is the starting point of the magnificent worldwide spread of our movement for human revolution, or inner transformation.

Tsunesaburo Makiguchi, the Soka Gakkai's founding president, often described his struggle as being as challenging as "making a landing in the face of the enemy." Ever undaunted, he stood up alone as a genuine practitioner of Nichiren Buddhism at a time when its teachings were all but lost to society and when the country as a whole was rushing headlong to war. He set an example of what it means to dedicate one's life to the Law without hesitation.

TRUE CAUSE AND TRUE EFFECT

In the "Life Span" chapter of the Lotus Sutra, Shakyamuni Buddha reveals that although people have long believed he attained enlightenment for the first time in his present life, that is not the case. Rather, he says, "It has been immeasurable, boundless hundreds, thousands, ten thousands, millions of nayutas of kalpas since I in fact attained Buddhahood" (*The Lotus Sutra*, p. 225). Thus he says that he first attained Buddhahood at a time in the past too remote to imagine.

Until this statement, his disciples thought he had attained enlightenment in this life as an effect of past virtuous practices carried out over previous lifetimes. But now it appeared Shakyamuni had already been enlightened while carrying out those benevolent practices. Thus, such acts were expressions of his Buddhahood rather than the means to attain Buddhahood. He says that in the extremely remote past he had carried out the "bodhisattva way" and at that distant time attained an enduring life-state of Buddhahood.

In light of this revelation, Shakyamuni's original enlightenment in the remote past came to be known as the "true effect."

Nichiren Daishonin identified the Law of Nam-myoho-renge-kyo as the "true cause," explaining that it enabled not only Shakyamuni, but all Buddhas, to attain enlightenment; moreover, it makes it possible for all human beings to do so. It is the fundamental Law that has existed in the universe and in all life since "time without beginning."

From the viewpoint of the true effect, Buddhahood is still a result of causes piled up over time. The "effect" of Buddhahood comes in some distant lifetime.

But from the standpoint of true cause, Buddhahood is recognized as an eternally present potential within human life at each moment. Chanting Nam-myoho-renge-kyo with faith and determination immediately invokes the true cause, bringing forth one's innate Buddha nature. This is called the "simultaneity of cause and effect." Both true cause and true effect exist together in a single moment. The present moment and every moment thereafter are transformed for the better by the wisdom and vitality of one's emerging Buddhahood.

In Nichiren Buddhism, Nichiren and his teaching are referred to respectively as the teacher and the Buddhism of true cause, while Shakyamuni and his teachings are referred to as the teacher and the Buddhism of true effect.

Second Soka Gakkai president Josei Toda, who inherited the legacy his mentor, Mr. Makiguchi, awoke to his own mission in prison. [Both had been jailed by the wartime militarist authorities who saw their peace-oriented Buddhist activities as a threat to the authority of Shintoism, the state religion used to rally support for the war.] On his release, Mr. Toda stood up alone in the desolate, war-torn landscape of Japan to rebuild the Soka Gakkai. Mr. Toda's self-reliant practice marked the full-fledged start of a movement for the victory of the people.

I, too, as a disciple who inherited the Soka spirit, embarked on a voyage into the vast uncharted waters of global *kosen-rufu.*

Through their noble spiritual struggles, Mr. Makiguchi and Mr. Toda showed us how much an individual human being can accomplish. They will go down in history as teachers who serve as an inspiration for all humankind. It could be said that the tributes they are today receiving from countries near and far are proof of the victory of the mentors and disciples of Soka.

As disciples around the world—who share this noble mentor-disciple spirit—continue to open wide the great path of a humanistic religion that truly enriches and elevates people, the ideals and endeavors of our Soka movement will be applauded all the more in this century.

Humanity today is earnestly seeking living examples and role models. In particular, people yearn to find those who embody a humanistic philosophy, one that will usher in a happier and more hopeful future. The time has now arrived for our valiant members across the globe to be respected as Bodhisattvas of the Earth. This is because they are carrying out the very practice those Bodhisattvas vowed to pursue.

There is absolutely no doubt that Nichiren is praising our efforts in transmitting the heritage for attaining Buddhahood on a global scale, and that Shakyamuni, Many Treasures and all Buddhas throughout the three existences are applauding the impressive development of our SGI movement.

1. Bodhisattvas of the Earth: An innumerable host of bodhisattvas who emerge from beneath the earth and to whom Shakyamuni Buddha entrusts the propagation of the Mystic Law, or the essence of the Lotus Sutra, in the Latter Day of the Law. They are led by four bodhisattvas—Superior Practices, Boundless Practices, Pure Practices, Firmly Established Practices—and Superior Practices is the leader of them all.

2. Ceremony of entrustment: also, ceremony of transmission. A ceremony that takes place centering around the treasure tower, which is suspended in the air, as described in the "Treasure Tower" and "Entrustment" chapters of the Lotus Sutra. While it represents the transmission of the Law to the Bodhisattvas of the Earth as a whole, in the "Supernatural Powers" chapter, Shakyamuni expounds the essence of the Lotus Sutra and specifically entrusts their leader, Bodhisattva Superior Practices, with its propagation in the Latter Day of the Law.

3. "But good men, it has been immeasurable, boundless hundreds, thousands, ten thousands, millions of nayutas of kalpas since I in fact attained Buddhahood" (LS, 225).

SGI PRESIDENT IKEDA ON TRUE CAUSE AND TRUE EFFECT

In his *Lectures on the "Expedient Means" and "Life Span" Chapters of the Lotus Sutra*, vol. 3, SGI President Ikeda refers to the practice of the bodhisattva way as the practice of true cause.

He states: "Our Buddhist practice is not one of revering true effect. Since embracing the Mystic Law is in itself enlightenment, when we embrace the Gohonzon we can immediately manifest the world of Buddhahood in our lives. The bodhisattva practice of the Buddhism of true cause is to direct ourselves toward the nine worlds while basing ourselves on the life of Buddhahood. It is, it might be said, to dive headlong into the mundane reality of society dominated by the nine worlds, based on the life of Buddhahood.

"In other words, our practice entails constantly going back and forth between the practice for oneself of [reciting the sutra] and chanting [Nam-myoho-renge-kyo] and the practice for others of spreading the Mystic Law. The key to manifesting the world of Buddhahood lies in this continuing activity.

"Accordingly, the Buddhism of true cause exists in the way of life, the practice, of ceaselessly striving to improve one's immediate, everyday surroundings and to carry the age and society forward" (p. 21).

4. Nichiren Daishonin writes: "The meaning of the earlier sutras is that clarity of mind is like the moon, and that purity of mind is like a flower. But it is not so with the Lotus Sutra. It is the teaching that the moon itself is mind, and the flower itself is mind" ("The Gift of Rice," WND-1, 1126).

5. Perfect enlightenment: also, supreme perfect enlightenment. The enlightenment of a Buddha. "Perfect enlightenment" also refers to the last and highest of the 52 stages of bodhisattva practice, or Buddhahood.

6. This refers to the principle of "casting off the transient and revealing the true"—the revealing of a Buddha's true status as a Buddha, and the setting aside of that Buddha's provisional or transient identity. Nichiren Daishonin indicates in his writing "The Opening of the Eyes" that, in surviving the execution attempt of the Tatsunokuchi Persecution, he cast off his transient status as an ordinary person and revealed his true identity as the Buddha of the Latter Day of the Law (see WND-1, 269).

7. Three Great Secret Laws: The core principles of Nichiren Buddhism: (1) the object of devotion, (2) the invocation, or *daimoku* of Nam-myoho-renge-kyo and (3) the sanctuary or the place where one chants the *daimoku* before the object of devotion.

8. Three powerful enemies: The three types of people who persecute those who propagate the Lotus Sutra are: 1) Arrogant lay people; 2) arrogant priests; and 3) arrogant false sages.

9. Three obstacles and four devils: Various obstacles and hindrances to the practice of Buddhism. The three obstacles are: (1) the obstacle of earthly desires, (2) the obstacle of karma and (3) the obstacle of retribution. The four devils are: (1) the hindrance of the five components, (2) the hindrance of earthly desires, (3) the hindrance of death and (4) the hindrance of the devil king.

10. From "Oko kikigaki" (The Recorded Lectures); not included in *The Writings of Nichiren*, vols. 1 and 2.

STUDY GUIDE

The following is a summary of key points from SGI President Ikeda's lecture.

We can only spur others to embark on inner change through our conduct as people who are ourselves undertaking this same change by challenging our Buddhist practice. This is the mission of the Bodhisattvas of the Earth, led by Bodhisattva Superior Practices.

The Significance of the Transmission From Shakyamuni and Many Treasures to Bodhisattva Superior Practices

In "The Heritage of the Ultimate Law of Life," Nichiren Daishonin clarifies the practice of chanting Nam-myoho-renge-kyo as the way to receive the heritage of the Law of life and death. He writes, "The important point is to carry out your practice confident that Nam-myoho-renge-kyo alone is the heritage that was transferred from Shakyamuni and Many Treasures to Bodhisattva Superior Practices" (WND-1, 217).

Asserting that Nam-myoho-renge-kyo is the Law entrusted to Superior Practices by Shakyamuni and Many Treasures, Nichiren later affirms that he himself is Superior Practices.

In addition, this entrustment, which is the crux of the teachings of the Lotus Sutra, marks the transition from the teaching and teacher of true effect, to those of true cause—a radical change in the framework of the Buddhist teachings that is necessary for the realization of the Buddha's vow for universal enlightenment.

From the Buddha of True Effect to the Buddha of True Cause

True effect refers to the enlightenment Shakyamuni attained in the remote past, while true cause is the practice he carried out to attain that enlightenment.

Bodhisattva Superior Practices appeared in the real world as an ordinary human being who embodied the Buddhism of true cause in his own life and conveyed it to others.

What distinguishes the Buddhism of true cause from the Buddhism of true effect is that in the former, cause and effect are simultaneously present in the Mystic Law. This Mystic Law is the true seed of Buddhahood. Based on this law of causality, ordinary people can attain enlightenment just as they are by chanting Nam-myoho-renge-kyo.

Nichiren states: "Shakyamuni Buddha, who has attained perfect enlightenment, is our own flesh and blood. His practices and the resulting virtues are our bones and marrow" ("The Object of Devotion for Observing the Mind," WND-1, 365). In other words, when we firmly establish in our lives Buddhist practice and the benefit of Buddhahood, we can manifest the life-state of the Buddha of perfect enlightenment.

Unlike the Buddhism of true effect in which enlightenment is viewed as something distant and unattainable, the Buddhism of true cause inspires action for the happiness of self and others.

The Essence of the Buddhism of True Cause—A Struggle Against Devilish Functions

Nichiren lived based on his lifelong vow for the enlightenment, peace and happiness of all people—the aspirations of the Lotus Sutra—and infused his faith into the chanting of Nam-myoho-renge-kyo, which he taught others. For his belief and actions as a votary of the Lotus Sutra, he was persecuted. He battled and triumphed over the attacks by the ruling authorities and their supporters.

At Tatsunokuchi, having almost been executed, he demonstrated the merit and practice of Buddhahood as an individual confronting and resolutely prevailing over the hindrances of death and the "devil king," the epitome of destructive and manipulative forces. It was during this Tatsunokuchi Persecution that he discarded his transient status and revealed his true identity.

Nichiren writes, "Superior Practices, the leader of the Bodhisattvas of the Earth, has already made his advent in this world, so the great Law, the essence of the Lotus Sutra that was entrusted to him, will spread without fail" ("The Teaching, Practice, and Proof," WND-1, 482). His words resound with his awareness as the teacher of true cause of the Latter Day, who has proven the power of the Law as a "bodhisattva-Buddha," an enlightened human being.

Nichiren Buddhism is grounded on the relationship of mentor and disciple. Human beings in a sense are weak and find it extremely hard to break through their fundamental darkness. But they also have the capacity for great nobility through belief in their innate power and that of others. Through contact with the life of a great victor like Nichiren, we discover our own limitless potential. By carrying on Nichiren's teachings and helping others become happy, we actualize our enlightenment.

Moreover, because Nichiren successfully established the philosophy of ultimate humanism and empowerment, we consider him the teacher of all humankind.

The Great Path of a Humanistic Religion

The Lotus Sutra is a teaching of revitalization, celebrating the limitless potential and dignity of life of each person. Nichiren distilled this essence in Nam-myoho-renge-kyo, and the SGI extends this humanistic religion to the world.

The three founding presidents of the Soka Gakkai—Tsunesaburo Makiguchi, Josei Toda and Daisaku Ikeda—have actualized the Buddhist practice of Shakyamuni and Nichiren based on their shared commitment to *kosen-rufu.* Their practice as mentors and disciples is the starting point for spreading this movement for human revolution. It is our mission and function as SGI members, as Bodhisattvas of the Earth, to continue this legacy and become living examples of this humanistic philosophy.

Lectures on
The HERITAGE *of the* ULTIMATE LAW *of* LIFE

SGI PRESIDENT IKEDA'S STUDY LECTURE SERIES

(12)

"EARTHLY DESIRES ARE ENLIGHTENMENT" AND "THE SUFFERINGS OF BIRTH AND DEATH ARE NIRVANA"

Transforming Illusion and Suffering Into Confidence, Joy and Hope

Be resolved to summon forth the great power of faith, and chant Nam-myoho-renge-kyo with the prayer that your faith will be steadfast and correct at the moment of death. Never seek any other way to inherit the ultimate Law of life and death, and manifest it in your life. Only then will you realize that earthly desires are enlightenment, and that the sufferings of birth and death are nirvana. Even embracing the Lotus Sutra would be useless without the heritage of faith.

I will go into particulars again on another occasion.

With my deep respect,
Nichiren,
the shramana[1] of Japan

The eleventh day of the second month in the ninth year of Bun'ei (1272), cyclical sign *mizunoe-saru.*

Reply to the Honorable Sairen-bo
(*The Writings of Nichiren Daishonin*, vol. 1, p. 218)

Lecture

The beneficial power of the Mystic Law is immeasurable. If we continue to practice correctly just as Nichiren Daishonin teaches, we can achieve the supreme state of attaining Buddhahood in this present, irreplaceable lifetime. In the final passage of "The Heritage of the Ultimate Law of Life," Nichiren clarifies the key to correct faith for inheriting the Law and calls on us to lead truly unsurpassed lives.

The Soka Gakkai alone has inherited the ultimate Law of life and death from Nichiren, correctly upholding and practicing his teaching and spreading it widely throughout the world in accord with his instructions. That is why the infinite power of the Mystic Law emerges powerfully in the lives of each of us who exert ourselves for *kosen-rufu.*

When we bring forth from within us the great joy that comes from realizing that we are entities of the Mystic Law, we can change even the most intractable problems and sufferings into wisdom, and freely utilize the struggle as a force for value creation. We inherently possess the fundamental power to overcome any seemingly impossible deadlock. When we believe with unshakable certainty in our innate power to "change poison into medicine"—the power to turn any hardship into a springboard to absolute happiness—we have nothing to fear.

The Mystic Law is the fundamental principle that allows us to draw forth the limitless power we inherently possess. It enables us to change earthly desires, or deluded impulses, into wisdom, just as a fire burns firewood to produce light. We can also transform a life that has been filled with the sufferings of birth and death into one pervaded by vibrant and unbounded joy—just as spring sunshine can melt ice and snow to create a flowing stream.

Self-transformation—this is the main theme of Buddhism. Nichiren Buddhism is a teaching that actually transforms lives. Everything starts with us, with our own human revolution. This forms the basic underpinning of Nichiren Buddhism and the activities of the Soka Gakkai.

Again, in this closing passage of "The Heritage of the Ultimate Law of Life," Nichiren seems to be calling out to us: "Awaken to the vast power you possess! Chant Nam-myoho-renge-kyo with the firm belief that you will achieve a wonderful life of great fulfillment! This itself is the true heritage." He concludes this writing by clarifying that the heritage of faith is the sole means through which we, and indeed all people, can share in the heritage for attaining Buddhahood.

The Essence of Faith for Inheriting the Law

"The Heritage of the Ultimate Law of Life" brims throughout with the fundamental Buddhist spirit to enable all people to realize enlightenment. Pervading it is Nichiren Daishonin's great compassionate wish to make it possible for all human beings to lead lives of supreme happiness.

In the previous installment, we studied the passage in which Nichiren declares that he has been carrying out the mission of Bodhisattva Superior Practices, who inherited the Law of life and death and vowed to appear in the Latter Day. As is evident from this fact, it is none other than Nichiren Daishonin who established the great Law for the enlightenment of all people. He is the "teacher of true cause."

The final passage, which follows, sets forth the essential elements of faith necessary for people of the Latter Day to inherit from Nichiren the Law for attaining Buddhahood. These are summed up as: "the great power of faith," "a correct and steadfast mind at the moment of death,"[2] "the realization that earthly desires are enlightenment and the sufferings of birth and death are nirvana," and "the heritage of faith" (see WND-1, 218). In this and the next installment, I will discuss these principles and their practice.

First, Nichiren says, "Be resolved to summon forth the great power of faith." "Be resolved" implies a conscious commitment and determination. It could be said that "the great power of faith" means the ability to continually rededicate ourselves and summon fresh faith in our hearts.

Next, he explains what we need to do in concrete terms of our Buddhist practice, saying, "Chant Nam-myoho-renge-kyo with the prayer that your faith will be steadfast and correct at the moment of death."

We have already discussed at length earlier in this series the concept of having a correct and steadfast mind, or attitude in faith, at the moment of death. [See September–October 2007 *Living Buddhism*, pp. 54–61.] Bringing one's life to a close with a sense of great fulfillment and serenity as a result of our faith in the Mystic Law, without being perturbed by the hindrance of death or other devilish functions, leads to the attainment of a boundless and enduring state of happiness.

In order to have a correct and steadfast mind at the moment of death, it is crucial that we strive day after day, month after month, with the spirit of faith that "now is the last moment"—always living in such a way that we have no regrets. In order for us to attain this state of mind, Nichiren teaches us to deepen our prayers each day, and persevere with a resolve to practice faith wholeheartedly. He also informs us that there is no way to inherit the ultimate Law of life and death apart from correctly practicing Buddhism. This

CHANGING POISON INTO MEDICINE

This principle demonstrates that earthly desires and suffering can be transformed into benefit and enlightenment by virtue of the power of the Mystic Law. This phrase is found in a passage from Nagarjuna's *Treatise on the Great Perfection of Wisdom*, which mentions "a great physician who can change poison into medicine." In this passage, Nagarjuna compares the Lotus Sutra to a "great physician" because the sutra opens the possibility of attaining Buddhahood to persons of the two vehicles, or voice-hearers and cause-awakened ones. Other sutras condemned such persons as having "scorched the seeds of Buddhahood," denying them the possibility of ever attaining enlightenment. T'ient'ai (538–97) says in *The Profound Meaning of the Lotus Sutra*, "That persons of the two vehicles were given the prophecy of their enlightenment in this [Lotus] sutra means that it can change poison into medicine." This phrase is often cited to show that any limitation, problem or suffering can be transformed eventually into the greatest happiness and fulfillment in life.

(Adapted from *The Soka Gakkai Dictionary of Buddhism*)

means summoning forth "the great power of faith" and chanting Nam-myoho-renge-kyo for the happiness of ourselves and others, confident that we will have a correct and steadfast mind at the moment of death.

Inner Transformation Lies at the Heart of Inheriting the Law

In his conclusion to this writing, Nichiren Daishonin focuses on what each of us needs to do to achieve enlightenment.

The Buddhism of true cause propagated by Nichiren is a teaching for people to actualize the causality for attaining Buddhahood. People are the foundation. Each person is important. Unless the spirit of valuing each individual is put into practice, any theorizing on the heritage of the Law, no matter how exalted, will be empty.

This also means that those who practice Nichiren Buddhism must have the awareness and confidence that they can definitely change their lives on a profound level. The reason Nichiren says, "Never seek any other way [than this] to inherit the ultimate Law of life and death, and manifest it in your life," is that the heritage of the Law does not exist apart from faith in the Buddhism of true cause, which enables each person to transform themselves inside and attain Buddhahood in this lifetime based on chanting Nam-myoho-renge-kyo.

In what way, then, are our lives actually transformed? What kind of life-state can we attain through faith? In relation to this, Nichiren writes, "Only then will you realize that earthly desires are enlightenment, and that the sufferings of birth and death are nirvana." Summoning the great power of faith and chanting Nam-myoho-renge-kyo with the prayer that our faith will be steadfast and correct at the moment of death in itself constitutes the realization that "earthly desires are enlightenment" and "the sufferings of birth and death are nirvana." Attaining this state of life is the true benefit of Nichiren Buddhism.

What this means is that, through the power of strong and unshakable faith and chanting Nam-myoho-renge-kyo, we can turn illusions and sufferings into the means for developing value-creating wisdom and establish an inner state of complete assurance and joy.

The state of mind that can perceive earthly desires as enlightenment and the sufferings of birth and death as nirvana is synonymous with the attainment of Buddhahood in one's present form. This is also the great benefit of "changing poison into medicine." In the Buddhism of true cause, all people, through the power of faith, can forge in the depths of their lives the great and indestructible state of Buddhahood.

The Life-State and Benefit of Attaining Buddhahood in One's Present Form

The concepts "earthly desires are enlightenment" and "the sufferings of birth and death are nirvana" both describe transformative functions inherent in life. "Earthly desires are enlightenment" means that the wisdom for attaining Buddhahood (i.e., enlightenment) appears in lives dominated by earthly desires, or deluded impulses. "The sufferings of birth and death are nirvana" means that the state of true peace and tranquillity of the Buddha (i.e., nirvana) manifests in lives that are wracked by the sufferings of birth and death.

In Nichiren Daishonin's writings, we find that there are very few instances where one of these two principles is mentioned alone without the other. They appear together to express either the life-state or the benefit of attaining Buddhahood in one's present form.

The Causality of the "Seeds of Opposites" and the Mystic Law of "Changing Poison Into Medicine"

Taken in a literal sense, "earthly desires" and "enlightenment" are diametric opposites and cannot be identified with one another. The same can be said of "the sufferings of birth and death" and "nirvana." Rather, it is "earthly desires" and "the sufferings of birth and death"

EARTHLY DESIRES ARE ENLIGHTENMENT

From "The Doctrine of Three Thousand Realms in a Single Moment of Life"

"But when, through the Lotus Sutra, we meditate moment by moment on the meaning of threefold contemplation in a single mind and the principle of three thousand realms in a single moment of life, then we come to realize that we ourselves are Thus Come Ones of original enlightenment. Then the clouds of ignorance part and the moon of the essential nature of phenomena shines forth. We wake from dreams of delusion and the round moon of original enlightenment is seen in all its brilliance. We see that this fleshy form received in birth from our parents, this body bound by earthly desires, is none other than the Thus Come One who has existed always and is ever-abiding. This is what is called the attainment of Buddhahood in one's present form, the realization that earthly desires are none other than enlightenment and that the sufferings of birth and death are none other than nirvana" (WND-2, 85).

that are similar. As is well known, Shakyamuni Buddha deeply perceived the causal role that earthly desires such as greed, anger and foolishness play in creating the sufferings of birth and death.

This view of causality led to the Hinayana Buddhist practice of striving to eradicate earthly desires in order to free oneself from these fundamental sufferings. This way of practicing Buddhism, however, caused people to despise and seek to escape the sufferings of birth and death. That was because it was focused solely on eliminating earthly desires (evil), based on a partial concept of causality that held that evil is the only possible outcome of evil. With such a view, efforts to completely eradicate evil were destined to be frustrating and ultimately futile.

Although the provisional Mahayana teachings subsequently taught the principles of "earthly desires are enlightenment" and "the sufferings of birth and death are nirvana," the actual practice of these teachings comprised aspiring for the attainment of Buddhahood by either endlessly accumulating good causes, as seen for example in the idea of carrying out austere practices throughout many lifetimes, or depending for salvation on an absolute Buddha that transcends this world.[3]

Ultimately, however, such Mahayana practices and beliefs also caused people to abhor the sufferings of birth and death and seek to escape this world.

This was because these practices and beliefs were based on a partial concept of causality that held that good can only be produced by good. What happened was that those who carried out a self-reliant bodhisattva practice could only hope to attain enlightenment in the inconceivably distant future. Those who practiced with a dependent faith had no choice but to rely on the agency of an absolute Buddha, such as Amida, to free themselves from the *saha* world and be reborn in the "good" circumstances of a pure land, where they could resume their efforts to accumulate good causes. Either way, there was no guarantee of attaining the fruit of practice in this lifetime. Ultimately, this causal perspective is merely the reverse of the belief that evil only produces evil.

Be that as it may, people whose lives were shackled by the illusions of earthly desires and the sufferings of birth and death naturally were unable to gain the true joy of being liberated from those chains, and there was nothing to give them any real hope or confidence of attaining enlightenment.

Nichiren Daishonin has the following to say with regard to the erroneous approaches of the pre-Lotus Sutra teachings toward earthly desires and the sufferings of birth and death and their relationship to enlightenment and nirvana: "The heart of the pre-Lotus Sutra teachings is that one should discard earthly desires, despise the sufferings of birth and death, and seek enlightenment and nirvana elsewhere. The spirit of the Lotus Sutra is that earthly desires are enlightenment and that the sufferings of birth and death are nirvana"[4] (*Gosho zenshu*, p. 821).

What, then, does it mean to regard earthly desires and the sufferings of birth and death as inseparable from enlightenment and nirvana? In a writing titled "What It Means to Hear the Buddha Vehicle for the First Time,"[5] addressed to his lay disciple Toki Jonin, Nichiren says that the essence of ordinary people practicing the Lotus Sutra is found in the concept of the "seeds of opposites" (WND-2, 741). The "seeds of opposites" means that that which is the opposite of the effect, or fruit, of attaining Buddhahood—namely, earthly desires and the sufferings of birth and death—becomes the cause, or seed, for attaining Buddhahood.

Both these partial concepts of causality—of viewing evil as the only possible outcome of evil or viewing good as the only possible outcome of good—are inadequate for enabling ordinary people to gain enlightenment. In the final analysis, an approach that draws a hard and fast distinction between good and evil cannot but cause people—who have no choice but to live in the midst of evil—to lose hope.

Many of the Buddhist schools in Nichiren's day had grown divorced from reality or had succumbed to a narrow elitism with a focus on a small group of practitioners or priests. A probable reason for this is that, viewing good and

NICHIREN DAISHONIN ON DEATH

"If you wish to free yourself from the sufferings of birth and death you have endured since time without beginning and to attain without fail unsurpassed enlightenment in this lifetime, you must perceive the mystic truth that is originally inherent in all living beings. This truth is Myoho-renge-kyo" ("On Attaining Buddhahood in This Lifetime," WND-1, 3).

"The aspect or characteristics of the threefold world are birth, aging, sickness, and death. But if we look at birth and death in terms of their true nature, then there is no birth or death. And if there is no birth or death, then there is no ebb or flow. Not only do birth and death not exist. To look on birth and death with repulsion and try to escape from them is termed delusion" (*The Record of the Orally Transmitted Teachings*, p. 127).

"One who listens to even a sentence or phrase of the sutra and cherishes it deep in one's heart may be likened to a ship that crosses the sea of the sufferings of birth and death" ("A Ship to Cross the Sea of Suffering," WND-1, 33).

"When he was alive, he was a Buddha in life, and now he is a Buddha in death. He is a Buddha in both life and death. This is what is meant by that most important doctrine called attaining Buddhahood in one's present form" ("Hell Is the Land of Tranquil Light," WND-1, 456).

evil as distinct and separate, they were unable to give hope to people living in an evil and defiled age.

It seems likely that Nichiren emphasized the "seeds of opposites" because he realized, if people were to have genuine hope in life, it was vital for them to have a view of causality that offers the possibility of good coming out of evil—the possibility that something negative can be transformed into something positive.

In "What It Means to Hear the Buddha Vehicle for the First Time," Nichiren describes this causality of the "seeds of opposites" as "changing poison into medicine." This principle teaches that, just as a skilled physician can use even a poison or toxic substance as medicine, through the power of the Mystic Law we can transform the three paths of earthly desires, karma and suffering[6] into the three virtues of the Dharma body, wisdom and emancipation.[7] Truly, earthly desires become enlightenment and the sufferings of birth and death become nirvana.

In the same writing, Nichiren

concludes by saying that only when we have deep faith that the three paths are themselves the three virtues can we overcome the sufferings of birth and death and be said to have heard the Lotus Sutra in a true sense.[8] Put another way, when we believe from the depths of our hearts that earthly desires are enlightenment and the sufferings of birth and death are nirvana, birth and death are no longer a source of suffering. We are then able to truly "hear the Lotus Sutra."

The principle of the "seeds of opposites," which is also referred to as "the opening up and merging of the seeds of opposites," means unifying things that are in opposition and revealing their broader significance by understanding them in a larger context. In the case of "earthly desires are enlightenment" and "the sufferings of birth and death are nirvana," "earthly desires" and "the sufferings of birth and death," which are in opposition to "enlightenment" and "nirvana," certainly take on a new meaning.

It is precisely because we have sufferings that we can earnestly chant to the Gohonzon. The determination to seriously confront our sufferings causes the fundamental power inherent in our lives to emerge that much more strongly.

At the moment we chant, our sufferings—our earthly desires—have already become causes for enlightenment. It could even be said that our earthly desires in fact contain enlightenment. In a sense, earthly desires themselves undergo a qualitative change from "earthly desires that cause suffering" into "earthly desires that can be transformed into enlightenment." It is the power of Nam-myoho-renge-kyo—the Mystic Law of the simultaneity of cause and effect—that makes this possible.

We Are Buddhas Just As We Are

There is no attainment of Buddhahood separate from the earthly desires and the sufferings of birth and death of ordinary people. Attaining Buddhahood does not mean becoming some kind of superhuman being who transcends all else. This is a point that second Soka Gakkai president Josei Toda consistently emphasized. He once remarked: "'Earthly desires are enlightenment' and 'the sufferings of birth and death are nirvana' describe a life in which we savor a state of happiness and complete peace of mind, while living with our earthly desires just as they are.... Enlightenment is nothing particularly out of the ordinary. Because we have earthly desires, we can experience fulfillment, and because we have fulfillment, we experience happiness. To wake up each morning with a sense of physical well-being, to have a good appetite, to enjoy what we do each day and to not feel worried or anxious about life—to live in this way is enlightenment. It is nothing exceptional. We should not misconstrue 'earthly desires are enlightenment' as meaning

A COMPARISON OF HINAYANA AND MAHAYANA

Hinayana and Mahayana are two names given to major streams of Buddhist thought. Teachings classified as Hinayana view desire and illusion as the cause of suffering and seek to extinguish them as the way to nirvana. Hinayana practice has as its goal the attainment of the state of *arhat*, a state in which one is free from the cycle of death and rebirth and attains nirvana. There is no recognition that it is possible to attain the supreme state of Buddhahood, as the Buddha is seen as being inherently superior to ordinary people.

Mahayana, or greater vehicle, does not seek to completely extinguish desire, which it views as a natural function of life. Instead, it focuses on the role of the bodhisattva to lead a great many people to supreme enlightenment. It is thought that early Mahayanists considered Buddhism as it was practiced by existing monastic orders to be limited, calling them Hinayana (lesser vehicle). Such teachings focused on the emancipation of a limited class of monks, and therefore were seen as able to transport far fewer people to the destination of enlightenment. This is why some view the designation *Hinayana* as originally pejorative.

The Lotus Sutra, highest of the Mahayana teachings and the doctrinal basis of Nichiren Buddhism, reveals that Buddhahood is eternally present in all life and does not focus on rebirth in a pure land (as emphasized in other Mahayana sutras). Rather, it focuses on the continuation of bodhisattva practice in the realm of ordinary beings referred to as the *saha* world (i.e., Earth).

T'ien-t'ai and Nichiren Daishonin clearly held Mahayana to be superior to Hinayana. But it should be understood that Hinayana in this case refers to a category of scriptural content, doctrines and principles rather than to any particular Buddhist school or present-day tradition.

Such doctrines as "earthly desires are enlightenment" and "the sufferings of birth and death are nirvana" epitomize the difference between the Hinayana and Mahayana teachings. The former views earthly desires and even the cycle of birth and death as the cause of suffering and as obstacles to attaining enlightenment, whereas the latter views Buddhahood as inherent within all of life's functions.

that we will turn into some truly extraordinary being."[9]

Mr. Toda was always utterly himself, natural and unpretentious. Outwardly, he was in every way an ordinary person, but his mind was always keenly focused on the advance of the Soka Gakkai. Above all, his sense of responsibility for *kosen-rufu* was truly a reflection of his towering state of enlightenment. Cherishing a fervent "earthly desire" to achieve *kosen-rufu*, Mr. Toda demonstrated a commitment to this cause that transcended life and death. He based himself on a vast state of life I would describe as "enlightenment manifesting as responsibility."

To be truly oneself means to continually polish and develop our lives just as we are, without trying to become someone we are not. In other words, it means that the essence of achieving human revolution is none other than showing actual proof of attaining Buddhahood in one's present form. That is, the principles of "earthly desires are enlightenment" and "the sufferings of birth and death are nirvana" are actualized in our lives in the midst of our Buddhist practice to keep challenging ourselves through faith.

The Greatest of All Joys

Striving with the spirit that "earthly desires are enlightenment" and "the sufferings of birth and death are nirvana" is a source of joy. There is no greater joy than developing the profound awareness that "ordinary people are identical with the highest level of being" (OTT, 22), and "one is a Buddha in both life and death" ("Hell Is the Land of Tranquil Light," WND-1, 456).

Our efforts to attain Buddhahood in our present form are always filled with joy. When we tackle our problems head-on and summon the wisdom to find a way to surmount them, almost without realizing it we come to savor a state of immense joy, our lives overflowing with a powerful life force that enables us to put everything that has happened into perspective and to take it all in stride.

The life-state of the Buddha inherently abounds with immense joy. It is pervaded by the joy of the Law that comes from having arrived at the ultimate truth. Having attained a state of "deathlessness,"[10] the Buddha's life overflows eternally with the joy of being alive. Manifesting Buddhahood means bringing forth the joy of the Buddha from the depths of our beings.

If we uphold the Mystic Law with courage, the life force of Buddhahood that enables us to take on any hardship will reveal itself within us. If we have invincible hope shining undaunted by even the bitterest setbacks, then this life force will never be exhausted.

Through the power of the Mystic Law, we come to recognize that, though we may once have been overwhelmed by difficulties, we actually have the inner strength to address and overcome them.

THE THREE VIRTUES

The three virtues are three attributes with which a Buddha is endowed: the Dharma body, wisdom and emancipation. The Dharma body is the essential truth or principle to which the Buddha is enlightened. Wisdom refers to the Buddha's ability to perceive and understand that truth. Emancipation is the condition in which that truth and the wisdom to perceive it are essentially one, and the person is free from the realm of the sufferings of birth and death.

The three virtues correlate with various other Buddhist concepts, such as the Buddha's three bodies, the three truths and the three paths (see the *Soka Gakkai Dictionary of Buddhism* for descriptions of these terms). In particular, T'ien-t'ai taught that the three paths—earthly desires, karma and suffering—are in themselves the three virtues. That is, within the cycle that gives rise to suffering can be found the qualities or causes for enlightenment, absolute happiness. In this way, suffering itself can give rise to happiness. The principle called "changing poison into medicine" also refers to the transformation of the three paths into the three virtues.

Nichiren Daishonin writes: "In explaining the word *myo*. . .[Nagarjuna] says it is 'like a great physician who can change poison into medicine.'

"What is the poison? It is the three paths of earthly desires, karma, and suffering that are our lot. What is the medicine? It is the [three virtues of the] Dharma body, wisdom, and emancipation. And what does it mean to change poison into medicine? It means to transform the three paths into the three virtues" ("What It Means to Hear the Buddha Vehicle for the First Time," WND-2, 743). Nichiren goes on to associate this transformation with the principle of attaining Buddhahood in one's present form.

By dedicating ourselves to the great objective of *kosen-rufu*, we come to realize that our own problems and worries can serve as the driving force for changing our lives for the better and thereby prove the validity of Nichiren Buddhism. We come to appreciate that our refusal to be defeated by suffering can be a source of inspiration and encouragement to many others. And by maintaining a fighting spirit for *kosen-rufu*, we can arrive at the realization that we ourselves are originally Buddhas.

The Lotus Sutra speaks of "hearts filled with great joy" (*The Lotus Sutra*, p. 152). In *The Record of the Orally*

Transmitted Teachings, the phrase "great joy" is annotated with the words "earthly desires are enlightenment, the sufferings of birth and death are nirvana" (OTT, 211). The life-state of attaining Buddhahood in one's present form, the realization that "earthly desires are enlightenment" and "the sufferings of birth and death are nirvana," is itself the greatest of all joys.

The Record of the Orally Transmitted Teachings continues: "This passage refers to the great joy that one experiences when one understands for the first time that one's mind from the very beginning has been the Buddha. Nam-myoho-renge-kyo is the greatest of all joys" (OTT, 211–12).

The principles of "earthly desires are enlightenment" and "the sufferings of birth and death are nirvana" indicate that we can lead strong, fulfilling lives characterized by joy so broad and enduring it can embrace any kind of suffering or sorrow.

I recall the following words of Tolstoy: "Rejoice! Rejoice! One's life's work, one's mission, is a joy. Rejoice to the sky, to the sun, to the stars, to the grass, to the trees, to the animals, and to one's fellow human beings. Be ever vigilant that nothing destroys this happiness. Should it be destroyed, it means that you have somewhere made a mistake. Find that mistake and correct it."[11]

The stance of the great author that "one's life's work, one's mission, is a joy" certainly resonates with the profound philosophy of Buddhism. Our Buddhist practice enables us to feel a deep and abiding joy in our lives. Tolstoy further says that we should find any mistake that destroys this happiness and take action to correct it. From the standpoint of Buddhism, this corresponds to the practice of positively transforming earthly desires and the sufferings of birth and death—that is, to internalizing the principles of "earthly desires are enlightenment" and "the sufferings of birth and death are nirvana," and striving to change our karma.

We of the SGI who embrace and practice the Mystic Law, though we may experience periods of suffering or illusion, are truly walking the path of champions of unsurpassed wisdom and philosophy. Through our faith in Nichiren Buddhism, we can positively transform all poison through the great beneficial medicine of the Mystic Law.

Nichiren Daishonin writes, "Through the extraordinary power of the character *myo,* or 'wonderful,' this poison [of earthly desires and the sufferings of birth and death] is changed into the understanding that the sufferings of birth and death are nirvana, that earthly desires are enlightenment" ("On Attaining Buddhahood in One's Present Form," WND-2, 585–86).

The Mystic Law is a precious principle for achieving a life of absolute victory. By basing themselves on the

Mystic Law, each individual can lead a life of triumph in which "earthly desires are enlightenment" and "the sufferings of birth and death are nirvana." That ever-increasing numbers of people are living with such brilliance as they share in the heritage of the ultimate Law of life and death demonstrates the success of Nichiren Buddhism.

1. *Shramana*: (Skt) A seeker of the way. In India, the word originally referred to any ascetic, recluse, mendicant or other religious practitioner who renounced secular life and left home to seek the truth. Later, it came to mean chiefly one who renounces the world to practice Buddhism.
2. "A correct and steadfast mind at the moment of death" is the same term (Jpn *rinju shonen*) as "faith that is steadfast and correct at the moment of death" in the text of the passage from Nichiren Daishonin's writing. It refers to a condition in which, even when faced with death, one's mind is not consumed with erroneous thoughts arising from the three poisons of greed, anger and foolishness, but instead is characterized by unshakable confidence in one's own Buddhahood and firm belief in the Mystic Law. While this principle describes one's condition at the moment of death, it also represents a state the practitioner aims to make prevalent at each moment, so that one can lead a life of no regrets.
3. The prime example of this is found in the Pure Land teachings, which speak of a transcendent Buddha called Amida, whose compassion is considered absolute and all-encompassing. By relying on that absolute compassion, one is said to gain rebirth in that Buddha's pure land, after which one can carry out Buddhist practice and attain Buddhahood.
4. "Oko kikigaki" (The Recorded Lectures); not translated in WND, vols. 1 and 2.
5. In this writing, Nichiren Daishonin states that there are two types of practice of the Lotus Sutra: the "opening up and merging of the seeds of similar species," and the "opening up and merging of the seeds of opposites." He indicates that by embracing the Lotus Sutra one can change the three paths of earthly desires, karma and suffering into the three virtues of the Dharma body, wisdom and emancipation, and can attain Buddhahood in one's present form.
6. Three paths of earthly desires, karma and suffering: They are called "paths" because one leads to the other. Earthly desires, which include greed, anger, foolishness, arrogance and doubt, give rise to actions that create evil karma. The effect of this evil karma then manifests itself as suffering. Suffering aggravates earthly desires, leading to further misguided action, which in turn brings on more evil karma and suffering.
7. Three virtues of the Dharma body, wisdom and emancipation: Three attributes of a Buddha. The Dharma body means the truth that the Buddha has realized, or the true aspect of all phenomena; wisdom is the capacity to realize this truth; and emancipation means the state of being free from the sufferings of birth and death.
8. Nichiren Daishonin writes: "Question: What benefit do we gain by hearing this doctrine [that the three paths are themselves the three virtues]? Answer: This is what it means to hear the Lotus Sutra for the first time. Miao-lo says: 'If one has faith in the teaching that the three paths of earthly desires, karma and suffering are none other than the three virtues of the Dharma body, wisdom and emancipation, then one can cross the two rivers of transmigration, to say nothing of making one's way in the threefold world. And when ordinary people in the latter age hear this doctrine, not only will they themselves attain Buddhahood, but also their fathers and mothers will attain Buddhahood in their present forms" ("What It Means to Hear the Buddha Vehicle for the First Time," WND-2, 744).
9. Translated from Japanese. Josei Toda, *Toda Josei zenshu* (Collected Writings of Josei Toda) (Tokyo: Seikyo Shimbunsha, 1982), vol. 2, p. 162.
10. Deathlessness: A term derived from the statement in the "Medicine King" chapter of the Lotus Sutra that reads "he will know neither old age or death" (LS, 288). "Deathlessness" refers to a state in which one perceives that life and death are two phases of the eternal aspect of life itself, which is one with the Mystic Law.
11. Translated from Japanese. Leo Tolstoy, *Torusutoi no kotoba* (Words of Tolstoy), translated and edited by Fumihiko Konuma (Tokyo: Yayoi Shobo, 1997), p. 94.

STUDY GUIDE

The following is a summary of key points from SGI President Ikeda's lecture.

In the closing passage of "The Heritage of the Ultimate Law of Life," Nichiren Daishonin calls upon us to muster the limitless power within ourselves to transform suffering into wisdom, confidence, joy and hope. The ongoing effort to uncover this innate limitless power—this self-transformation or human revolution—is the essential theme of Nichiren Buddhism. Nichiren clarifies that it is only through the "great power of faith" that we can share in the heritage for attaining Buddhahood. We, SGI members, have inherited the ultimate Law of life and death from Nichiren, practicing and spreading his teachings throughout the world.

The Essence of Faith for Inheriting the Law

Nichiren outlines the essentials of faith, stating: "Be resolved to summon forth the great power of faith, and chant Nam-myoho-renge-kyo with the prayer that your faith will be steadfast and correct at the moment of death" (WND-1, 218).

In this statement, "be resolved" implies commitment and determination and "the great power of faith" is the ability to continually refresh our faith and rededicate ourselves. To have faith that is "steadfast and correct at the moment of death" indicates that in basing our lives on the Mystic Law and striving each day as if "now is our last moment," we can create a victorious state of being and bring our lives to a close with great fulfillment and peace.

Inner Transformation Lies at the Heart of Inheriting the Law

The spirit to value each individual and the confidence that one's life will change on a profound level are key to attaining enlightenment. Nichiren says, "Never seek any other way [than this] to inherit the ultimate Law of life and death, and manifest it in your life" (WND-1, 218). The heritage exists in faith in the Buddhism of true cause, which enables inner transformation based on chanting Nam-myoho-renge-kyo.

Nichiren continues, "Only then will you realize that earthly desires are enlightenment, and that the sufferings of birth and death are nirvana" (WND-1, 218). In other words, illusions and sufferings become the means for developing wisdom, complete assurance and joy.

The Causality of the "Seeds of Opposites" and the Mystic Law of "Changing Poison Into Medicine"

Nichiren teaches that our sufferings can serve as a catalyst for the fundamental power inherent in our lives to emerge. However, prior to the Lotus Sutra, Shakyamuni Buddha had explained that suffering was caused by desires. This led to the Hinayana Buddhist practice of trying to eradicate earthly desires to free oneself from suffering, which caused people to despise and seek to escape the sufferings of birth and death. But coming from a partial concept of causality, the view that evil is the only possible outcome of evil, efforts to completely eradicate evil are destined to be futile.

Provisional Mahayana Buddhism then taught the principles "earthly desires are enlightenment" and "the sufferings of birth and death are nirvana." But attaining Buddhahood was thought to require austere practices carried out over many lifetimes; or people depended on the saving grace of a godlike, transcendent Buddha, like Amida. These views also arise from a partial concept of causality—in this case, the view that good can only be produced by good.

Therefore, neither the Hinayana teaching of achieving nirvana through eradicating desires nor the provisional Mahayana teachings of reward through rebirth in a paradise or countless lifetimes of austere practice helped people to rid themselves of suffering, truly transform karma or have any real hope of attaining enlightenment in one's present form.

On the other hand, Nichiren explains that the essence of ordinary people practicing the Lotus Sutra is found in the concept of the "seeds of opposites" (see "What It Means to Hear the Buddha Vehicle for the First Time," WND-2, 741). This means the seed, or cause, is the opposite of the fruit, or effect, it produces. Namely, it means that earthly desires and the sufferings of birth and death become the cause, or seed, for attaining Buddhahood.

Nichiren describes this as "changing poison into medicine." Just as a skilled physician can use even a toxic substance as medicine, the Mystic Law can transform the three paths of earthly desires, karma and suffering into the three virtues of the Dharma body, wisdom and emancipation. The moment we chant Nam-myoho-renge-kyo, our desires themselves change from "earthly desires that cause suffering" to "earthly desires that can be transformed into enlightenment." The power of the Mystic Law that is the simultaneity of cause and effect makes this possible.

We Are Buddhas Just As We Are

Without earthly desires and sufferings there is no enlightenment for ordinary people. To be "just as we are" means to constantly challenge ourselves in faith to polish our lives while remaining true to ourselves.

True joy emerges when, through the power of the Mystic Law, we realize our innate power and wisdom to win over the problems that had once overwhelmed us. Our refusal to be defeated by suffering can be a source of inspiration to many others. This fighting spirit for *kosen-rufu* brings the realization that we ourselves are originally Buddhas, and this is the source of greatest joy.

Lectures on *The* HERITAGE *of the* ULTIMATE LAW *of* LIFE

SGI PRESIDENT IKEDA'S STUDY LECTURE SERIES

(13)

THE HERITAGE OF FAITH

The Heritage for Attaining Buddhahood Flows in the Lives of Disciples Who Strive Selflessly for Others' Happiness in the Same Spirit As the Mentor

Be resolved to summon forth the great power of faith, and chant Nam-myoho-renge-kyo with the prayer that your faith will be steadfast and correct at the moment of death. Never seek any other way to inherit the ultimate Law of life and death, and manifest it in your life. Only then will you realize that earthly desires are enlightenment, and that the sufferings of birth and death are nirvana. Even embracing the Lotus Sutra would be useless without the heritage of faith.

I will go into particulars again on another occasion.

With my deep respect,
Nichiren,
the shramana[1] of Japan

The eleventh day of the second month in the ninth year of Bun'ei (1272), cyclical sign *mizunoe-saru*

Reply to the Honorable Sairen-bo
(*The Writings of Nichiren Daishonin,* vol. 1, p. 218)

Lecture

The Heritage of Faith in All Its Aspects

This writing, Nichiren Daishonin's response to Sairen-bo's question about the transmission of the ultimate Law of life and death, clarifies that Myoho-renge-kyo is the supreme Law that can free all people of the sufferings of birth and death. In addition to outlining on several different levels what it means to embrace and uphold this Law, this letter stresses the importance of taking Nichiren—who functions as Bodhisattva Superior Practices[2] in the Latter Day of the Law—as one's teacher and practicing faith with the same spirit as he does in order to overcome the sufferings of birth and death. The final passage concludes by stating that the heritage of faith is the only true means by which all people can inherit the Law of Myoho-renge-kyo, the ultimate Law of life and death (see *The Writings of Nichiren Daishonin*, vol. 1, p. 218).

This conclusion addresses the very heart of Buddhism. The question of life and death is a fundamental source of human suffering, and the transmission of the ultimate Law of life and death is a means for resolving that suffering. No matter how wonderful a teaching may seem, unless it explains to individuals the key to surmounting the sufferings of birth and death, it has no real substance.

The best and surest way to convey the supreme Law to others is through faith. The Law cannot be transmitted by such transitory and illusory phenomena as priestly authority or religious rituals and ceremonies. Faith is of foremost importance in transmitting the true, supreme Law.

Only faith can break through the darkness of ignorance shrouding our lives and enable us to tap the infinite power of the Mystic Law we inherently possess. To share in the heritage of the Law means to bring forth within us this boundless power of the Law.

That is why in this writing Nichiren has gone to great lengths to offer a full, multidimensional explanation of the heritage of faith, which we have discussed in detail over the course of this series. In this final installment, let us reconfirm the main points.

First, correct faith is grounded in the realization that "Shakyamuni Buddha who attained enlightenment countless kalpas ago,[3] the Lotus Sutra that leads all people to Buddhahood,[4] and we ordinary human beings are in no way different or separate from one another" (WND-1, 216). This is a crucial point concerning the substance of faith in the Mystic Law. In this writing, Nichiren states that chanting Nam-myoho-renge-kyo with this belief is a "matter of

Seikyo Press

SGI President Ikeda and others applaud as Universidad Autonoma de Santa Domingo Rector Roberta A. Reyna Tejada delivers a congratulatory message at the 5th Nationwide Youth Leaders Meeting, Hachioji, Tokyo, January 19, 2008.

the utmost importance" for his disciples (WND-1, 216). The core message of this statement is to believe that our present self is an entity of Myoho-renge-kyo and that we can attain Buddhahood in our present form in this lifetime.

Second is the aspect of striving fully in faith so that we have no regrets, based on the spirit that "now is the last moment of one's life" (WND-1, 216), and achieving "a correct and steadfast mind at the moment of death"[5] (see WND-1, 218). Wholeheartedly practicing faith day after day and month after month, and continuing to do so throughout our lives, assures us of attaining Buddhahood in this lifetime. Here, Nichiren explains the heritage of faith in terms of one's own depth of faith and the continuing of one's Buddhist practice.

Moreover, when we attain Buddhahood in this existence, the life-and-death cycle we continually undergo throughout past, present and future becomes "life and death as functions of Myoho-renge-kyo"[6] and follows the rhythm of birth and death in the realm of Buddhahood.[7] This present lifetime in which we have been born as human beings is an irreplaceable existence; it will determine the direction of our lives throughout the eternal cycle of birth and death.

Third is the importance of unity in faith, a commitment to the widespread propagation of the Law in the spirit of "many in body but one in mind" (WND-1, 217). The heritage of Myoho-renge-kyo is not just there for us alone. All people are entities of Myoho-renge-kyo and as such can partake in the heritage for attaining Buddhahood. Actions to help others gain access to this heritage is the way of *kosen-rufu*, the great wish or vow of the Buddha. And *kosen-rufu* is made a reality by the harmonious community of practitioners united in faith toward that shared objective. Here, Nichiren clarifies the heritage of faith in terms of *kosen-rufu* and the harmonious community of practitioners.

As I have summarized above, Nichiren explains the heritage of faith on different levels, addressing 1) the substance of faith; 2) the depth of faith and continuing in Buddhist practice; and 3) *kosen-rufu* and the harmonious community of practitioners. He thus gives us a full picture of the kind of faith needed to share in the heritage of the ultimate Law of life and death.

Sharing the Same Commitment As the Teacher Is the Key

Nichiren Daishonin references Bodhisattva Superior Practices—the teacher who embodies all of these aspects of the heritage of faith.

The multifaceted meaning of the heritage of faith has been explained in words, but if many people are to actually share in this heritage in their own lives, it is necessary to have a teacher who embodies it in its entirety. Whereas words merely explain each aspect of the heritage of faith separately, a teacher whose character and behavior embody the Law of Myoho-renge-kyo can convey and awaken people to this heritage in one stroke.

Accordingly, in this writing, Nichiren urges us to chant and practice Nam-myoho-renge-kyo, the Law transmitted by Bodhisattva Superior Practices, and he implies that his own efforts in propagating this teaching correspond to the appearance of Superior Practices as predicted in the Lotus Sutra.

After these remarks concerning the teacher, Nichiren concludes by emphasizing the importance of the heritage of faith. In other words, striving in faith with the same commitment as the teacher is the key and the ultimate path to sharing in the heritage of faith.

We can regard this entire writing as a detailed exposition of the heritage of faith.

The View of Life and Death in Nichiren Buddhism: A Wellspring of Hope for Humankind

Since my youth, I have been confident that a change in the way of looking at life and death, based on the teachings of Nichiren Buddhism, would give untold hope to humankind. I have also felt that this would form an indispensable foundation for actualizing world peace. And I have discussed this in

SGI PRESIDENT IKEDA ON FAITH

To break through the shell of the lesser self and focus on the eternal thought in the innermost depths of our lives—that is what it means to have faith in the Mystic Law.

Ultimately, it comes down to awareness. We need to awaken to the fact that we are the Mystic Law to establish the awareness that we are living out our lives based on the Mystic Law over the three existences—past, present and future.

Second Soka Gakkai president Josei Toda said: "Our existence as ordinary common mortals is the secret and mystic expedient; the truth is that we are Buddhas. The Gohonzon is also enshrined in our hearts. In other words, the core of Nichiren Buddhism lies in the conviction that the Gohonzon enshrined in our Buddhist altar is identical to our own lives."

We experience one suffering after another. We are assailed by hardships. That is the reality of life. But each of us possesses the power to solemnly face and overcome all these obstacles. The point is whether we believe this and can actually manifest this strength. That is the key to victory.

It is precisely by challenging and overcoming difficulties as ordinary people that we can demonstrate the greatness of the Mystic Law. Our being ordinary people is an expedient means that enables us to fulfill this mission.

To be defeated by suffering and filled with complaint is to be shackled by our karma. When we are squarely facing our suffering, we are able to transform it into our mission. Everything depends on our determination.

Opening our eyes to the Buddha within, to the Mystic Law within—that is the linchpin of faith and the foundation of Buddhism.

(see *The World of Nichiren Daishonin's Writings*, vol. 1, pp. 128–29)

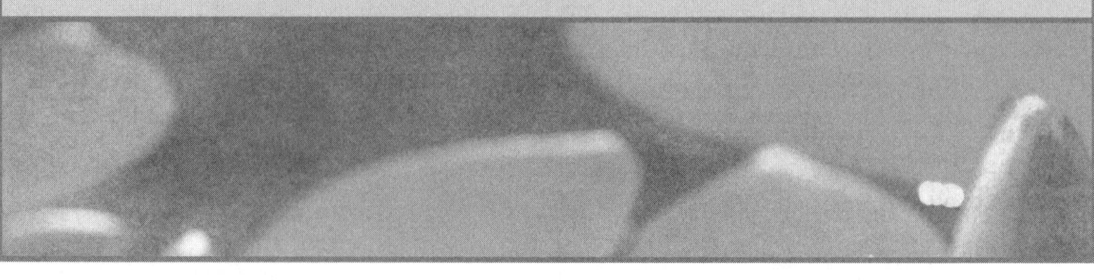

various ways, whenever the opportunity has arisen.

In *Choose Life*, my dialogue with British historian Arnold J. Toynbee,[8] the first of my many dialogues with scholars and leaders around the globe, we squarely took up and discussed this theme of life and death.

"Does life persist after death, or does it belong only to this world? If it does continue beyond death, is it eternal or finite, and in what state does it persist?"[9] Dr. Toynbee earnestly listened to my candid questions. And he offered the restrained comments of a scholar, responding, "The possible eternal nature of life is an important question that arouses points insusceptible of actual proof."[10] But he also went on to say, "I believe that these questions can be answered in terms of *ku* [the Buddhist concept of non-substantiality] or of eternity, but not in terms of space-time."[11]

He inferred that the question of life and death is a fundamental issue not so much of scholarship but of religion, and he turned the question back on me, suggesting that it would fall to me as a Buddhist to provide an answer.

The insightful conclusion of this leading intellectual is that the answer lies in the domain of religion. The problem of life and death poses an eternal riddle for humankind, and at the same time is a central focus of religion. It is no exaggeration to say that this is precisely where religion's raison d'être is found.

In his work *The System of Value-Creating Education*,[12] first Soka Gakkai president Tsunesaburo Makiguchi makes the following observation: "With reference to our life activities as they relate to the universe as a whole, when we directly confront the problem of life and death—even if we are a person of great wisdom or scholarship, or a person of great heroism or enterprise—we realize how miniscule our own power is in comparison. At that time, we have to face up to the power of the universe itself, which is truly awesome in its immensity. Our activities on a religious or spiritual sphere arise from this recognition. Our life activities as they relate to society, too, can in fact be regarded as part of such activities."[13]

He is saying that if we wish to resolve the problem of life and death, we must acknowledge the immense power of the universe and open up our lives to the spiritual or religious impulse within. His point that our activities in society are part of our spiritual or religious activities also bears close consideration.

As practitioners of Nichiren Buddhism, the powerful life force we develop through our activities in the spiritual realm serves as the engine that enables us to lead positive and valuable lives in society. Here, the heritage of faith is the key to a spiritual life in which we are in tune with the vast power of the universe that encompasses both life and death.

NICHIREN DAISHONIN'S DISCIPLE: ABUTSU-BO

Endo Tamemori changed his name to Abutsu-bo upon becoming a lay priest of the Pure Land sect (Abutsu is derived from *Amida-butsu*, or Amida Buddha). How he came to live on Sado is uncertain. Most likely he was a native, though there is speculation he was exiled there for political reasons.

Nichiren Daishonin openly criticized the Pure Land teachings, earning himself numerous enemies in the process. When Nichiren came to Sado, Abutsu-bo met with him in debate, intent on disproving Nichiren's views. But Nichiren defeated him, and Abutsu-bo and his wife, the lay nun Sennichi, moved by Nichiren's character, immediately became his disciples.

The couple would frequently support Nichiren with food and clothing throughout the two years of the Sado exile, and they continued to do so even after Nichiren moved to the Minobu area. Abutsu-bo even made the long journey to Minobu to visit Nichiren three times. He was 91 years old when he died.

Abutsu-bo and the lay nun Sennichi received several letters from Nichiren. Perhaps the most famous of these is "On the Treasure Tower" (*The Writings of Nichiren Daishonin*, vol. 1, p. 299), in which Nichiren states: "Abutsu-bo is therefore the treasure tower itself, and the treasure tower is Abutsu-bo himself. No other knowledge is purpose," indicating his strong confidence in Abutsu-bo's Buddha nature.

Abutsu-bo's Seeking Spirit Toward Nichiren

Here, based on guidance Nichiren gave to his followers, I will highlight the decisive importance of the heritage of faith in overcoming the sufferings of birth and death, especially the aspect of striving with the same commitment as the mentor.

Abutsu-bo can be considered a leading representative of the followers, one who shared in the heritage of faith during Nichiren's day and thereby overcame the sufferings of birth and death and attained Buddhahood in his lifetime. In a letter to the lay nun Sennichi about her deceased husband, Abutsu-bo, Nichiren writes: "Some may wonder where the spirit of the late Abutsu-bo may be at this moment. But by using the clear mirror of the Lotus Sutra to reflect his image, I, Nichiren, can see him among the assembly on Eagle Peak, seated within the treasure tower of Many Treasures Buddha and facing toward the east" ("The Treasure of a Filial Child," WND-1, 1042).

Here, Nichiren describes Abutsu-bo as "facing toward the east," meaning he is seated directly opposite the Buddhas Shakyamuni and Many Treasures, who are seated side by side within the treasure tower at the pure land of Eagle Peak.[14] This is certainly the correct way to view Abutsu-bo, who had risked his own life to support and aid Nichiren.

For instance, during the harsh winter on Sado Island, without a thought for his own safety, Abutsu-bo repeatedly visited Nichiren under cover of darkness at the Sammai-do, his dwelling in Tsukahara, to bring him food. And even after Nichiren's exile and subsequent move to Mount Minobu, Abutsu-bo, despite his advanced age, made the long and arduous journey from Sado to visit him at least three times over the course of several years.

The deceased Abutsu-bo, we are told, now resides in the pure land of Eagle Peak and is facing the Buddhas inside the treasure tower with the same earnest spirit with which he sought out Nichiren during his life. We can take this to mean that disciples are certain to attain Buddhahood if they strive in faith with a seeking spirit toward the teacher who expounds and practices the Mystic Law.

Guidance to Nanjo Hyoe Shichiro

Next, I'll cite a passage from "Encouragement to a Sick Person," a letter Nichiren Daishonin wrote in 1264 to Nanjo Hyoe Shichiro, [15] the father of Nanjo Tokimitsu[16]—both of whom embraced faith in the Mystic Law. Shichiro had fallen ill and died the following year. This writing can be viewed as Nichiren's heartfelt guidance to a disciple who was approaching death, clarifying the essential path for attaining Buddhahood.

Nichiren writes: "Should you depart from this life before I do, you must report to Brahma, Shakra, the four heavenly kings, and King Yama.[17] Declare yourself to be a disciple of the priest Nichiren, the foremost votary of the Lotus Sutra in Japan. Then they cannot possibly treat you discourteously. But if you should be of two minds, alternately chanting the Nembutsu[18] and reciting the Lotus Sutra, and fear what others may say about you, then even though you identify yourself as Nichiren's disciple, they will never accept your word. Do not resent me later" (WND-1, 82).

In this letter, Nichiren teaches Shichiro the spirit and practice of the votary of the Lotus Sutra based on the five guides for propagation. Nichiren indicates elsewhere that the five guides represent the "attitude of mind that should characterize the votary of the Lotus Sutra when he strives to propagate

KEY CONCEPTS FROM THE "LIFE SPAN" CHAPTER

Before the Lotus Sutra, it was believed that Shakyamuni attained enlightenment under the *bodhi* tree after having spent countless lifetimes as a bodhisattva in the service of various Buddhas. The sutra states, however, that it had been an immeasurable length of time since he had "in fact attained Buddhahood" (*The Lotus Sutra*, p. 225).

When Shakyamuni revealed this, the whole notion of bodhisattva practice as a means to attaining enlightenment was turned on its head. Now Shakyamuni's bodhisattva practice could be seen as his Buddhahood manifested in "his behavior as a human being" ("The Three Kinds of Treasure," *The Writings of Nichiren Daishonin*, vol. 1, p. 852).

The clarification of Shakyamuni's innate Buddhahood is the basis for the concept of "the mutual possession of the Ten Worlds," which teaches that the states of life from the suffering of hell to the joy of Buddhahood exist in all people.

It was once believed that upon death a Buddha would enter the extinction of nirvana or go to a pure Buddha land. But the "Life Span" chapter reverses this notion as well in its depiction of Shakyamuni saying to his disciples, "Ever since [attaining Buddhahood in the remote past], I have been constantly in this *saha* world, preaching the Law, teaching and converting" (LS, 225).

Shakyamuni also states that were he to remain in the world in his present form, his disciples would grow too reliant upon him. Instead, he appears to enter nirvana so that his disciples will arouse a desire to seek his teachings.

The Buddha's intent—the desire to save living beings from suffering and to lead them to enlightenment—is mentioned in other sutras. But without the mutual possession of the Ten Worlds, the goal of attaining enlightenment in one's present form could not be achieved. Thus, the Buddha's true intent to "cause living beings / to gain entry into the unsurpassed way / and quickly acquire the body of a Buddha" (LS, 232) would not have been elucidated without the "Life Span" chapter of the Lotus Sutra. Nichiren Daishonin emphasizes the importance of this chapter, stating: "Were it not for the presence of the 'Life Span' chapter among all the teachings of Shakyamuni, they would be like the heavens without the sun and moon, a kingdom without a king, the mountains and seas without treasures, or a person without a soul. This being so, without the 'Life Span' chapter, all the sutras would be meaningless" ("The Essence of the 'Life Span' Chapter," WND-1, 183–84).

its teachings" ("What It Means to Slander the Law," WND-2, 246). They are five important points to which practitioners must pay attention when spreading the Mystic Law. Here, Nichiren, the teacher of *kosen-rufu,* is in fact describing his own spirit and actions as the votary of the Lotus Sutra.

Through this letter, he is trying to explain to Shichiro, who has fallen ill and is facing death, the importance of striving in faith with the same spirit that Nichiren has. This illustrates how practicing faith with the same commitment as the teacher who is the votary of the Lotus Sutra can assist us enormously in overcoming the sufferings of birth and death and in attaining Buddhahood in this lifetime.

Nichiren offers Shichiro advice to this effect: "If you should die, proudly tell the heavenly deities that you are a disciple of the votary of the Lotus Sutra. They are sure to protect you. But if you allow yourself to be swayed by the sufferings of sickness and death, and traces of your past belief in the Nembutsu should resurface, leaving you conflicted about faith, I can't be held responsible for the outcome." Nichiren poured his whole heart into these words, genuinely wishing for his disciple to attain Buddhahood. This encouragement enabled Shichiro to break through his doubts and summon strong faith in the Lotus Sutra. Nichiren later learned how the following year Shichiro had died while maintaining "a correct and steadfast mind at the moment of death."[19]

The Pride of Leading a Life of Unsurpassed Value

The path of mentor and disciple in the Soka Gakkai has also been characterized by a shared commitment and dedicated efforts to widely propagate Nichiren Buddhism in society. And I am confident that the valiant struggles of our members since the pioneering days of our movement are actions that carry on the humanistic legacy of the Lotus Sutra.

On the evening of August 14, 1947, some 60 years ago, I first met President Toda at a discussion meeting in the Kojiya area of Kamata in Tokyo. The man who was to become my mentor was 47 at the time, and I was 19. When I entered the room on that fateful day, President Toda was giving a lecture on Nichiren Daishonin's treatise "On Establishing the Correct Teaching for the Peace of the Land." He declared: "I want to rid the world of all suffering and misery. Won't you join me?" That was the first time I heard him speak. I believe his words were also a cry heralding the dawn of a great new people's movement.

On that day, I asked him what was the true way of life for a human being. President Toda's response was entirely free of any intellectual game-playing or deceit. Each of his answers shone with

FIVE GUIDES FOR PROPAGATION

Nichiren Daishonin established five criteria for correctly propagating his teaching of Nam-myoho-renge-kyo.

Teaching: Nichiren emphasizes a correct understanding of the teaching, recognizing the differences among the many Buddhist teachings, and discerning which are profound and which are superficial, while maintaining the awareness that the Lotus Sutra stands supreme among all the sutras. This is because Nam-myoho-renge-kyo, implicit in the "Life Span" chapter of the Lotus Sutra, is the teaching that enables all people in the Latter Day of the Law to attain Buddhahood.

Capacity: This refers to the life tendency of the people, the nature of their connection to Buddhism (or lack thereof), and their ability to understand and believe in the Buddhist teachings. In short, to understand the people's capacity means knowing by what teaching they can attain Buddhahood.

Time: The development of Buddhism following Shakyamuni's death is divided into three periods known as the Former, Middle and Latter Days of the Law (see January–February 2008 *Living Buddhism,* p. 65). The Law that is to spread in the Latter Day of the Law, the present time period, is Nam-myoho-renge-kyo, the essence of the Lotus Sutra.

Country: This refers to discerning the nature of a particular nation's or society's connection to Buddhism. Nichiren states that some countries actively slander the correct teaching, some are completely ignorant of it, some are exclusively Hinayana, some exclusively Mahayana, and others both Hinayana and Mahayana. He concludes that the Mystic Law of Nam-myoho-renge-kyo can save all people, even including those who oppose it.

Sequence: The point of this criterion is that one should not propagate a teaching inferior to those that have already spread.

(Excerpted and adapted from *The Soka Gakkai Dictionary of Buddhism*)

Nam-myoho-renge-kyo is the key to awakening the Buddhahood of all people, but the most effective means for introducing someone to Buddhist practice will vary from person to person. Nichiren's primary intent in creating these criteria was to indicate why he considered chanting Nam-myoho-renge-kyo to be the correct practice for the Latter Day of the Law. These guides also apply to sharing Buddhism with people around us, reminding us to develop the wisdom necessary to understand each person's needs. We should be aware of what forms of Buddhism, if any, people have encountered, as well as their cultural and religious background. We should take heed of how best to encourage people in terms of what they know and understand about the causes of the problems they face, confident that we can bring them to awaken their Buddhahood through chanting Nam-myoho-renge-kyo.

genuine humanity. He was truly a person grounded in the Lotus Sutra and had risen above the sufferings of birth, aging, sickness and death.

That day marked the start of my journey of shared commitment with my mentor. Mr. Toda taught me about the true nature of life and death. And as time went by, I felt it was my duty as a disciple to clarify and show actual proof of overcoming the sufferings of birth and death.

When disciples strive in a spirit of oneness with the mentor, sharing the same commitment to *kosen-rufu*, they can summon infinite strength. The mentor, based on a profound understanding of the fundamental question of life and death, ponders deeply and takes action to help all people manifest their innate potential and lead happy and successful lives.

I learned the way of faith in Nichiren Buddhism, the key to absolute victory, from Mr. Toda. Mr. Toda learned it from Mr. Makiguchi. And Mr. Makiguchi learned it from Nichiren and from chanting to the Gohonzon. This is the heritage of mentor and disciple in the Soka Gakkai.

When disciples unite in spirit with the mentor, they can overcome the sufferings of birth and death and, in this lifetime, attain a state in which they savor the boundless joy of the Law that continues eternally throughout past, present and future. That is the purpose of Buddhism.

Accordingly, the key to inheriting the ultimate Law of life and death lies in faith that embodies the spirit of not begrudging one's life in striving for *kosen-rufu* and the happiness of others, united in spirit with the mentor.

I once dedicated the following poem to some fellow members who had joined me in pledging to wage a selfless struggle.

> ***The oneness of mentor and disciple—***
> ***the fundamental principle of Soka***
> ***and Nichiren Buddhism,***
> ***the heritage of life***
> ***that exists within you.***

The brilliant second act of worldwide *kosen-rufu* has now opened. An age when the heritage of the ultimate Law of life and death flows throughout the world has now arrived. We have only just begun.

There is no nobler or more valuable way of life than to enable people across the globe to share in this supreme heritage and to savor a state of being in which they can feel joy in both life and death.

The world is waiting for the advance of Soka humanism, which has the power to elevate people's lives to a state pervaded by eternity, happiness, true self and purity. The world is closely watching the victorious achievements of mentor and disciple in the SGI.

This concludes the series "Lectures on 'The Heritage of the Ultimate Law of Life.'"

1. *Shramana*: (Skt) A seeker of the way. In India, the word originally referred to any ascetic or other religious practitioner who renounced secular life and left home to seek the truth. Later, it came to mean chiefly one who renounces the world to practice Buddhism.

2. Superior Practices: The leader of the Bodhisattvas of the Earth. In the "Supernatural Powers" chapter of the Lotus Sutra, Shakyamuni Buddha transfers the essentials of the sutra to Bodhisattva Superior Practices. Several of Nichiren Daishonin's writings refer to his own propagation efforts as the work of Bodhisattva Superior Practices.

3. This refers to the Buddha who eternally undergoes the cycle of birth and death in the realm of Buddhahood in order to teach and convert living beings in the *saha* world.

4. The Lotus Sutra is the teaching that reveals that all people inherently possess the Buddha nature and that expounds the path whereby they can enter the Buddha way and attain enlightenment.

5. "A correct and steadfast mind at the moment of death" is the same term as "faith that is steadfast and correct at the moment of death" in the text of the passage from Nichiren Daishonin's writing. It refers to a condition in which, even when one is faced with death, one's mind is not consumed with erroneous thoughts arising from the three poisons of greed, anger and foolishness, but instead is characterized by unshakable confidence in one's own Buddhahood and firm belief in the Mystic Law.

6. Life and death are originally inherent aspects of Myoho-renge-kyo, which is the fundamental Law pervading the universe and all life. Since Myoho-renge-kyo encompasses the Ten Worlds, all things, as entities of Myoho-renge-kyo, undergo the phases of life and death in the Ten Worlds. Accordingly, by embracing the Mystic Law, we can transform birth and death in the realm of delusion of the nine worlds into birth and death in the realm of Buddhahood.

7. Birth and death in the realm of Buddhahood: To freely undergo the cycle of birth and death based on the realization that our lives are entities of the all-pervasive Law of Myoho-renge-kyo and that life and death are inherent functions of Myoho-renge-kyo. Further, it is to embody the immense compassion and life force inherent in the universe and practice the Buddha way in lifetime after lifetime in order to lead all living beings to enlightenment.

8. Arnold Toynbee (1889–1975)—British historian and author of a 12-volume history of the world focusing on the rise and fall of civilizations in terms of failing or succeeding to grow in the face of challenging situations.

9. Arnold Toynbee and Daisaku Ikeda, *Choose Life: A Dialogue*, edited by Richard L. Gage (London: I.B. Tauris & Co., Ltd., 2007), p. 248.

10. *Choose Hope*, p. 248.

11. *Choose Hope*, p. 256.

12. *The System of Value-Creating Education*: A work in which Soka Gakkai founding president Tsunesaburo Makiguchi set forth the practical educational methods that he developed and advocated. The first volume of the work was published on November 18, 1930, and marked the official start of the Soka Gakkai.

13. Translated from Japanese. Tsunesaburo Makiguchi, *Soka Kyoikugaku taikei* (The System of Value-Creating Education), in *Makiguchi Tsunesaburo zenshu* (Collected Writings of Tsunesaburo Makiguchi) (Tokyo: Daisanbunmei-sha, 1982), vol. 5, p. 189.

14. Eagle Peak is the place where Shakyamuni preached the Lotus Sutra. It also symbolizes the Buddha land or the state of Buddhahood, as in the expression "the pure land of Eagle Peak."

15. Nanjo Hyoe Shichiro (d. 1265): A lay follower of Nichiren Daishonin and the father of Nanjo Tokimitsu. A retainer of the Kamakura shogunate, he governed Nanjo Village in Izu Province. As steward of the village, he was also called Ueno. Originally a believer in the Pure Land (Nembutsu) teaching, he became Nichiren's follower after hearing him preach. He is thought to have fallen ill near the end of 1264, and he passed away the following year.

16. Nanjo Tokimitsu (1259–1332): A lay follower of Nichiren Daishonin. In addition to supporting Nichiren, Tokimitsu aided Nikko Shonin, Nichiren's direct disciple and subsequent successor, in his propagation efforts in the Fuji area. He also provided crucial assistance to fellow practitioners at the time of the Atsuhara Persecution (1278 onward).

17. These are gods and kings depicted in Buddhist mythology. Brahma and Shakra are the two principal tutelary gods of Buddhism. The four heavenly kings serve Shakra and protect the four quarters of the world. King Yama is king of the world of the dead who judges and determines the rewards and punishments of the deceased.

18. To chant the Nembutsu means to chant the name of Amida Buddha, the practice of the Pure Land school of Buddhism.

19. Nichiren Daishonin writes: "Although your late father was a warrior, he had an abiding faith in the Lotus Sutra, and thus . . . I know that he ended his life in the frame of mind of a true believer [with a correct and steadfast mind at the moment of death]" ("On the Offering of a Mud Pie," WND-2, 499).

STUDY GUIDE

The following is a summary of key points from SGI President Ikeda's lecture.

The final passage of this writing addresses the very heart of Buddhism, stating that the heritage of faith is the only means by which all people can inherit the ultimate Law of life and death.

Only through faith can we break through the darkness of ignorance shrouding our lives and tap the infinite power of the Mystic Law we inherently possess. In his writings, Nichiren Daishonin examines various dimensions of faith.

First, correct faith is grounded in the realization that "Shakyamuni Buddha who attained enlightenment countless kalpas ago, the Lotus Sutra that leads all people to Buddhahood, and we ordinary human beings are in no way different or separate from one another" (WND-1, 216). To have faith in Nichiren Buddhism is to be certain that our present self is an entity of Myoho-renge-kyo and that we can attain Buddhahood in our present form.

Second, to strive fully to deepen our faith and to live fully without any regret is to have the spirit that "now is the last moment of one's life" and "a correct and steadfast mind at the moment of death." Nichiren emphasizes the importance of having such steadfast faith and of maintaining this effort.

Third, unity in faith is expressed as the spirit of "many in body, one in mind." Because all people are entities of Myoho-renge-kyo, everyone can partake in the heritage for attaining Buddhahood. Unity in faith is the commitment to widely propagate the Law. This is the vow of the Buddha and is expressed and made a reality by the harmonious community of practitioners united in faith toward this shared objective.

Sharing the Same Commitment As the Teacher Is the Key

Bodhisattva Superior Practices is the teacher who embodies all aspects of the heritage of faith. Nichiren identifies with and fulfills the role of Bodhisattva Superior Practices, urging us to chant and practice Nam-myoho-renge-kyo. Striving with the same commitment as the teacher is the key and the ultimate path to sharing in the heritage of faith.

The View of Life and Death in Nichiren Buddhism: A Wellspring of Hope for Humankind

Contemplating the eternal riddle of birth and death is one of religion's essential tasks.

A change in the way of looking at life and death, based on the teachings of Nichiren Buddhism, would give untold hope to humankind.

As practitioners of Nichiren Buddhism, the powerful life force that we develop through our activities in the spiritual realm serves as the engine that enables us to lead positive and valuable lives in society.

Abutsu-bo's Seeking Spirit Toward Nichiren

Abutsu-bo can be considered a leading representative of the followers, who shared in the heritage of faith during Nichiren Daishonin's day and thereby overcame the sufferings of birth and death and attained Buddhahood in his lifetime.

During the harsh winter on Sado Island, without a thought for his own safety, Abutsu-bo repeatedly visited Nichiren under cover of darkness at the Sammai-do, his dwelling in Tsukahara, to bring him food. And even after Nichiren's pardon from exile and subsequent move to Mount Minobu, Abutsu-bo, despite his advanced age, made the long and arduous journey from Sado to visit him at least three times during the course of several years.

In a letter to the lay nun Sennichi about her deceased husband, Nichiren writes, "By using the clear mirror of the Lotus Sutra to reflect his image, I, Nichiren, can see [Abutsu-bo] among the assembly on Eagle Peak, seated within the treasure tower of Many Treasures Buddha and facing toward the east" ("The Treasure of a Filial Child," WND-1, 1042).

We can take this passage to mean that disciples are certain to attain Buddhahood if they persevere in their Buddhist practice with a seeking spirit toward the teacher who expounds and practices the Mystic Law.

The Pride of Leading a Life of Unsurpassed Value

When disciples strive in a spirit of oneness with the mentor, sharing the same commitment to *kosen-rufu*, they can summon infinite strength. The mentor, based on a profound understanding of the fundamental question of life and death, ponders deeply and takes action to help all people manifest their innate potential and lead happy and successful lives. Accordingly, the key to inheriting the ultimate Law of life and death lies in faith that embodies this effort to strive together with the mentor for *kosen-rufu* and for the happiness of others without begrudging one's life.

There is no nobler or more valuable way of life than enabling people across the globe to share in this supreme heritage and savor a state of being in which they can feel joy in both life and death.

The world is awaiting the advance of Soka humanism, which has the power to elevate people's lives to a state pervaded by the virtues of eternity, happiness, true self and purity. The world is closely watching the victorious achievements of mentor and disciple in the SGI.

Key Points of

SGI PRESIDENT IKEDA'S LECTURE SERIES ON *The* HERITAGE *of the* ULTIMATE LAW *of* LIFE

SGI President Ikeda has written an in-depth 13-part lecture series on Nichiren Daishonin's letter, "The Heritage of the Ultimate Law of Life" (*The Writings of Nichiren Daishonin,* vol. 1, p. 216), which began in the May–June 2007 *Living Buddhism* and concludes in the May–June 2008 issue. *Living Buddhism* presents an overview of key points from President Ikeda's lecture series.

Nichiren wrote this letter to answer a question from his disciple Sairen-bo, a priest formerly of the Tendai school exiled to Sado Island. He met Nichiren and converted to his teachings in 1272, not long after attending the Tsukahara Debate (a public debate with priests of the Pure Land and True Word schools, held at Nichiren's lodgings on Sado). Sairen-bo was a scholar of Buddhism and seems to have asked very profound questions, such as the inquiry that led to this letter. Nichiren writes: "How admirable that you have asked about the transmission of the ultimate Law of life and death! I have never heard of anyone who has asked such a question. I have answered in complete detail in this letter, so please take it deeply to heart" (WND-1, 217).

In his lecture series, President Ikeda emphasizes and revisits several key points Nichiren made in his answer to Sairen-bo, namely the Buddhist view of death, the transmission of the teachings between mentor and disciple, the shared vow of the Buddha and the Bodhisattvas of the Earth and the concept of unity in fulfilling that vow.

THE BUDDHIST VIEW OF DEATH

Death is an inevitable state common to all life. All people must face death, and yet there is no tangible way of knowing what it holds. The question of life and death is central to most religions, each seeking to understand death and to explain this universal yet mysterious occurrence.

Buddhism rejects two common views of death, opting instead for the view that life and death are not opposites, but are aspects of the same Law. In the first installment of the series, President Ikeda writes: "The Buddha rejected the two most common views of death, which represented two extremes, and both of which he considered erroneous. Neither could fully enable people to transcend the fear and uncertainty of death. One of these was the view of death as the annihilation or complete cessation of self (the view of annihilation), while the other was the view of death as the self continuing in the form of an unchanging immortal soul or spirit (the view of permanence). Both views consider the question of life and death only from the point of birth onward until one's demise, with life and death seen as opposites. As such, neither view embodies the wisdom that correctly perceives the true reality of life and death" (May–June 2007 *Living Buddhism*, p. 70).

In the third installment, President Ikeda likens an individual life span to a wave appearing on the surface of the ocean and then submerging back into the ocean again. "The ocean represents the Mystic Law," he writes, "and the wave, an individual life or phenomenon. The pattern of waves arising from the ocean and then returning to it corresponds to the cycle of birth and death. It must be noted, however, that individual lives do not get swallowed up upon death in the ocean of the Mystic Law and disappear in the same way that a casual observer may see ordinary waves disappearing into the ocean.

"If we consider that there are various currents flowing through the ocean not visible from the surface, the difference between life and death could be likened to that between surface waves and the undulating currents within the ocean's depths. The life essence of an individual is certainly not extinguished at death. Life and death are simply the undulations of the Mystic Law itself" (July–August 2007 *Living Buddhism*, pp. 50–51).

Shakyamuni was enlightened to the true nature of life and death, seeing neither death as a cessation of existence nor life as a state of absolute and unique being. Understanding this, he employed various methods to detach people from either view. However, it was not until the "Life Span" chapter of the Lotus Sutra that the true nature of life and death was fully expounded.

The commonly held view of Shakyamuni was that he'd passed countless lifetimes in bodhisattva practice, purifying himself through good causes in service of various Buddhas until finally attaining the state of Buddhahood under the *bodhi* tree. In the "Life Span" chapter, he says otherwise: "In all the worlds the heavenly and human beings and asuras all believe that the present Shakyamuni Buddha, after leaving the palace of the Shakyas, seated himself in the place of practice not far from the city of Gaya and there attained anuttara-samyak-sambodhi. But good men, it has been immeasurable, boundless hundreds, thousands, ten thousands, millions of nayutas of kalpas since I in fact attained Buddhahood" (*The Lotus Sutra*, p. 225).

This revelation radically altered the way Shakyamuni's enlightenment was understood by his disciples. Bodhisattva practice no longer fit the definition of a gradual means of attaining Buddhahood, but became understood instead as the means by which a Buddha manifests compassion through action (through practicing for oneself and others). Bodhisattva practice is thus the actualization of the Buddha's vow to make all people equal to him.

Viewed in conjunction with the general Buddhist view of life and death, this means that since all life is one with the Mystic Law throughout birth and death, life contains Buddhahood at all times. The practice of a bodhisattva is not to gradually work toward attaining Buddhahood in the future nor wiping out desire (i.e. the Hinayana concept of nirvana). Nor is the goal of Buddhism rebirth in a pure Buddha land. Rather, the Buddha exists in the bodhisattva who carries out Buddhist practice in the real world to remove suffering and delusion from all people.

Teaching others the true nature of birth and death is of greatest importance in Buddhism. The transmission of this teaching is the heritage of the ultimate law of life and death, about which Sairen-bo had inquired.

Bodhisattva practice is thus the actualization of the Buddha's vow to make all people equal to him.

THE VOW OF THE BODHISATTVAS OF THE EARTH

In the "Expedient Means" chapter of the Lotus Sutra, Shakyamuni states that he has fulfilled his vow to make all persons "equal to me, without any distinction between us" (LS, 36).

Nichiren writes in this letter: "Shakyamuni Buddha who attained enlightenment countless kalpas ago, the Lotus Sutra that leads all people to Buddhahood, and we ordinary human beings are in no way different or separate from one another. To chant Myoho-renge-kyo with this realization is to inherit the ultimate Law of life and death" (WND-1, 216).

President Ikeda further stresses this point in the fifth installment. He writes: "Nichiren Daishonin says we must chant Myoho-renge-kyo with the realization that we are in no way different or separate from the Buddha and the Law. Here, *realization* does not simply mean an intellectual appreciation but rather *belief and understanding* [see *The Record of the Orally Transmitted Teachings*, pp. 54–55]—that is, an understanding based on belief, or a heartfelt acceptance and conviction in the depths of one's life. This is essential" (September–October 2007 *Living Buddhism*, p. 50).

To have faith that one's life is Myoho-renge-kyo is essential to practicing Nichiren Buddhism. Spreading this teaching is the role of the Bodhisattvas of the Earth.

In the Lotus Sutra, the Bodhisattvas of the Earth are disciples of Shakyamuni from the infinite past. Awakened to the ultimate Law of life, they vow to Shakyamuni to widely spread the Lotus Sutra in the Latter Day of the Law, a future time (corresponding to the present age) in which the Buddha's teachings have become obscured and provisional teachings have lost their power to save people. Nichiren considered his disciples—who chant Nam-myoho-renge-kyo with faith that their lives are endowed with Buddhahood—to be Bodhisattvas of the Earth.

In *The Record of the Orally Transmitted Teachings*, Nichiren states: "Thus we may say that the bodhisattvas who emerge from the earth are the bodhisattvas of the essential teaching. The word 'essential' or 'original' represents the merits [blessings] handed down from the past of numberless major world system dust particle kalpas ago, the merits [blessings] that are without beginning and without end.

"These bodhisattvas are possessors of the essential or original Law. The original Law is Nam-myoho-renge-kyo" (p. 119).

In the Lotus Sutra, the Bodhisattvas of the Earth have four leaders: Superior Practices, Boundless Practices, Pure Practices and Firmly Established Practices (for more information see January–February 2008 *Living Buddhism*, p. 71).

In the "Supernatural Powers of the Thus Come One" chapter of the Lotus Sutra, the Bodhisattvas of the Earth make the following vow: "World-Honored One, after the Buddha has entered extinction, in the lands where the emanations of the World-Honored One are present, and in the place where the Buddha has passed into extinction, we will preach this sutra far and wide" (LS, 272).

In his letter to Sairen-bo, Nichiren clarifies the role of Superior Practices and his relationship to the heritage of the ultimate Law of life. "The important point is to carry out your practice confident that Nam-myoho-renge-kyo alone is the heritage that was transferred from Shakyamuni and Many Treasures to Bodhisattva Superior Practices" (WND-1, 217). Later in the letter, he writes: "Whether or not Bodhisattva Superior Practices has appeared in this world, Nichiren has already made a start in propagating this teaching" (WND-1, 218).

The great desire of the Buddha to make all people equal to him, the vow of the Bodhisattvas of the Earth to widely spread the teachings and the SGI's noble mission for *kosen-rufu* are ultimately one and the same.

President Ikeda writes: "The Lotus Sutra is permeated by the Buddha's great vow to enable all people to attain Buddhahood. Shakyamuni teaches that a person who inherits and carries on this vow is a genuine bodhisattva and true disciple of the Buddha. He also calls on his followers to widely propagate the Law throughout the world after his passing, stressing the importance of winning in the struggle against negative forces that seek to obstruct the flow of *kosen-rufu*" (January–February 2008 *Living Buddhism*, p. 48).

The great desire of the Buddha to make all people equal to him, the vow of the Bodhisattvas of the Earth to widely spread the teachings and the SGI's noble mission for kosen-rufu *are ultimately one and the same.*

MANY IN BODY BUT ONE IN MIND

Nichiren Daishonin explains to Sairen-bo that unity is of utmost importance in fulfilling the vow of the Bodhisattvas of the Earth and transmitting the heritage of the ultimate Law of life.

President Ikeda writes that Nichiren "urges his followers to transcend all differences among themselves, to become as inseparable as fish and water, and to unite in the spirit of 'many in body but one in mind.' The heritage of the ultimate Law of life and death, he says, flows in the lives of those who chant Nam-myoho-renge-kyo—a practice for both oneself and others—based on this spirit of equality and unity" (November–December *Living Buddhism* 2007, p. 47).

It is important to note that "differences" refers to antagonism and the sense of self-importance that arises from failing to see the connection inherent in all life. It serves as a warning that egotism can harm unity and common purpose. Nichiren cautions, "But if any of Nichiren's disciples disrupt the unity of many in body but one in mind, they would be like warriors who destroy their own castle from within" (WND-1, 217).

"Many in body" indicates the diversity of human life, as seen in the various personalities, interests and backgrounds of Buddhist practitioners. This is partiularly true of the SGI, an organization transcending cultural, geographic and economic factors.

"One in mind" refers to the shared goal of *kosen-rufu*. As Nichiren writes in "The True Aspect of All Phenomena," which was also addressed to Sairen-bo: "If you are of the same mind as Nichiren, you must be a Bodhisattva of the Earth. And if you are a Bodhisattva of the Earth, there is not the slightest doubt that you have been a disciple of Shakyamuni Buddha from the remote past" (WND-1, 385). Being "one in mind" can therefore be said to mean "of the same mind as Nichiren."

Just as Shakyamuni was concerned with the future of Buddhism after his death, Nichiren gave encouragement to ensure the longevity of his teachings. In the eighth installment of his lecture series, President Ikeda writes: "Nichiren realized that, after his passing, for there to be a solidly united gathering of followers in which his spirit lived on would mean that people of future generations who had never personally met him could still embrace faith and practice as his disciples. They would share the same commitment for *kosen-rufu* and thus permit the heritage of faith for attaining Buddhahood to flow on indefinitely. Therefore, he writes, when his followers are united in the spirit of 'many in body but one in mind,' 'even the great desire for widespread propagation [*kosen-rufu*] can be fulfilled.' It is a declaration that the Buddha's great desire or vow for *kosen-rufu* will be passed on without interruption and *kosen-rufu* will certainly be achieved as long as there is a unified gathering of practitioners who uphold the Mystic Law. Unity is the most crucial ingredient in fulfilling this great aspiration" (November–December 2007 *Living Buddhism*, pp. 49–50).

Also implicit in the idea of "many in body but one in mind" is the importance of respect among Nichiren's disciples. It stands to reason that a group of believers with dictatorial leadership or in which some people are exalted and others considered inferior, could in no way constitute "many in body but one in mind." Only when practitioners uphold the shared vow and respect one another's inherent Buddhahood can they truly unite.

THE SUFFERINGS OF BIRTH AND DEATH ARE NIRVANA, EARTHLY DESIRES ARE ENLIGHTENMENT

Nichiren Daishonin writes: "Be resolved to summon forth the great power of faith, and chant Nam-myoho-renge-kyo with the prayer that your faith will be steadfast and correct at the moment of death. Never seek any other way to inherit the ultimate Law of life and death, and manifest it in your life. Only then will you realize that earthly desires are enlightenment, and that the sufferings of birth and death are nirvana. Even embracing the Lotus Sutra would be useless without the heritage of faith" (WND-1, 218).

"The sufferings of birth and death are nirvana" and "earthly desires are enlightenment" are two principles declaring that, since the essential nature of one's life is Myoho-renge-kyo, and life and death are functions of the Law, it follows that when one awakens to this truth, the entirety of one's experiences throughout life and death can be sources of joy.

The Buddhist teachings classified as Hinayana focus on eradicating desires, which are seen as the cause of suffering. If desires are wiped out, suffering would be as well, they reason. Such a view, however, led people to despise and seek to escape from the sufferings of birth and death. President Ikeda points out that such practices were "focused solely on eliminating earthly desires (evil), based on a partial concept of causality that held that evil is the only possible outcome of evil. With such a view, efforts to completely eradicate evil were destined to be frustrating and ultimately futile" (March–April 2008 *Living Buddhism*, p. 69).

The provisional Mahayana teachings either espouse attaining Buddhahood through austere practices designed to create good fortune over many lifetimes, or seeking salvation from an absolute and transcendent Buddha such as Amida. These practices, too, result in a desire to avoid the sufferings of birth and death. The provisional Mahayana teachings conclude that good can only come from good. They find no hope for good among the sufferings and evils of the *saha* world. As President Ikeda points out, this perspective is "merely the reverse of the belief that evil only produces evil" (March–April 2008 *Living Buddhism*, p. 70).

In Nichiren's view, neither of these approaches leads to revealing one's innate enlightenment. He states, "To look on birth and death with repulsion and try to escape from them is termed delusion" (OTT, 127). He follows this by saying, "Now when Nichiren and his followers chant Nam-myoho-renge-kyo, they realize the originally inherent nature of birth and death" (OTT, 127).

In the 10th installment of his lecture series, President Ikeda states: "When we bring forth from within us the great joy that comes from realizing that we are entities of the Mystic Law, we can change even the most intractable problems and sufferings into wisdom, and freely utilize the struggle as a force for value creation. We inherently possess the fundamental power to overcome any seemingly impossible deadlock. When we believe with unshakable certainty in our innate power to 'change poison into medicine'—the power to turn any hardship into a springboard to absolute happiness—we have nothing to fear.

"The Mystic Law is the fundamental principle for drawing forth the limitless power we inherently possess. It enables us to change earthly desires, or deluded impulses, into wisdom, just as a fire burns firewood to produce light. We can also transform a life that has been filled with the sufferings of birth and death into one pervaded by a vibrant and unbounded joy—just as spring sunshine can melt ice and snow to create a flowing stream" (March–April 2008 *Living Buddhism*, p. 65).

Nichiren's emphasis on faith is significant. Faith—the unshakable confidence that chanting Nam-myoho-renge-kyo awakens one's true nature as a Buddha—is required to transform suffering and delusion into the means for developing profound wisdom and joy. In reminding his disciple Sairen-bo to "be resolved to summon forth the great power of faith," he is in effect restating the importance of continuous dedication to the vow of the Bodhisattvas of the Earth to spread the essential teaching of the Lotus Sutra to all people.

We inherently possess the fundamental power to overcome any seemingly impossible deadlock.

MENTOR AND DISCIPLE

Sairen-bo's question about the transmission of the heritage of the ultimate Law of life can be understood as a question about the nature of the mentor-disciple relationship. In his response, Nichiren Daishonin says, "The important point is to carry out your practice confident that Nam-myoho-renge-kyo alone is the heritage that was transferred from Shakyamuni and Many Treasures to Bodhisattva Superior Practices" (WND-1, 217).

The transfer of the heritage to which Nichiren alludes began in the infinite past and culminates in the "Supernatural Powers of the Thus Come One" chapter of the Lotus Sutra. Superior Practices and the other Bodhisattvas of the Earth were disciples of Shakyamuni in lifetime after lifetime due to their powerful bond with their mentor.

Encapsulating this transfer, Shakyamuni says to Superior Practices and the other Bodhisattvas of the Earth: "To put it briefly, all the doctrines possessed by the Thus Come One, all the freely exercised supernatural powers of the Thus Come One, the storehouse of all the secret essentials of the Thus Come One, all the most profound matters of the Thus Come One—all these are proclaimed, revealed and clearly expounded in this sutra.

"For this reason, after the Thus Come One has entered extinction, you must single-mindedly accept, uphold, read, recite, explain, preach and transcribe it, and practice it as directed" (LS, 274).

Nichiren understood the essence of the sutra transferred from Shakyamuni to Superior Practices to be Nam-myoho-renge-kyo. In the Latter Day of the Law, Nichiren alone, functioning as Superior Practices, widely declared and spread this Law to his disciples. In the relationship between Shakyamuni and Superior Practices and then Nichiren and his disciples, we see a model of the mentor-disciple relationship, the paradigm of instruction for the essential Law.

In the ninth installment of his series, President Ikeda speaks at length of the significance of the mentor and disciple relationship. He writes: "Buddhism is a teaching conveyed through the mentor-disciple relationship. The oneness, or shared commitment, of mentor and disciple forms the essence of Buddhist practice. If we forget the mentor-disciple relationship, we cannot attain Buddhahood. Nor can we achieve eternal happiness or realize *kosen-rufu.* It is through the bond of mentor and disciple that the Law is transmitted. Buddhism is the Law of life; and the Law of life cannot be transmitted through words or concepts alone.

"The heritage of the ultimate Law of

life and death flows in the lives of those who strive for *kosen-rufu* based on the path of mentor and disciple. Please remember that without the mentor-disciple relationship, the flow of this heritage will be cut off" (January–February 2008 *Living Buddhism*, p. 47).

In other schools of Buddhism, the heritage of the teachings is often transferred through obscure or esoteric ceremonies or the inheritance of particular objects. But in Nichiren Buddhism, the heritage of the ultimate Law of life and death is open to everyone and transferred through the shared vow of mentor and disciple, the vow for *kosen-rufu,* the widespread propagation of the Law to secure the happiness and peace of humanity.

The deification of Shakyamuni that occurred in many Buddhist schools after his death can be viewed as a collapse of the mentor-disciple relationship. The great wish of the Buddha becomes impossible when the Buddha is erroneously given a transcendent and non-human status, a status that common mortals cannot achieve. In such schools, the veneration of the Buddha replaces the desire to attain Buddhahood in one's present form, and the vow of the bodhisattva to lead all people to enlightenment is also rendered impossible.

In contrast to this, Nichiren Buddhism—the Buddhism of mentor and disciple—understands that Buddhahood is inherent in all life. The Buddha is not deified, nor is the object of devotion a transcendent or supernatural Buddha. Rather, enlightenment in one's present form is available to all and the object of devotion is the Law itself, Myoho-renge-kyo, of which life and death are functions.

It is well established in the Lotus Sutra and in Nichiren's writings that those who are dedicated to the spread of the Law will face persecution and hardship. Through the shared vow of mentor and disciple, though, the spread of *kosen-rufu* goes on regardless of the obstacles and enmity that arise.

President Ikeda writes, "This lofty mentor-disciple relationship is the vital spirit of the Soka Gakkai. If this spirit lives on, our movement will continue to develop eternally. The mentor-disciple spirit of the first three presidents is key to securing the foundation of the *kosen-rufu* movement for the future.

"Mr. Toda states that by going to prison with his mentor, he was able to realize his former existence as a Bodhisattva of the Earth and the sutra's meaning. He found the key in the sutra passage concerning being reborn in lifetime after lifetime with one's mentor.

"Both mentor and disciple dedicate their lives eternally to bodhisattva practice—this point is crucial to understanding the Lotus Sutra's essence" (January–February 2008 *Living Buddhism*, pp. 56–57).

INDEX

C

G

H

L

O

P

R

S

U